*Battles and Massacres on the
Southwestern Frontier*

Battles and Massacres on the Southwestern Frontier

Historical and Archaeological Perspectives

Edited by
RONALD K. WETHERINGTON
and FRANCES LEVINE

UNIVERSITY OF OKLAHOMA PRESS : NORMAN

Library of Congress Cataloging-in-Publication Data

Battles and massacres on the Southwestern frontier : historical and archaeological perspectives / edited by Ronald K. Wetherington and Frances Levine.
   pages cm
Includes bibliographical references and index.
ISBN 978-0-8061-4440-5 (pbk. : alk. paper)
1. Indians of North America—Southwest, New—Wars. 2. Massacres—South West, New—History—19th century. 3. Historic sites—Southwest, New. 4. Excavations (Archaeology)—Southwest, New. 5. Southwest, New—History—19th century. I. Wetherington, Ronald K. II. Levine, Frances.
E78.S7B345 2014
979'.02—dc23   2013027319

The paper in this book meets the guidelines for permanence and durability of the Committee on Production Guidelines for Book Longevity of the Council on Library Resources, Inc. ∞

Copyright © 2014 by the University of Oklahoma Press, Norman, Publishing Division of the University. Manufactured in the U.S.A.

All rights reserved. No part of this publication may be reproduced, stored in a retrieval system, or transmitted, in any form or by any means, electronic, mechanical, photocopying, recording, or otherwise—except as permitted under Section 107 or 108 of the United States Copyright Act—without the prior written permission of the University of Oklahoma Press. To request permission to reproduce selections from this book, write to Permissions, University of Oklahoma Press, 2800 Venture Drive, Norman, OK 73069, or email rights.oupress@ou.edu.

Contents

List of Figures   vii

Acknowledgments   ix

Introduction   1
    Ronald K. Wetherington and Frances Levine

The Battle of Cieneguilla

Commentary   9
    Frances Levine

The Historical Record   12
    Will Gorenfeld

The Archaeological Record   43
    David M. Johnson

The Battle of Adobe Walls

Commentary   79
    Ronald K. Wetherington

Historical Perspectives   82
    T. Lindsay Baker

Archaeology at Adobe Walls   93
    J. Brett Cruse

The Sand Creek Massacre

Commentary 113
Frances Levine

What's in a Name? The Fight to Call Sand Creek
a Battle or a Massacre 116
Ari Kelman

Reassessing the Meaning of Artifact Patterning 134
Douglas D. Scott

The Mountain Meadows Massacre

Commentary 153
Ronald K. Wetherington

Understanding the Mountain Meadows Massacre 156
Glenn M. Leonard

Placing the Dead at Mountain Meadows 190
Lars Rodseth and Shannon A. Novak

Afterword: American Indians and the
Formalities of History 209
Joe Watkins

References 221
List of Contributors 239
Index 243

Figures

1. Map showing locations of Cieneguilla, Adobe Walls, Sand Creek, and Mountain Meadows — x–xi

The Battle of Cieneguilla

2. View of the Cieneguilla battle site — 44
3. Surveyors using metal detectors — 47
4. Site boundary — 49
5. Sample of artifacts — 52
6. Artifact distribution — 53
7. 1856 sketch map of battle — 54
8. Trail of artifacts — 56
9. Dismount location — 58
10. Apache camp — 60–61
11. Horse position — 64
12. Fallback position — 65
13. Location of ascent — 67
14. Final retreat — 68
15. Dropped vs. fired caps at horse position — 72
16. Dropped vs. fired ammunition at final retreat — 74

The Battle of Adobe Walls

17.	Topography of the Adobe Walls site	101
18.	Artifacts recovered from the Adobe Walls site	103

The Sand Creek Massacre

19.	Aerial photograph of Sand Creek site	136
20.	Altered iron objects	137
21.	Bullets and cartridge cases from Bowen find area	142
22.	Lead case shot balls, cannonball shrapnel, and Bormann fuses	143

The Mountain Meadows Massacre

23.	Brigham Young, 1858	159
24.	Aerial photograph of Mountain Meadows	166
25.	Map of southern Utah, showing Mountain Meadows location	166
26.	Isaac C. Haight	170
27.	William H. Dame	170
28.	John D. Lee	170
29.	Etching of the Mountain Meadows Massacre	175
30.	George A. Smith	183

Acknowledgments

This book emerged from a conference convened by the editors at the Fort Burgwin Research Center in Taos, New Mexico, in the fall of 2008. We wish to express our gratitude to the Center for providing the amenities for that conference. Further financial support was provided by the Clements Center for Southwest Studies at Southern Methodist University in Dallas, Texas. We sincerely appreciate the support and encouragement of the Clements Center's late director, David J. Weber, in making this project possible.

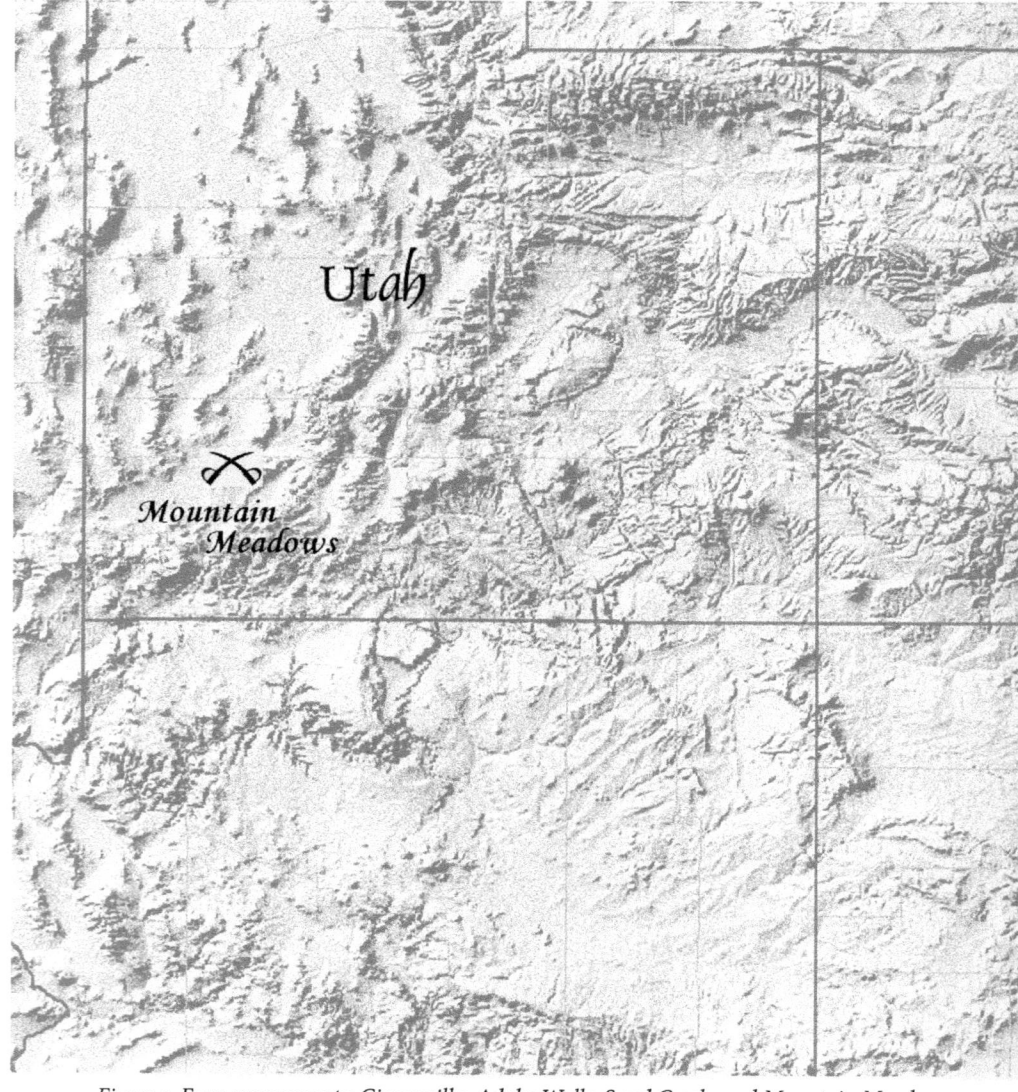

Figure 1. Four engagements: Cieneguilla, Adobe Walls, Sand Creek, and Mountain Meadows.

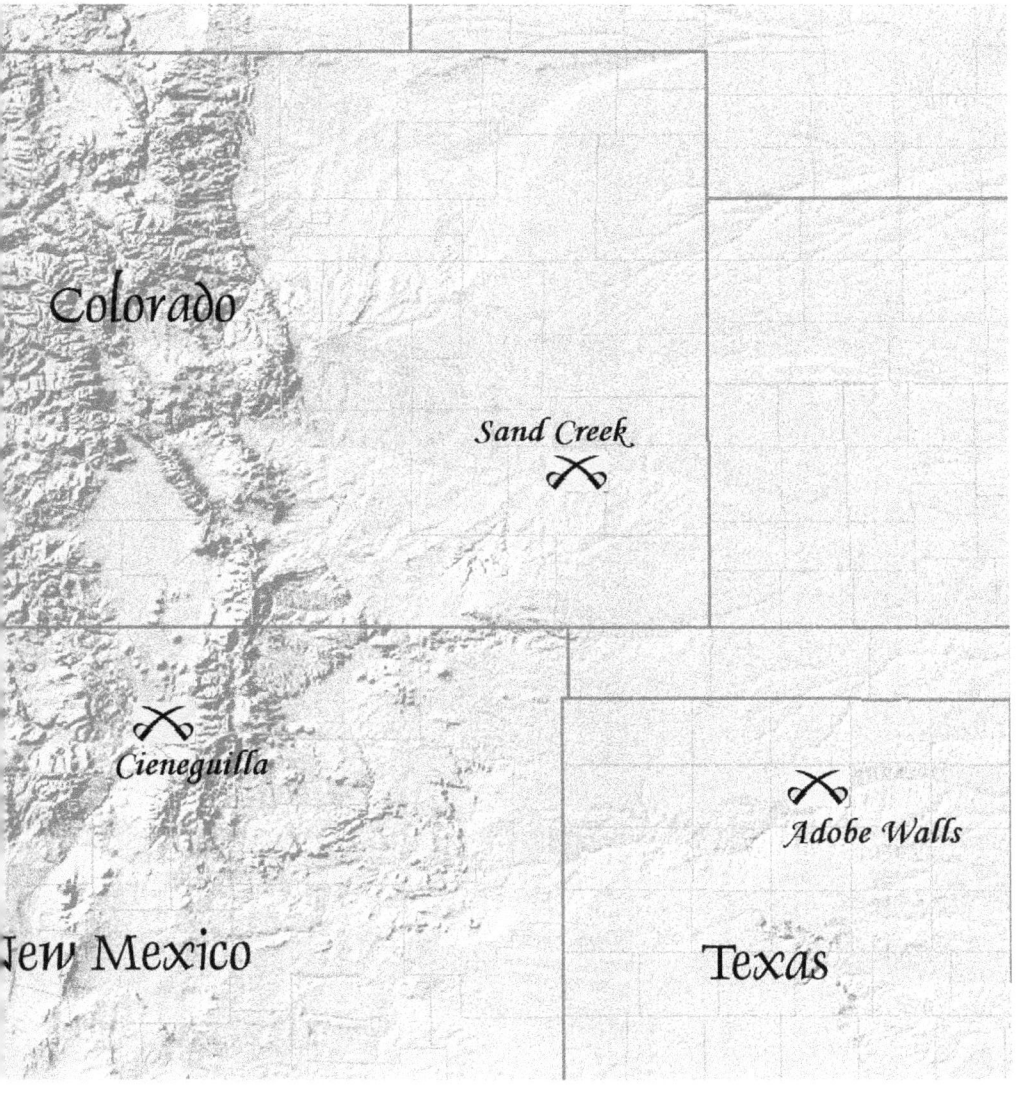

Introduction

Ronald K. Wetherington and Frances Levine

It might appear to some readers incongruous to combine treatises on battles with others on massacres in a single volume. It is only mass killing that they appear to have in common, whereas their contrasts are profound. Battles are, after all, between armed forces—usually military—with a cursory understanding that the killing field is equally engaged, or thought to be. Massacres, on the other hand, involve one-sided events in which the dead are mostly innocent victims who are suddenly thrust onto the killing field involuntarily.

We believe that there is meaning in identifying threads of commonality among the two battles and two massacres described here, and exploring these threads is one purpose of this book. Both massacres and battles—before twentieth-century weapons technology invited distant killing—are intimate affairs. The emotional and physical violence of both often stems from the common sources of fervor and fear, each of which stirs up deeper and often masked feelings of prejudice or outright hate. Most important for our purpose, the so-called fog of war shrouds both massacre and battle in functional amnesia or denial so dense that it cannot always be amended by later clarity. This is because, in the human brain, neither organized nor impulsive killing is guided by the neocortex. The centers of reason and rationality are well subordinated in the heat of killing, dying, and surviving by the ancient limbic brain, what Loren Eisley calls "the nose brain of our reptile past."[1] We remember it imperfectly, if at all, after the killing event is finished. We detect both the common causes of violence and the ensuing sublimation of facts in most of the accounts that follow.

A second purpose of this book is to compare historical and archaeological perspectives. This approach will be found less unusual by most readers: historical archaeology has commonly addressed the role of excavation and historical documentation as two important sources for understanding the recent past. However, historical archaeology is an amalgam that draws from two disciplines in a single effort; what we found intriguing was to invite a specialist in history and another in archaeology to address a single engagement, in order to reveal the sometimes subtle interpretations that can arise from different methodologies and different theoretical perspectives. The disagreement over the alleged involvement of Paiutes in the Mountain Meadows massacre is a good example. More often, however, we find that the differences lie more in focus than in interpretation. In both the Sand Creek and Adobe Walls accounts, for instance, the separate foci on artifact distribution discerned by the archaeologists and eyewitness accounts available to the historians yield powerful details and narratives but little interpretive dispute.

These four engagements all involve American whites and American Indians, although the Mountain Meadows massacre is more problematic in the nature of Indian involvement. It was our original idea to include the Native American perspective alongside the archaeological and historical. Much of the reason for failure in this effort is discussed in the final comments by Joe Watkins. Watkins argues, for example, that many Indians are reluctant to speak (or write) for their tribes or their cultures for reasons imbedded in the collectivism of native societies. Furthermore, he notes that, although American written history represents what is largely a consensus account among white Americans, for Indians it is not *their* history and they may have little interest in commenting on it.

The period during which these four events took place—the three decades of the 1850s through the '70s—marks the first half of the long conflict between the U.S. Army, acting to protect pioneer settlers from Indian attack, and the tribes whose land and resources were being alienated by them. In the Mountain Meadows disaster, whether or not the Paiute tribe participated, they had a tenuous relationship with the Mormon settlers and a distrust of whites.

This period witnessed increasing desperation among Indians and heightened fear among settlers. It also experienced systematic breakdown of agreements and peace treaties by both the government and the Indians.

Confrontation and misunderstanding on both sides were inevitable, as was the fervor bordering on fanaticism that often drove the confrontations and the uncompromising resolve that characterized both sides. Religious passion powered some of these confrontations, Mountain Meadows for example, or the conviction that God or reason was on the side of settlers, as we see in Colonel Chivington's lack of remorse at Sand Creek. For the tribes attacking Adobe Walls, the fervor was reinforced by the promise that the Great Spirit would protect them from the white man's bullets.

But the obsession has the same qualities whether driven by religious fervor or a reasoned passion. For the fanatic, Krakauer tells us, "[a] delicious rage quickens his pulse.... Ambiguity vanishes from the fanatic's worldview; a narcissistic sense of self-assurance displaces all doubt."[2] It was such an internal fire that likely led Lieutenant Davidson over the edge of reason at Cieneguilla (he often bragged that his superior training and his troops could easily "wipe out" the primitive Apaches), as may also have been the case with Chivington at Sand Creek, who obsessed for revenge over "mutilated bodies" of whites.

For both the battles and massacres discussed here, we would do well not to minimize the power of fear derived from uncertainty on the part of Indians and settlers alike. Neither side was always infused with goodwill and faith in peaceful resolution, and the resulting unpredictability of what either side would do next brought palpable fear into each settlement, each wagon train, each Indian camp and reservation. "This deep, constant *apprehension*, which neither the pioneers nor the Indians escaped," writes McMurtry, "has, it seems to me, been too seldom factored in by historians of the settlement era.... In my opinion this grinding, long-sustained apprehension played its part in the ultimate resort to massacre."[3] Terrorized settlers, particularly in the more remote and less populated areas, often lived in constant fear, sometimes bordering on panic. After the Colorado gold discoveries in 1860–61, for example, the increasing settlements on the eastern Colorado piedmont encroached on Indian bison lands, leading to increased attacks by Plains tribes—particularly Kiowas—and the so-called Colorado War culminated in the Sand Creek massacre. Even relatively secure locations, as the Rath settlement at Adobe Walls appeared to be, could quickly be shaken from complacency by the realization that few places in the emerging West were ever truly safe.

Finally, still another common thread to understanding both battles and massacres, those here included, is the ambiguity or deliberate dissembling and controversy that inevitably follows the confrontation. Only for Adobe Walls is there little ambiguity over the sequence of unfolding events, but even here body counts and positions of the participants remain uncertain, and the alleged early warning from the collapsed ridgepole is still debated. For all of the others the conflicting accounts and the rancor over assignation of blame or guilt have been constant sources of contention. Reliability of testimony, bias in reporting, difficulty in acquiring precise historical or archaeological data, even the predispositions of scholars who interpret these events, are subject to question. The authors of this volume have attempted to reconcile at least some of these. Rodseth and Novak, for example, seek to "slow down the narrative" in order to sort out the precise sequence of events—and the distance between them—at Mountain Meadows, enabling us to cast a clearer light on what happened. Johnson's mapping of the artifactual evidence at Cieneguilla performs a similar service—separating time into segments defined by the distribution of the event's empirical elements. These represent, in effect, human behavior frozen in time and capable of deliberative interpretation.

The topics of wartime reporting and command failures also turned out to be surprisingly and even disturbingly pertinent to our times. Daily reports from war zones throughout the world have remarkable similarities to these nineteenth-century events. Afghanistan, Croatia, Iraq, Darfur, Rwanda, Syria, Benghazi, to name only a few recent cases, have shown us that the explanation of cause and effect is often too shrouded by the pall of political and social complexity to be comprehended immediately. This ambiguity in our final understanding can be seen in the contradictory testimonies at Sand Creek, Cieneguilla, and even Mountain Meadows.

The lessons of these nineteenth-century battles and massacres are still relevant: real-time killings have causes and motivations that go beyond any fog of battle or uncontrollable ferocity. The application of historical and archaeological disciplines to untangling the contexts of contemporary social problems has much to offer as case studies in the failures of command leadership.

This untangling is perhaps the most significant role of the historian and the investigative archaeologist, as displayed in the accounts that follow. They differ less in their final interpretations than in the methods through which they try to untangle all the brambles of social complexity out of which emerge those final, violent acts.

The historian has the obligation to repeal the sometimes hysterical consensus of the immediate aftermath by revealing the layers of frustration, fear, and anger as they build up slowly in advance of—and as causal antecedents of—the events: the history of broken treaties and peremptory Indian raids in Colorado, in New Mexico, and in Texas. These are powerful social contexts that build, collectively through time, a stronger motive than any immediate incident can foster.

The archaeologist and bioarchaeologist, on the other hand, must seek to identify and evaluate evidence for the inadequacy of military or paramilitary discipline in the confrontations that pepper the historical landscape of the Southwest. The pattern of different ordnance at Sand Creek, the geographic distribution of ballistic and blunt trauma wounds at Mountain Meadows, and the dropped ammunition at Cieneguilla provide narratives analogous to those of historians in understanding these events, and every bit as poignant.

We must confess that, going into this project, we expected disagreements between the interpretations of historians and archaeologists to dominate the dialogue. We anticipated that conflicts between the documentary and archaeological record would characterize much of the data. We found quite the opposite. This prevalence of interpretive agreement may be due to a tendency for dispassionate investigation to minimize subjective bias. It may also be due in part to the role of time's passage in changing the nature of objectivity itself.

NOTES

1. Eisley 1973:23.
2. Krakauer 2004:xxii.
3. McMurtry 2005:6.

The Battle of Cieneguilla

Commentary

Frances Levine

Cieneguilla may not be a battle that has seared its way into the American psyche, as have those at Sand Creek and Little Bighorn. But it ought to have been so. In this section, the Battle of Cieneguilla emerges from the obscurity of our history as an object lesson about the ultimate value of knowing the truth, however difficult it may be to determine and however long it takes to emerge.

Will Gorenfeld sets out the chronology of events that led to and followed from the battle, which took place on a steep-sided ridge in the Rio Grande drainage, near Taos, New Mexico Territory, on March 30, 1854. The historical record allows us to slow the events, to lay out the tactics and decisions that officers took in planning and responding to what they understood as provocation by Jicarilla Apaches. Deeper than that, we see how the preconceptions and prejudices among the officers about the Jicarilla people led them to underestimate their opponents. Gorenfeld steps back from the immediate events of the day to show how U.S. Army training and equipment contributed to the incompetence of the battle tactics. But ultimately it was poor command leadership that sealed the fate of the troopers killed that day. Lt. John W. Davidson of the 1st U.S. Army Dragoons produced the official record of the battle. His inflated and inaccurate report of the battle fueled national reaction against the Jicarilla people and led to more drastic positions in U.S. Indian policy. Ultimately, the Jicarillas were defeated in strategies as well as in spirit. But through Gorenfeld's skillful assembling of contemporaneous sources and later reflections on the battle, we gain insight into the way that the close bonds among officers obscured the official reports of the battle. "Mistakes were made, but reputations were preserved," might be one way to characterize the official reporting about Cieneguilla. And those same official reports preserved reputations for generations.

Dave Johnson's archaeological mapping of the ridgetop Jicarilla village, the steep sides of the battle area, the dismount location of the dragoons, and the troops' retreat path make the actions of the battle and the understanding of how these locations and logistics contributed to the day's fatalities nearly palpable. Archaeological sites formed by temporary uses, like an Apache campsite, often do not have much left in terms of structures, and no deep deposits that warrant archaeological excavation. In recent years, archaeologists have applied intensive mapping strategies to the recovery of archaeological information. The pattern of refuse disposal visible on campsites and battlefields leads to a surprisingly deep understanding of the actions that took place in the pitch of battle. In the case of Cieneguilla, even 150 years after the battle, the surface of the site is protected by its land use as a National Forest, in an area that was fortunately not logged or crossed by a roadway.

Johnson isolates the action of each side in the battle by mapping the Jicarilla and military artifacts separately. In each case, these distribution patterns show us intentional decisions and, perhaps, the unintended results of the participants' responses in battle. When the artifact distribution patterns are plotted and combined in a map, they create an idea of the fury and panic that must have set in as the battle raged throughout the day and the number of dead on both sides mounted.

If only the participants knew what lay ahead for them, as we do from the distance of time. With the added perspective of more objective reports, and the details of the archaeological evidence, perhaps the army command would have altered its decisions and actions. Then again, maybe not. Lt. David Bell tried to raise the issues of Davidson's inflated reports during a subsequent court of inquiry and was denied the opportunity to participate in the inquiry by his superiors. Bell accused Davidson of trying to "transform an unskillful attack, a feeble resistance, a disorderly and disastrous flight" into a glorious triumph. Others knew about the drunkenness of army troops and the disasters of judgment and decorum that drunken officers swirled into the crucible of the American frontier. Failures such as those at Cieneguilla were made over and over in nineteenth-century Indian wars. If the truth were known at the time, perhaps this failure of leadership would have been corrected the next time and altered the course that led to the often-disastrous engagements between nineteenth-century army commanders and Indian tribes. Failures of leadership continue to be a part of the records of command in more recent events as well, perhaps pleading a cause for a greater place for historical perspectives in the training of present and future leaders.

The Historical Record

Will Gorenfeld

A contemptuous opinion of the prowess of these ferocious prairie Indians has been generally entertained by those who knew nothing about the matter—a consequence, probably, of the thousand exaggerated stories which Western adventurers have told of their own feats, and of the cowardly and thieving propensities of the savages.

—*New York Times, May 24, 1854*

For more than 150 years historians have accepted the U.S. Army's official explanation of a battle that took place north of Santa Fe, New Mexico Territory, in which a small band of Jicarilla Apaches killed or wounded nearly all of a patrol of sixty dragoons. The responsible commander, 1st Lt. John W. Davidson, spun the March 30, 1854, fiasco as a heroic escape, claiming to have survived an attack by a group much larger than the one he had actually encountered. Appalled, a fellow officer accused Davidson of trying "to transform an unskillful attack, a feeble resistance, [and] a disastrous flight . . . [into] a glorious triumph." To clear his name, Davidson requested an army court of inquiry. Two years after the fight, the board of inquiry acquitted him of blame for the near-massacre of his men, concluding that he "could not under the circumstances, with honor have avoided the battle . . . [and] . . . exhibited skill in his mode of attacking a superior force of hostile Indians." Reliance by generations of historians on the board of inquiry's finding resulted in a succession of inaccurate accounts of the battle.

The evidence of what actually happened lay quietly reposed beneath the soil of the battle site, below the sands of a ridgeline in the Sangre de Cristo Mountains of northern New Mexico. Then, in 2002, a detailed survey map of the site produced by archaeologist Dave Johnson of the U.S. Forest Service refuted the widely accepted accounts of the battle.[1] A truthful picture emerges when Johnson's findings are combined with a reevaluation of flawed primary sources: the army's self-serving government reports; inaccurate newspaper articles; and subjective, confused, or biased personal accounts. It is now clear that Lieutenant Davidson disobeyed orders, permitted many of his men to become intoxicated, placed his command in tactically unsound positions, and allowed his force to be routed by one smaller than his own, resulting in a significant defeat of the frontier army.

Fear and Loathing in the Sangre de Cristo Mountains

Some inexperienced people have charged Indians with possessing less courage than white men. There was never a greater mistake.

—Percival Lowe, *Five Years a Dragoon and Other Adventures on the Great Plains*

Between the fourteenth and sixteenth centuries, the Jicarillas migrated from Canada with other Athabascan Apaches and settled in the plains region of the American Southwest. Driven from the plains by the Comanches, by 1850 they numbered about eight hundred members in six scattered bands, loosely organized into two groups living in northern New Mexico: the agricultural Olleros of the Sangre de Cristo Mountains, and the Llaneros, hunter-gatherers of the plains.[2] United by a common language, Jicarilla bands were semiautonomous, their leaders acquiring influence "through skill and wisdom."[3]

After the conquest of the New Mexico Territory by the United States in 1846, territorial governor Charles Bent disdainfully described the Jicarillas as an "indolent and cowardly people, living principally by thefts committed on the Mexicans." The lack of adequate game in their lands, together with their fear of powerful tribes on the plains, prevented the Jicarillas from securing sufficient food.[4] Forced by American settlers off their hunting grounds, they had become dependent on federal food subsidies and stealing cattle.[5]

In 1852, Indian agent John Greiner described the Jicarillas as "very poor, very hard to govern, and from their continually roving through the settlements, there is danger to be apprehended from collisions between them and the citizens."[6] On December 4, 1852, however, Secretary of War Charles M. Conrad proudly reported to Congress that Indian violence in the territory had ended. He wrote that the Navajos and Apaches were "completely overawed, and manifest every desire to be at peace with the whites."[7] The Santa Fe *Gazette* chimed in with the observation that this was the "first year of peace this unfortunate section of the country has enjoyed for more than a period of a quarter century—its continuance is a fit subject of Hope, but not of faith."[8] Owing, in part, to the peace, the U.S. Army presence in central and northern New Mexico Territory was comparatively light, with only 760 soldiers in the region and many officers absent.[9]

When the Department of Indian Affairs halted the provision of food in 1854, the Jicarillas were left with no option but to resume the theft of cattle.[10] Raids and violence intensified, and an outcry for punishment was heard from settlers. 2nd Lt. David Bell, commanding a troop of 2nd U.S. Dragoons, was ordered to intercept Jicarilla raiders reported to be raiding near the headwaters of the Cimarron River in northeastern New Mexico. On March 5, 1854, Bell encountered Llanero warriors led by Lobo Blanco. It was widely believed in the territory that Lobo Blanco and his band were responsible for numerous outrages including the notorious murders in 1849 of the James White party.[11] When Bell moved to arrest Blanco, a fight broke out. The bloodshed cost the lives of Blanco, four tribesmen, and two dragoons.[12] In retaliation on the following day, Jicarillas raided cattle and slew two herdsmen.

White and Hispanic settlers of New Mexico mistakenly mistook the act for an uprising by all Jicarillas.[13] Kit Carson, the Indian subagent in Taos, sought to calm tempers by holding a council with Ollero leaders. They told him that they wanted no violence, that their band had not attacked Bell but feared whites would punish them for hunting. Carson was familiar with the tensions besetting the famished band and pleaded in a March 27 letter to Governor W. S. Messervy to trust the Apaches to "become quiet and contented" if supplied with food.[14] Carson then headed to Santa Fe to meet with Messervy and obtain the much needed wheat and corn.

The Olleros, alarmed by army patrols in nearby valleys, moved their encampment. Maj. George A. H. Blake sent his troops on what turned out to be a clumsy effort to capture a quartet of Ollero leaders, but the tribesmen fled.[15] Slipping into the mountains, the Olleros awaited Carson's return. The fleeing by the Jicarillas convinced Blake that the Olleros were joining other bands in a general uprising.

It is here that Lt. John W. Davidson enters the story. On March 21, 1854, he boasted to his fellow officers at Fort Union that, having recently encountered Jicarilla Apache warriors on the trail, he pronounced them "overwhelmed by fear" at the sight of his dragoons. Davidson observed that, having bows along with a few obsolete firearms, they were puny opponents and, had there been pretext, he would have "wiped them out." Another officer knew better. Lt. David Bell, recently touted in the territory as defeating Lobo Blanco's "daring band of outlaws," called the Jicarillas "not cowardly, to say the least." Disastrously for Davidson's command, Bell's insights would be ignored.[16]

Davidson was ordered by Major Blake to find the Olleros, "control their movement," and prevent them from fleeing west across the Rio Grande. Blake instructed Davidson to avoid a fight. That some soldiers were issued as little as twenty rounds of musketoon ammunition suggests that Blake anticipated no battle.[17]

Davidson's past had included little combat experience but he, nonetheless, clung to a view shared by most officers: a well-armed force of regulars led by a West Point officer was certain to defeat "primitive" Indians. Descended from a line of officers, he had graduated in 1845 from the U.S. Military Academy at West Point, New York.[18] While attached to Brig. Gen. Stephen W. Kearny's Army of the West in August 1846, Davidson had participated in the "bloodless" conquest of Santa Fe, and he later fought Californios (early Spanish-speaking residents of California) at the Battle of San Pascual.[19] It was in California that Davidson and Carson filched Californio horses and formed a friendship that would serve the young officer well. In 1850, Davidson participated in a massacre of a Pomo village at Clear

Lake in northern California.[20] After serving a year as regimental adjutant at Fort Leavenworth, Lt. Davidson was ordered to report to take field command of Company I, 1st Dragoons, at Cantonment Burgwin.[21] Because of his longevity in the service as a senior first lieutenant, he expected the army to promote him soon to the rank of captain.[22]

Davidson's orders to find the Olleros offered a chance to escape the tedium of garrison duty and, possibly, to cover himself in glory by capturing their village.[23] A few hours after departure, as if anticipating a fight, he requested reinforcements and a surgeon. Major Blake complied by sending Asst. Surgeon David Magruder, Corp. John Davis, and fifteen troopers from Company F.[24] After a fifteen-mile ride down the wagon road to Santa Fe, the troops paused the night in Cieneguilla—a village consisting of a Catholic chapel and some scattered ranchos.[25] While most of the dragoons slept, scouts scoured the banks of the Rio Grande for signs of a crossing by the Jicarillas.[26]

The dragoon of 1854 was an arsenal on horseback. Secured by a leather sling over his left shoulder hung a .69-caliber Springfield musketoon—a percussion muzzle-loading, smooth-bore carbine. In his pommel holster was either a single-shot Model 1842 percussion horse pistol in .54 caliber or a .44 Colt Dragoon revolver.[27] The foot-long horse pistol was wildly inaccurate, and it was said that "in practicing marksmanship it was never wise to choose for a mark anything smaller than a good sized barn."[28] The Dragoon revolver was clumsy to use and not very accurate, but its ability to fire six shots rapidly made it a prized weapon. From his buff belt the dragoon carried a heavy saber derisively known as a "wrist breaker," a purse-size leather cartridge box, and a small pouch of percussion caps. Slung over his right shoulder was a haversack for rations and a wooden canteen. Attempting to mount or skirmish on foot in rugged terrain while encumbered by all of this unwieldy weaponry and equipage, especially while under fire, was daunting.[29]

Stylish new uniforms patterned on a French design had been adopted by army brass in 1851, but the men stationed in New Mexico were still being issued surplus uniforms from the Mexican War. Most of the men had spent much of their time in the West at work building military posts and, since ammunition was scarce, the troops did not take target practice.[30]

The Rio Grande flows from snow packs high in the Rocky Mountains of Colorado, enters the northeast corner of New Mexico, and courses south across the middle of what is now the state before sharply turning southeast toward Texas.[31] Near Cieneguilla the river's deep gorge made for few crossings; one was nearby in the village of Embudo, about forty miles north of Santa Fe.

On March 30, 1854, standing amid a sparse forest and large boulders, civilian scout Jesus Silva and dragoon Jeremiah Maloney, of Cantonment Burgwin, searched the predawn darkness for traces of Jicarillas. All was silent save the gushing of the brisk mountain waters slicing through the chasm and the occasional shriek of a nighthawk. Looking to the northeast, Silva and Maloney spotted campfires twinkling brightly atop a ridgeline of the Embudo Mountains on the eastern side of the Rio Grande. Suspecting they had found the Jicarillas, the two men rode back to alert Davidson.

Half a League, Half a League Onward: The Advance through the Gorge

Of all arms, cavalry is the most difficult to handle in the field. It cannot engage the enemy except where the ground is favorable.

—*Louis Nolan, Cavalry: Its History and Tactics*

On the morning of March 30, 1854, Kit Carson met in Santa Fe with acting governor William S. Messervy to obtain food for the Olleros. Later in the day Major Blake, confident that Davidson had the Olleros well in hand, paid an unofficial visit to St. Vrain's mill, located a few miles north of the cantonment, to sample some of the liquid spirits there.[32] In the early morning Davidson's dragoons broke camp and traveled about a mile north on the Santa Fe–Taos trail, along the east side of the Rio Grande, then turned eastward to enter a narrow and winding gorge carved by the waters of Agua Caliente Creek.

As historian Victor David Hanson observed, "Mountainous terrain is the haunt of herdsmen who with slings, bows and javelins master the arts of ambush and guarding routes of transit."[33] Inspector general George McCall reported in 1850 that the Taos Valley region, "as a base of operations of a strong cavalry force against either the Utahs or Jicarilla Apaches . . . has nothing to recommend it; but, on the contrary many obstacles of serious character interpose themselves among the surrounding mountains."[34] Two years later, John Greiner, an Indian agent in New Mexico, wrote, "A dragoon mounted will weigh 225 pounds. Their horses are all as poor as carrion. The Indians have nothing but their bows and arrows and their ponies are as fleet as deer. Cipher it up. Heavy dragoons on poor horses, who know nothing of the county, sent after Indians who are at home any where and who always have some hours start, how long will it take to catch them?"[35] In 1853, Lt. Col. Edwin Sumner, the commanding officer of New Mexico Territory, recommended the withdrawal of all regular troops from the region, and, if any federal force remain, that it not include any mounted troops.[36]

Recall that Davidson's orders were to locate the Jicarillas and keep them from crossing the Rio Grande. This order might have easily been accomplished had he sent some of his men to approach the suspected encampment from the south and leave the bulk of his force to block the crossing of the river. Instead, Davidson decided to lead his entire command into a narrow canyon and to approach the village from the north. Like a stethoscope, the gorge echoed the clatter of iron-shod hooves, rattling of weaponry, and clank of tin cups, plates and implements. Miles away villagers heard it, denying Davidson the element of surprise. In all likelihood he was obsessed with the worry, as were most officers of the period, that the tribesmen would run away.[37] Davidson could not have been more mistaken, for as the first rays of sunlight warmed the hilltop the Jicarillas were not taking flight but making plans to defend the village. The narrowing chasm further limited Davidson's tactical options, forcing the dragoons to ride single file. Had the Jicarillas planned an ambush, this would have been the perfect place for it.

Corp. Richard Byrnes rode cautiously ahead of the troop with a detachment of six men. He soon located the Jicarilla camp, perched on a bluff a hundred feet above the south wall of the canyon, and reported back to Lieutenant Davidson. It was now eight o'clock in the morning, and as the soldiers neared the village they heard war chants. Sgt. William Holbrook, a seasoned Mexican War veteran, turned in his saddle and exclaimed, "Look out men, that is a war whoop and we've got to fight."[38] Having found the village, Davidson might have had his command turn around and leave terrain too steep and rocky for crossing on horseback. Instead, he marched his men southward into a small hollow and halted the troop. From the southern ridge, a tribesman taunted in English: "Come on up if you want to fight."[39] Here was the provocation Davidson had longed for—now he could "wipe them out." In Davidson's official report he wrote, "There was but one thing to do," having been challenged. "I . . . attacked."[40]

Disregarding both orders to avoid combat and prudent military tactics, Davidson barked out the order to dismount and prepare to fight on foot. Tying their horses to trees, the troops formed ranks. A small detachment consisting of about fifteen men and Dr. Magruder remained behind to guard the horses. First Sergeant Holbrook's platoon of about twenty men advanced southward up the wooded slope. Sgt. William Kent's twenty men formed to the left of Holbrook and pressed forward uphill to attack the right flank of the village.[41] Attacking on foot uphill over broken terrain put the dragoons at a decided disadvantage: their advance was slowed by the incline, slippery soil, weight of weapons, and the ability of the Jicarillas to fire down on them. The dragoons were trained to fight on foot as skirmishers, but what remains baffling is Davidson's mounted advance into the narrow gorge, leaving his command open to ambush, and then the dismounting of it, thus sacrificing the raison d'etre of a mounted force: shock and mobility.[42] Moreover, Davidson necessarily reduced his skirmish-line firepower by 25 percent when he deployed fifteen men to guard the horses. Some troopers, no longer close to their horses, likely worried about the prospect of retreat as they got moved away from their mounts and closer to the enemy.

If Davidson's tactic of attacking uphill with a mounted force in mountainous terrain was flawed, so was his weaponry. A dragoon relied chiefly on his musketoon, a carbine with an effective range of less than sixty yards. This meant that a dragoon was unlikely to wound an attacker who fired at him from a distance of more than 75 or so yards. Inspector general Joseph Mansfield reported in 1854 that the musketoon presented "no probable certainty of hitting the object aimed at, and the recoil is too great to be fired with ease," and concluded that the weapon was "a worthless arm" that had "no advocates that [he was] aware of."[43] This weapon had only recently been issued to the dragoons, and its defects would contribute to a series of defeats.[44]

The effectiveness of Davidson's forces may have been impaired by another factor: alcohol. If the abuse of alcohol was a major problem among soldiers out west, the problem was especially acute among Company F.[45] Major Blake had a keen fondness for spirits and Maj. Philip Thompson, nearly incapacitated by drink, would be soon cashiered for his drunkenness.[46] It was not unusual for troops in this region to fill their canteens with liquor.[47] A young Jicarilla later recalled seeing, prior to the fight, the dragoons pass "about their canteens and drink whiskey, becoming drunk."[48] Although no other mention is made of the possibility of drunkenness, on this cold March morning it would not be remarkable for many troopers to have consumed a sizable amount of whiskey before and during the fight.

The advanced elements awkwardly trudged up the slope at a near crawl.[49] Reaching the crest, the troopers caught their breath as they viewed the encampment. Unlike the teepees of the Great Plains, the Jicarilla homes were domed wikiups, covered with bark and thatch, or with skins in cold weather.[50] Sgt. William Kent formed his platoon into a ragged line and charged. Scattered shots rang from the village, killing him. The dragoons replied with an uneven volley that struck a few Jicarillas.[51] Within the space of two minutes the attackers were in control of the village, which they began to plunder as others tied Sergeant Kent's lifeless body to the back of a mule.[52] Davidson must have been pleased with what seemed an easy victory and anticipated a return to the fort with news of a glorious success and the opportunity to outshine Lieutenant Bell.

Counterattack

> In defensive warfare [cavalry] has seldom achieved great deeds, for to act a passive part in war is contrary to the spirit of Cavalry Tactics.
>
> —*Louis Nolan, Cavalry: Its History and Tactics*

Hearing shots and shouts from below, Davidson discovered that the Jicarillas had set upon his horse holders. His only choice was to order his men out of the village and down the slope to protect the horses.[53] Reaching the bottom of the hill, he formed his men into an elliptical skirmish line around the horses. Taking cover behind boulders and trees, the dragoons fired away with musketoons and pistols at small groups of warriors who dashed at them or fired from concealment.[54]

The army manual described the loading of the musketoon in ten distinct steps. At the command of "load," the butt of the weapon was placed under the trooper's right arm, the hammer half cocked while the left hand took a percussion cap from the cap box. The brass percussion cap, measuring a quarter inch in diameter, was placed on the nipple located under the hammer, and then pressed down. Next, a cigar-shaped paper cartridge was taken from the cartridge box and the trooper, using his teeth, tore it open. At the command of "cast about," the musketoon was brought to vertical position and the content of the cartridge was poured into the barrel. The swiveled ramrod was drawn from its slot under the barrel and "smartly" used to push the powder and bullet down the barrel. The ramrod was returned to its slot under the barrel, then the weapon was raised to a ready position awaiting the command to fire.[55]

When attempting to load under the confusing and terrifying conditions of combat, adhering to the ten-step loading routine was no easy task. Nervous and sweating fingers fumbled to draw a tiny percussion cap from the cap box, and placing it on the nipple resulted in many dropped caps. A shaking right hand attempting to pour the powder and ball of the cartridge into a barrel held by a left trembling hand, without exposing the shooter to enemy fire, could be also be daunting. Returning the swiveled rod under the barrel required a steady hand lest the swivel be broken and ramrod lost when an alarmed soldier madly attempted to return it. Less than a year prior to Cieneguilla, Inspector general Mansfield observed that a dragoon armed with a musketoon would be apprehensive because "it takes so long to load; he loses his ramrod, or his load out; he gets disconcerted and will probably be whipped if hard pressed."[56]

Most frustrating to the troops were Jicarilla archers positioned beyond the reach of the musketoons, who dispatched a "shower of arrows" down into the soldiers' defensive formation.[57] George McGunnegle, Davidson's brother-in-law who accompanied the expedition, wrote of the counterattack, "They commenced firing upon us, every shot taking effect either upon the horses or men."[58] Deftly darting from all sides and behind trees and boulders, their war hoops echoing off canyon walls, the Jicarillas gave the impression of superior numbers. Davidson would later report that he had encountered three hundred warriors. Estimations, however, by Carson and later by archaeologists concluded that Davidson's command met fewer than one hundred warriors that day.[59] The troops wasted their ammunition firing at elusive targets, flitting back and forth out of the dense cloud of gray gun smoke permeating the hollow, but it took some time for them to realize they were losing the battle. When trooper James Strawbridge asked Sergeant Holbrook whether he ought to remove the saddle from his dying horse, the veteran replied, "Wait until we whip the Indians and then it will be enough time to take the kits off of the dead horses."[60] Their limited supply of ammunition would not last long in a protracted firefight, and after an hour of fighting the ammunition was almost exhausted.

The ground was "strewn with arrows," nerves were wracked, and fatigue set in from the constant climbing, dodging, running, and fighting.[61] Peter Weldon, a soldier from Philadelphia, said that at this stage of the battle he "could stand up no longer."[62] By now the Jicarillas had wounded several men and killed two, and the bodies of several horses lay on the ground. With each casualty, each lost mount, and each spent cartridge, the dragoons became ever more impotent as a combat force.

Mount and Save Yourself

This order was calculated to strike terror to heart of the bravest soldier, for he would know that nothing but the utmost exertion could prevent his falling a prey to the merciless savage.

—*David Bell to Lt. Robert Williams, December 27, 1854*

Although never having seen combat out west, brother-in-law McGunnegle knew "we were in so bad a place that the Indians had great advantage of us."[63] Davidson and Holbrook consulted and decided their defensive position was untenable. Just then a rifle ball narrowly missed their faces and struck a tree behind them. The lieutenant ordered: "Mount and save yourself."[64] Bugler Henry McGrath brought up Lieutenant Davidson's horse and the troops mounted. With the loss of several mounts, some dragoons were forced to ride two to a saddle. Firing their Colt Dragoon revolvers and single-shot Aston horse pistols to good effect, a vanguard led the men out of the hollow. Five dead or dying soldiers were left behind.[65]

The command stopped briefly about 150 yards north of its original position.[66] Deciding that this was not a good defensible position, the troop splashed pell-mell across the shallow stream and headed up a steep embankment at the opposite side of the canyon. The Jicarillas did not appear to be following, and for the moment the battle seemed over. Halfway up the hill, trooper George Breenwald of Company F, seriously wounded, could no longer ride and pleaded, "Please don't leave me." Davidson ordered a halt to allow the soldiers to catch their breath, reload weapons, redistribute ammunition, tighten the cinches of the saddles, and allow the doctor to treat Breenwald, who, within moments, bled to death.[67] With difficulty, the dragoons gained the top of the ridge. The column of fifty-four men, many of them walking, moved along the ridgeline for about eight hundred yards and then, hoping to travel back through the canyon to Cieneguilla, descended from the ridge.[68]

In most victories over whites attempting to attack their villages, American Indians warriors were content to not pursue a defeated enemy, their basic tactical objective to repel an aggressor having been attained. To pursue meant to risk more deaths. And unlike the army, which could quickly replenish its manpower with eastern recruits, the tribes (Apaches in this case) could not replace fallen warriors. Each warrior, moreover, was vital as hunter, provider, and progenitor. Indeed, the very notion of a massed frontal attack—as in the Civil War—made no sense to Indians. On the other hand, when an enemy had been so thoroughly vanquished that further glory was in reach without risk of additional injury and where their casualties had been light, they would try to wipe out remaining survivors, as in the defeats of Lt. John Grattan (1854), Capt. William Fetterman (1866), and Lt. Col. George Custer (1876).[69] At Cieneguilla, the dragoons' command structure was badly broken and the men had depleted their ammunition; the troops were ripe for extermination.

As a rule, troops tend to bunch together on a battlefield. "Remaining close to comrades in combat is reportedly more important to the individual than avoiding enemy fire, and men will move through danger to be with their fellows rather than remain alone."[70] Officers and noncommissioned officers are responsible for seeing that the troops maintain their proper intervals between one another on the skirmish line.[71] Davidson had only two or three noncommissioned officers capable of exercising command— one NCO for each seventeen troopers—too few to prevent the tired, frightened men from bunching. As the troops attempted to descend the ridge, the Jicarillas attacked from all sides.[72] Under the command of Sergeant Holbrook, some soldiers scraped together a few rounds of ammunition and deployed as skirmishers to effect a series of rear-guard deployments. The Jicarilla warriors, safely positioned beyond the short range of dragoon firearms, continued to unleash volleys of arrows at the besieged dragoons. Silhouetted against the sky on a 25-foot-wide ridgeline and all but without ammunition, the troops were easy targets. It was at this stage of the battle that Davidson lost seventeen men.

Archaeologist Dave Johnson, nearly 150 years later, discovered the line of retreat, evidenced by piecing together bits and pieces of dropped bullets, spilled percussion caps, arrowheads, and other items, and concluded "that the soldiers were likely weary if not frantic during the push down the narrow ridge."[73] The soldiers fought desperately to escape the trap. When an arrow struck his right arm, trooper Weldon could fire his pistol only with his left hand.[74] All the while remaining cool, Davidson galloped along the line to rally his weary and panicked men, but an arrow struck him in the shoulder, and he fell wounded from his horse. Corp. Benjamin Dempsey promptly pulled the arrow out, only to be hit in the leg with a musket ball and then to lose a portion of his thumb to another shot. Dempsey somehow survived.[75]

His luck running out, Sergeant Holbrook was struck by two arrows, the shaft of one so deeply lodged that only the fletches could be seen. The sergeant faintly cried out, "I am shot and cannot go any further on foot." Weakened from the heavy loss of blood, he begged trooper Strawbridge to bring up his horse. While attempting to place his foot in the stirrup, the gallant Holbrook fell backward and died.[76]

Seeing their veteran sergeant dead, panicked dragoons searched for ammunition by madly spilling cartridge boxes of fallen comrades; others ran away.[77] A rifle ball, fired from below the ridge, entered the fleshy left thigh of Pvt. James Bronson and lodged in his right thigh near the groin. He attempted to run for his life but fainted from the extreme pain and loss of blood. Regaining consciousness, Bronson seized in each hand a stirrup of the saddles of two retreating troopers who dragged him for a half mile to safety.[78] The location of the bodies and artifacts unearthed by archaeologists reveal that most of the dragoon casualties occurred on this ridgeline.[79]

With forty-five of their sixty horses lost, the survivors—most without weapons and ammunition, virtually all wounded—walked, staggered, or rode two men to a horse. The Jicarillas ceased to follow and, with the ford at Embudo now unguarded, they began to move their village west across the river. It was midday when the first dragoon stragglers reached the relative safety of the settlement of Cieneguilla slightly over a mile from the battlefield on the ridge. Davidson promptly dispatched one of the few unwounded dragoons to Cantonment Burgwin with a request for help. Major Blake, spending this fine Thursday imbibing at St. Vrain's mill, hastily assembled a rescue party of twenty soldiers, a few civilians, and Pueblo Indians from Taos. Reaching Cieneguilla, they found the line of retreat strewn with the scattered bodies of seventeen men and abandoned equipage.[80] The searchers claimed to have discovered the bodies of nine dead Jicarillas on the battlefield.[81]

Although the Jicarillas had stripped the dead dragoons of clothes and equipment, they had scalped none. Kit Carson reasoned that, because they had received heavy casualties in the battle, their custom militated against any scalping.⁸² There was, however, a general prohibition among Jicarillas against taking scalps of vanquished enemies.⁸³

In terms of casualties, Cieneguilla was the worst defeat ever suffered by the 1st U.S. Dragoons. Twenty-four dragoons were killed in this action and another twenty-three wounded. A disproportionate number of wounded and dead were from Company F—all sixteen of them, largely recruits.⁸⁴

Lieutenant Davidson reported that his force had confronted 250–300 warriors and had killed fifty to sixty of them. Kit Carson opined that "the number of Indians who fell has never been ascertained, but there is no doubt that many of them were slain."⁸⁵ Chief Chacon later reportedly told the territorial governor, "The Americans killed a chief, Pecheco, and a ball [was] cut out of the entrails of a woman, who survived. A nephew of Lobo was also killed. About fifty Indians were killed at Cieneguilla."⁸⁶ Casa Maria, age fourteen at the time of the battle, told the anthropologist Pliny Goddard in 1911 that four warriors had been killed.⁸⁷

Fate of the Victors

What of the Jicarillas? A tribe Lieutenant Davidson had characterized as "cowardly" trounced one of the U.S. Army's finest regiments, demonstrating skillful tactics and superior courage. Even hard-bitten W. H. Davis, editor of the Santa Fe *Gazette,* acknowledged that the Jicarillas had fought bravely at Cieneguilla, expressing an opinion shared by many New Mexicans.⁸⁸ Nonetheless, in an editorial in the Gazette of April 29, 1854, the newspaperman called on the army to impose on the Jicarillas the severest punishment, "even to the extent of destroying the tribe entirely." And the eastern press, oft sympathetic to native peoples, demanded that "war, vigorously prosecuted, exterminating war if necessary, should be loosed upon these bloodthirsty barbarians."⁸⁹ An editorial in the Missouri *Republican* for May 27, 1854, foolishly expressed fear that Cieneguilla was an attempt by unified bands of American Indians to isolate New Mexico, California, and Oregon. Troops, civilian volunteers, and supplies were rushed to the region to subjugate the Jicarillas.

On April 4, 1854, a strong army column under the command of Lt. Col. Philip Cooke took to the field. Chief Chacon had fled west, hoping the rugged terrain in Rio Caliente Canyon would provide his band with a measure of protection. On April 8, Cooke attacked; the troops captured the pony herd, burned the village, and killed five warriors. In his report Cooke made special note of "the handsome charge of Lieutenant Bell, in which the superior instruction and discipline of his company seconded him well," and commended Bell's "second distinguished service under my orders, to the most favorable consideration."[90] A reporter wrote that fleeing Jicarilla "women and children were drowned in crossing a river, which was much swollen and ran with a rapid current."[91] In a letter of April 12, 1854, the ever-adaptable Kit Carson complained bitterly to acting governor Messervy that the Jicarillas had been "driven into war, by the action of officers & troops in that quarter."[92] Regardless of the injustice of the conflict, the flexible Carson believed chastisement of the tribe was in order and continued to scout for the army.[93]

Davidson quickly recovered from his shoulder wound. Within weeks of Cieneguilla, the battered Companies F and I were again taking the field in search of the even more battered Jicarilla fugitives—from Raton Pass down to the Pecos River country above Anton Chico.[94] By the end of June, Gen. John Garland proclaimed that the Jicarillas had been "most thoroughly humbled and beg for peace." This was far from the case.[95] In late December, Davidson's worn-out company had chased fugitive Jicarillas into southern New Mexico and staggered into Ft. Fillmore, the troops "destitute of clothing, the horse's appointments barely serviceable."[96] The war continued for another year, but one by one the scattered Jicarilla bands surrendered, dispossessed of their land and impoverished to starvation. Two years after Cieneguilla, Carson wrote that the Jicarillas had "experienced much suffering from the cold weather . . . and they are indeed in a very destitute condition."[97]

In 1873 the tribe was exiled to the Mescalero Apache Reservation in southeastern New Mexico.[98] A large number of starving Jicarillas, longing for their ancestral homeland, escaped from the reservation and returned there.[99] The tribe did not gain its own federal reservation until 1887.[100] Later years would witness the Jicarillas, though ravaged by the effects of bureaucratic indifference, poverty, and disease, pursuing their fight in the federal courts to gain legal redress against the government, preserving their culture, and securing a measure of financial independence for their members.[101]

Post-Battle Recriminations and Whistle Blowing

On April 1, 1854, two days after the battle at Cieneguilla, General Garland launched a preemptive attack in the media to douse criticism. Though the details of the battle supplied to him were "very unsatisfactory as regards particulars," the general mistakenly reported that Davidson's company had been "unexpectedly attacked." Despite gaps in knowledge, he praised the lieutenant's gallant leadership that saved the entire command from annihilation.[102] As word of the battle reached the East Coast, however, many came to wonder how a force of dragoons, "although accounted of the finest in the service and armed and equipped in the most complete manner, were utterly defeated" by primitively armed tribesmen.[103]

The Battle of Cieneguilla also became controversial in army circles. Lt. Davidson's loss of nearly half of his men raised many an eyebrow. It is here the shadowy hand of one Lt. Col. Philip Cooke may have been fast at work. The officer corps of the antebellum army was small in number, and every officer was aware of most secrets of brother officers.[104] One of the most competent soldiers to have ever served on the plains, Cooke served with the 1st Dragoons at the formation of the regiment in 1833. Akin to most West Point educated officers, he took a dim view of the competency of officers who gained their positions through the political appointment of civilians.[105] By 1854 three of the four senior officer grades in the 1st Dragoons were occupied by men who, in 1836, had been plucked from civilian life by President Andrew Jackson and made officers. Cooke likely believed that these unworthy political hacks had taken control of what was once an elite regiment and, as the disaster at Cieneguilla proved, was evidence of such. Rather than risk harm to reputation and his military career by personally criticizing his old regiment, he may have tapped Lieutenant Bell, Cooke's protégé and adjutant, to act as his cat's paw.[106]

On December 27, 1854, Lieutenant Bell, now stationed with Lieutenant Colonel Cooke at Fort Leavenworth, Kansas Territory, wrote to a former classmate at the military academy, Lt. Robert Williams of the 1st Dragoons, and criticized Davidson's actions. Claiming to have spoken to many participants in the battle, Bell concluded that Davidson had willfully disobeyed orders when he attacked the village, had made bad tactical decisions advancing uphill against the Jicarillas, allowed his command to panic under fire, and abandoned the wounded to their fate. Bell asserted: "If he [Davidson] had been under the command of almost any officer other than [Major] Blake he would have been tried for disobedience of orders." The lack of sufficient ammunition for a protracted firefight led Bell to question Davidson's claim that the battle lasted three hours. In this regard, he pointed out that the troops carried forty rounds of carbine ammunition and "in the excitement of action most men will lose a large portion of their ammunition." Finally, Bell believed that Davidson confronted far fewer Jicarilla warriors than the three hundred he had reported and that, according to what he was able to ascertain, the Jicarillas had possibly lost as few as two warriors.[107] In short, Bell called Davidson incompetent.

Court of Inquiry

When Williams shared Bell's letter with Davidson, the latter became furious. He demanded Bell be punished for conduct unbecoming an officer. The flap led to an army court of inquiry formed to investigate the Cieneguilla fight.[108]

One function of a court of inquiry is to investigate an incident to decide whether a court-martial is warranted.[109] The army, however, needed more to protect its honor and congressional funding than to uncover the truth about Cieneguilla—which was not the only embarrassing disaster suffered by the army in 1854. Another was the annihilation of the Grattan detachment near Fort Laramie, Nebraska Territory, by Lakota Sioux.[110] Both defeats stemmed from poor judgment and incompetent leadership on the part of junior officers. Add to the mix the loss of 160 artillery recruits who were swept overboard in late December 1853 when the overloaded streamer *San Francisco* foundered off Cape Hatteras.[111] The military was also under pressure from another embarrassing incident in which, on March 8, 1855, drunken members of Company F of the 1st Dragoons mutinied against Major Blake in the Taos plaza and beat him severely.[112] Finally, owing to the fact that Davidson was the senior 1st lieutenant in the mounted arm, the army had promoted him to the rank of captain, entrusting him with the command of Company B. Thus the prescribed fact-finding objective of the court of inquiry that convened in Santa Fe in March 1856 was flawed from the onset.

Col. Edwin V. Sumner, 1st Cavalry, Lieutenant Bell's commanding officer at Ft. Leavenworth and a former officer in the 1st Dragoons who had recently commanded the Department of New Mexico, refused to allow Bell to attend the hearing. Bell wrote to Winfield Scott, the army's commanding general, requesting permission to travel to New Mexico. He pointed out that he was "the only person cognizant of some of the circumstances, asserted in the letter in question, and other statements can only be substantiated by evidence of which I am in possession, and which is not known to any person in the Dept. of New Mexico otherwise than by my written statements." The young lieutenant also feared that "an investigation by a Court of Inquiry, with but a hearing upon the side of an accuser," would undoubtedly result if favorable to Davidson, in court martial charges being brought against him instead.[113]

On March 24, 1856, General Scott requested the adjutant general to issue an order directing Bell's presence at the court of inquiry—provided that the court was still in session.[114] But the hearing had concluded before this order was delivered and no one present at the hearing attempted to investigate or substantiate Bell's criticism. The court of inquiry took its cues from Davidson, who presented virtually all the evidence and conducted almost all the questioning of witnesses. Not only did the court fail to examine Davidson, it did not deign to visit the battlefield.

Also unmentioned in the record was that, at the time of the hearing, Major Blake's military career was on the line. He had taken up lodging in Taos, where he was more attentive to attending fandangos than to reviewing troops.[115] In 1856 he was being court-martialed for absenteeism, dereliction of duty, and causing a mutiny by some members of Company F to riot and attack him.[116] Bell had quoted Major Blake as remarking after the battle, "Davidson had done as well as could be expected." Davidson had preferred charges against Blake for daring to question the lieutenant's actions at Cieneguilla and for neglecting his duties as commander of the fort, but he dismissed these charges after Blake publicly toned down his disapproval. Blake's craven testimony contradicted Bell's assertion that the major was critical of Davidson's actions at Cieneguilla and denied that Davidson's dismissal of charges had anything to do with shaping his testimony.[117] Had Bell been allowed to attend the hearing, he may have gotten the judge advocate to cross-examine the major concerning his motive for changing his critical statement of Davidson's performance.

The pro-Davidson testimony of Sgt. James Bronson (aka Bennett), formerly of Company I and recently transferred to Company B, was also suspect. At the time of the hearing Bronson had recently been promoted to the rank of sergeant by Captain Davidson. He presented testimony that Davidson had kept his men in good order through the entire battle and had conducted a fighting withdrawal. The newly minted sergeant praised the captain's calm during the battle, dismissing any assertion that there was any panic among the men or that Davidson had abandoned the wounded.[118] Bronson's favorable testimony was no doubt also influenced by the gracious conduct of Davidson's wife, who in Bronson's words was "a very beautiful St. Louis lady" who had "been very kind to me in sending me a great many little niceties" during the two months in which he had been recuperating from wounds at the Cantonment Burgwin hospital.[119] It is also important to bear in mind that Bronson rode to the hearing in the company of Davidson as well as of two members of the court of inquiry: Capt. James H. Carleton, 1st Dragoons, and Col. Benjamin L. E. Bonneville, 3d Infantry.[120] Not surprisingly, these two officers would at the court-martial, as was too often the case in military hearings, "stand by [their colleague Davidson] like pickpockets."[121]

Testimony tendered by other enlisted participants supported Davidson's account—that is, that Davidson was forced into the fight, kept his men calm throughout the fight, did not abandon the wounded, and conducted an orderly retreat. The nearly identical accounts offered by each of the enlisted participants must be viewed with suspicion; although each man had fought on a different portion of the battlefield, their testimonies had a scripted quality to them and read suspiciously similar—unusual for a group of men engaged in combat.[122]

Davidson's star character witness was his good friend Kit Carson:

> [I am] intimately acquainted with Lieutenant Davidson and have been in engagements with him where he has taken a prominent part and can testify that he is as brave and discreet as it is possible for a man to be. Nearly every person engaged in and who survived that day's bloody battle had since told me that his commanding officer never once sought shelter, but stood manfully exposed to the aim of the Indians, encouraging his men and apparently entirely unmindful of his own life. It was, however, in the retreat they say that he acted

the most gallantly, for, when everything was going badly with the soldiers, he was as cool and collected as if under the guns of his fort. The only anxiety he exhibited was for the safety of his remaining men."[123]

Carson was not, however, cross-examined about having a motive to shade his version of the battle, being dependent as he was on the good graces of local army officers for scouting assignments.

On March 25 the court found Captain Davidson blameless. It concluded that he "could not under the circumstances, with honor have avoided the battle . . . [and] in the battle he exhibited skill in his mode of attacking a greatly superior force of hostile Indians."[124] The court's decision avoided the questions of Davidson's failure to follow orders and his poor tactical decisions.

Exit Dramatis Personae, Enter the Archaeologists

Sgt. James Bronson deserted the army soon after giving testimony at the court of inquiry. He avoided capture for desertion by traveling through the Mexican state of Chihuahua and ultimately returned to New York. He then (as Bennett) pursued the study of medicine and later honorably served as a surgeon with the Union Army.[125] Sergeant Strawbridge soldiered on with the 1st Dragoons for another six years. In 1859, while stationed with Company B at Fort Tejon, California, he wearied of army life and deserted.[126] Corp. Richard Byrnes, an Irish-born tough from the streets of New York, would survive his Cieneguilla arrow wound, only to fall at the battle of Cold Harbor, as colonel of the 28th Massachusetts Infantry.[127] George Blake, although later convicted by a court-martial panel for being one of the causes of the Taos mutiny of 1855, would be restored to duty, by General Garland, be promoted to the rank of colonel of the 1st Dragoons in 1861, fight with that regiment in the Civil War, and retire in 1870 as a colonel.[128] Surgeon David Magruder continued to serve with the army, performing heroically as a physician at Bull Run in 1861 and ultimately retiring in 1889 with the rank of colonel.[129]

Shortly after Lieutenant Bell's victory over Lobo Blanco, the Santa Fe *Weekly Gazette* wrote in glowing terms of his bravery, concluding, "If we had the matter in our own hands, he would be Capt. Bell tomorrow."[130] But this talented officer would never gain promotion to the rank of captain. Soon after writing his controversial letter, Bell had gained a first lieutenant's commission in the newly formed 1st Cavalry and participated in several skirmishes on the plains. In December 1860 he died while on recruiting duty at Fortress Monroe, Virginia.[131] Brevet Major General Cooke observed that Bell's "early death was a great loss to the whole service."[132] Criticism of the official account of the battle virtually ceased with Bell's death.[133]

In the weeks following the battle, one enlisted man described Lieutenant Davidson as acting as a petty despot. Specifically, Pvt. John Hutchinson complained that Davidson refused to obey the court decree ordering Hutchinson's release from duty. In retaliation for petitioning the court, the lieutenant accused Hutchinson of destroying company muster rolls and placed him in confinement.[134] Later years found Davidson a troubled soul, described by an enlisted man as being "a strict disciplinarian" who was "able though erratic . . . an opium and morphine eater under the strict leadership of his wife."[135] On the positive side, John W. Davidson's attitude toward American Indians would soften. In 1859, while pursuing cattle rustlers in California, Davidson determined that the falsely accused Paiute tribe was innocent of stealing livestock and concluded that they were "deserving of the watchful care & protection of our Government."[136]

In the Civil War, Davidson earned honors for heroism and gained the temporary rank of brigadier general. With war's end, he became lieutenant colonel of an African American regiment of cavalry, an assignment often rejected by most white officers for fear that it would hamper promotion. In 1879, Black Jack Davidson was promoted to the rank of colonel of the 2nd Cavalry. Two years later he died from injuries suffered when a horse he was riding fell on him.[137]

Archaeologist David Johnson's analysis of the battlefield site led him to agree with Bell's estimation that the number of warriors facing Davidson's unit was less than 130.[138] There may have been even fewer warriors than estimated by Johnson, and from what we know of their reported malnourishment these warriors were not likely in top form. Johnson also found the route of retreat littered with numerous dropped musket balls, unfired percussion caps, and other equipment. The archaeological evidence supports Bell's accusation that the Jicarillas entrapped the dragoons as they retreated along the ridgeline, shattering the discipline, cohesion, and combat effectiveness of Davidson's force. Johnson concluded that, contrary to all contemporary army reports, the troops, virtually out of ammunition, panicked on the ridge and were soundly routed by the Jicarillas.[139]

On a dreary December day in 1849, slightly over four years before the Battle of Cieneguilla, Sgt. William Kronig was busily copying an official account of his detachment's flawed attack of a Jicarilla village. He recalled, "I copied it and to my surprise I read of the wonders we had performed. The report went on to say that there were fifty-two Indians killed, and the balance of the two tribes frozen to death in the snowstorm. While at work on the report, Colonel [Benjamin] Beall stepped into the office and asked what I thought of it. I replied that, according to the report, our success had been a very brilliant one; to this he remarked, 'that it was paper talk.'"[140]

Historians, often necessarily, tend to rely on accounts given by participants to historical events and by government reports. Too frequently these reports are, in the words of Colonel Beall, nothing more than bureaucratically induced "paper talk." In the case of Cieneguilla, nearly all historical writings about the conflict assumed the court of inquiry to have been an accurate account of the sangfroid of an able commander who bravely led his men out of an ambush; these sources never raised the specters of direct disobedience of orders, drunken troops, inferior armaments, insufficient ammunition for the task at hand, incompetent command, and total panic. Sometimes human memory fails to reconstruct a historical event accurately. Other times a witness has an incentive not to tell the truth. The archaeological record, however, is not subject to human memory lapses or contemporary disincentives to the rendering of objective reporting.[141] The lesson to be learned from Cieneguilla is that historians must view the mass of material they gather in connection with a particular event with a degree of suspicion and with a willingness to embrace archaeological evidence, especially when it calls into question the written and oral record.

◦◦◦◦

The archaeological evidence largely sustains Lieutenant Bell's controversial assertion of foolish leadership that occasioned a military fiasco. The disciplines of history and archaeology demand that new attention be paid to Bell's long-overlooked report, revealing a whitewashing of a significant defeat of the frontier army.

NOTES

1. For mistaken historical accounts, see Brackett 1965:79; Carson 1966:149; Davidson 1974:69–74; Herr 1953:135; Michno 2003:24; Peters 1874:424; Sabin 1995:2.660–61; Urwin 1983:93; Utley 1967:144; Yenne 2006:74. Only a few writers have questioned the official version of the battle of Cieneguilla; see the foreword by Jerry Thompson in Bennett 1996:xxii–xxvii; Scott et al. 2007, 2:236–60; Taylor 1969:275–76.

2. Opler 1971:309, 317.

3. Ortiz 1983:459–60; Swanton 1969:372; Tiller 1983:4.

4. Governor Bent to Indian Commissioner William Medill, Nov. 10, 1846, Message of the President of the United States Transmitting Information in answer to a resolution of the House of the 31st of December, 1849, on the subject of California and New Mexico (Ex. Doc. no. 17, 1850), 191; see also Opler 1971:320.

5. See, generally, Frazer 1980.

6. Abel 1916:202.

7. Message of the President of the United States to the Two Houses of Congress at the Commencement of the Thirty-Second Congress, second session, Serial 674, Part II, Report of the Secretary of War (Washington: Robert Armstrong, Printer, 1852), 3.

8. Santa Fe *Gazette*, February 26, 1853.

9. U.S. Congress, House of Representatives, Message of the President, Report of the Secretary of War, Position and Distribution of Troops in the Western Division, Adjutant General's Office, Washington, D.C., Nov. 20, 1853. House Ex. Doc. No. 1, 33d Cong., 2d Sess. Serial 747, Part II (Washington: Robert Armstrong Press, 1853), 120.

10. Report from Dr. Michael Steck, Indian Agent, mentioned in Santa Fe *Weekly Gazette*, Feb. 13, 1853; Utley 1967:143.

11. Bennett 1996:xv; Taylor 1969:271.

12. Col. John Garland, Albuquerque, New Mexico, to Adj. Gen. Roger Jones, Mar. 29, 1854 (G177); Letters Received by the Office of the Adjutant General (Main Series), 1805–1889, Record Group 94, Microcopy 567, Roll 82, National Archives, Washington, D.C.; Rodenbough 2000:177. See also Taylor 1969:271–73 [hereafter, for National Archives (NA) citations, Record Group (RG), Microcopy (M), Roll (R)].

13. Tiller 1983:55, notes, "Had officials taken the time to acquaint themselves with the Jicarillas perhaps they would have realized . . . the Jicarillas were sincere in their attempts to find a peaceful solution to the economic problem of limited land and resources, which was the overriding cause of the political conflicts." See also Brackett 1965:135; Taylor 1969:273.

14. Carson to Messervy, Mar. 23, 1854, Letters Received, Office of Indian Affairs, New Mexico Superintendency, 1854–1855, RG 75, M243, R547, NA; Dunlay 2000:162–63.

15. Testimony of Maj. George Blake, Proceedings of Davidson Court of Inquiry convened at Santa Fe, New Mexico Territory, February 9, 1856, Judge Adjutant General's Office, RG 153, HH 751 [hereafter Davidson COI], 60–61, NA; Goddard 1911:242.

16. Specifically, Lt. Bell revealed:

> On the evening of the 21st of March, Lieut. Davidson [arrived] at Fort Union from Taos where he had left [with] his Company and reported to Col. Cooke for instructions. I was present when he arrived, and afterwards during several conversations between him and Col. Cooke in relation to the Indians, their mode of and ability for war &c. Col. Cooke and myself occupied the same house, and Lieut. D was our guest. He stated that on his way from Cantonment Burgwin to Fort Union, where he had been ordered by Col. Cooke, he met the Apaches in a canyon between the former place and Moro, that he had halted his command and, with Col. Brooks, had a talk with them; he described them as being overwhelmed with fear and protesting that they desired peace, stating also that he had made advantageous dispositions for battle in case they exhibited any signs of insolence or hostility. He also commented upon the miserable quality of their arms, and their mean, shrinking deportment, at the same time averring that he was sorry they did not show some signs of hostility, for that if they had, he would have 'wiped them out.' In the same conversation, he stated that the number of warriors counted at the time amounted to one hundred and seven. When informed that these same Indians had, two weeks previously, when attacked by a command of dragoons, evinced anything but a cowardly spirit; he reiterated his assertion, for rather brash, as to what he could do with them. (Bell to Williams, Dec. 27, 1854, Letters Received, Department of New Mexico, Office of the Adjutant General, RG 94, M1120, R3, NA)

17. Maj. George Blake to Lt. Col. P. S. G. Cooke, Mar. 30, 1854, Letters Received, Department of New Mexico, M1120, R3, NA; Testimony of Sgt. James Bronson, Davidson COI, 84. The troops may have taken as little as seventeen rounds of musketoon ammunition per man. See Asst. Surgeon David Magruder to Lt. John Davidson, Aug. 1, 1855, Davidson COI, exhibit I. Ammunition was issued in packets of ten cartridges.

18. "John W. Davidson," in Heitman 1903:1.355; Cullum 1850:266.

19. Carson 1966:113.

20. For details of this slaughter of Pomo tribesmen, see generally Michno 2003:6; Phillips 1990:66–70; Pritzker 2000:138.

21. Cullum 1858:2.128.

22. Altshuler 1991:93; Cullum 1850:76–77; Davidson 1974:68; Official Army Register 1856 (Washington: Adjutant General's Office 1856), 12.

23. Young officers often welcomed even the most routine of patrols as relief from the tedium of garrison duty; Skelton 1992:186–87.

24. Testimony of Peter Weldon, Davidson COI, 106; Testimony of Maj. Blake, Davidson COI, 63.

25. Whipple and Ives 1853–54:45.
26. Testimony of Private Edward Maher, Davidson COI, 100.
27. Ball 2001:30.
28. Pickerill 1865:12.
29. Brackett 1965:66; Steffen 1977:1.140.
30. Frazer 1963:39–41; Proceedings of the Capt. Philip Thompson Court of Inquiry convened at Santa Fe, New Mexico Territory, May 16, 1855, Judge Adjutant General's Office, RG 153, HH 496, NA.
31. Horgan 1954:1.5–6.
32. Testimony of Maj. George Blake, Davidson COI, 55.
33. Hanson 2001:158.
34. Frazer 1968:135. "On more than one occasion, the Apache have escaped from dragoons, when almost in their grasp, where fleetness of their horses was put to test by the troops on broken down animals."
35. *Journal of American History* 8 (4, 1909), 549, cited in Frazer 1968.
36. Ball 2001:30.
37. In 1849, Capt. William Grier, while in command of some of these same men, hesitating to attack a Jicarilla village, allowed the tribesmen time to kill Ann White, a captive, and then to escape. See Dunlay 2000:138–39.
38. Testimony of Sgt. Bronson, Davidson COI, 74; in 1850, Sgt. Holbrook had led a patrol that scalped some dead American Indians. Holbrook to McLaws, Apr. 7, 1850, Letters Received, 9 Military District, RG 393, M1102, 2, NA; and Munroe to Jones, Apr. 15, 1850, M269/1850, Letters Received, Office of the Adjutant General, RG 94, NA; Carson 1966:136–37. The report sent along to the War Department included a note from Sgt. Holbrook's commanding officer, Capt. Grier, stating that Mexican civilians who had accompanied the expedition performed the scalping. See Message of the President to the 31st Congress, Exec. Doc no. 1, Senate version, Report of the Secretary of War (Washington 1850), 70–71; and Bennett 1996:xxiii.
39. Testimony of Sgt. Strawbridge, Davidson COI, 88.
40. Davidson to Blake, Apr. 1, 1854, Letters Received, Department of New Mexico, Office of the Adjutant General, RG 94, M1120, R3, NA.
41. Testimony of Sgt. Bronson, Davidson COI, 74.
42. Von Clausewitz 1993:341.
43. Garavaglia and Worman 1998:1133–34.
44. Frazer 1963:40–41; Gorenfeld and Gorenfeld 1998; Worman 2005:34–36.
45. On Oct. 25, 1853, half of the F Company garrison stationed at Ft. Massachusetts became intoxicated and riotous. On Mar. 9, 1855, many of the men of Company F again became drunk and mutinied in Taos; see Court Martial of Major George A. H. Blake, convened at Santa Fe, New Mexico Territory, Jan. 21, 1856, Judge Adjutant General's Office, RG 153, HH 660, NA; see also Ball 2001:58.
46. Katie Bowen to Father and Mother, Nov. 2, 1851, and May 2, 1852, Arrott Collection, Donnelly Library, New Mexico Highlands University, Las Vegas, N.Mex.

47. As an example, prior to leaving on a campaign on Mar. 8, 1855, Maj. Thompson stopped at St. Vrain's mill in Talpa and in Taos, New Mexico Territory, for the purpose of allowing his men to obtain and consume a quantity of intoxicants for their comfort; Court Martial of Major Philip R. Thompson, convened at Santa Fe, New Mexico Territory, Jan. 21, 1856, Judge Adjutant General's Office, RG 153, HH 533, NA.

48. Goddard 1911:242.

49. Testimony of Sergeant Bronson, Davidson COI, 74.

50. Pritzker 2000:14.

51. "Buck and ball," commonly fired from the musketoon, consisted of one .63-caliber lead ball along with three .31-caliber balls. Scott 2007:2.243; Winders 1997:93.

52. Testimony of Sgt. Bronson, Davidson COI, 86; the mention of plundering shows up in an official history of the regiment. Capt. R. P. Page Wainwright, "The First Regiment of Cavalry," in Rodenbough and Harkin 1966:159. Although there are no known written accounts of looting at Cieneguilla, the fact that this disgraceful conduct had occurred may have been orally passed on among officers.

53. Testimony of Peter Weldon, Davidson COI, 108.

54. Testimony of Sgt. Bronson, Davidson COI, 75; A year after the battle, Asst. Surgeon Magruder wrote that the Model 1847 musketoon failed the troops at Cieneguilla (see note 57). Indeed, the weapon would continue to demonstrate its unsuitability for combat at locations such as near the Illinois River in southwestern Oregon and Steptoe's disaster near Tohatonimme Creek in southeastern Washington. In 1858, Army Ordnance finally replaced it with the reliable and accurate Sharps carbine. Gorenfeld and Gorenfeld 1998.

55. Poinsett 1856:106.

56. Frazer 1963:66.

57. Testimony of Sgt. Bronson, Davidson COI 78; Dr. Magruder later expressed his view: "Had they [the troops] been armed with an efficient weapon instead of the musketoon, I have no doubt we should have remained in possession of the field." Dr. Magruder to Davidson, Aug. 1, 1855, Davidson COI, exhibit I.

58. Missouri *Republican*, Apr. 29, 1854.

59. Scott et al. 2007:2.249.

60. Testimony of Sgt. James W. Strawbridge, Davidson COI, 89.

61. Typically, the thirty to forty rounds of carbine ammunition carried by a dragoon would be barely enough to last for a sustained fight of thirty minutes. See, e.g., Barbero 2003:80; Testimony of Sgt. Strawbridge, Davidson COI, 89. Dr. Magruder claimed that each dragoon carried but seventeen rounds into battle. Dr. Magruder to Davidson, Aug. 1, 1855.

62. Testimony of Trooper Peter Weldon, Davidson COI, 109.

63. Missouri *Republican*, Apr. 29, 1854.

64. Testimony of Trooper Peter Weldon, Davidson COI, 109; Testimony of Sgt. Strawbridge, Davidson COI, 103.

65. Testimony of J. M. Francisco, Davidson COI, 41.

66. Scott et al. 2007:2.248.
67. Testimony of Sgt. James Bronson, Davidson COI, 86.
68. Scott et al. 2007:2.248–49.
69. Utley 1967:113; 1973:107, 265.
70. Mawson 2007:221.
71. Marshall 1947:145.
72. Scott et al. 2007:2.249.
73. Ibid., 2.140.
74. Testimony of Trooper Peter Weldon, Davidson COI, 112.
75. Testimony of Sgt. James Strawbridge, Davidson COI, 94.
76. Ibid.
77. Testimony of Trooper Peter Weldon, Davidson COI, 112.
78. Bennett 1996:54.
79. Scott et al. 2007:2.249.
80. Garland to Jones, Apr. 1, 1854 (G178); Letters Received, Office of the Adjutant General, Microfilm Publication RG 94, M567, R82; NA; Testimony of Maj. Blake, Davidson COI, 64; see also Santa Fe Weekly *Gazette*, Apr. 15, 1854.
81. Testimony of J. M. Francisco, Davidson COI, 37–38, 41–43. Years later, a Jicarilla recalled the fight as follows:

> The Jicarilla moved their camp to a mountain east of Picuris. When they had been there four days the Americans came again on horseback early in the morning. They halted and one approached to pass the Apache a paper. An Apache took it from the hands of the officer and tore it up. Someone shot the person who had handed the paper, wounding him in the arm. Then the soldiers opened the fight. They had halted on the plain with their horses and were shooting in different directions, the Indians having surrounded them. The Apache kept on shooting and killing the soldiers until only two were left. Four of the Apache were killed. They took all the arms of the soldiers and the money from their clothes, a large sum. (Goddard 1911:243)

82. Testimony of C. Carson, Davidson COI, 33.
83. Goddard 1911:244; Pritzker 2000:14.
84. Company F, 1st Dragoons muster roll for Apr. 30, 1854, RG 94, NA.
85. Santa Fe *Gazette,* Apr. 15, 1854; Carson 1966:151.
86. Santa Fe *Gazette*, Oct. 21, 1854.
87. Goddard 1911:242.
88. Santa Fe *Gazette*, Apr. 15, 1854.
89. New York *Times*, May 24, 1854.
90. Garland to Lt. Col. Lorenzo Thomas, Apr. 30, 1854, Santa Fe, New Mexico, contained in Message of the President of the United States to the Two Houses of Congress at the Commencement of the Second Session of the Thirty-Third Congress, Report of the Secretary of War (Washington: A.O.P. Nicholson, 1854), 2:33–34; Rodenbough and Harkin 1966:179.

91. Christopher Carson, letter to New York *Tribune*, June 29, 1854; Goddard 1911:243.

92. Dunlay 2000:164.

93. Ibid.; Taylor 1969:279.

94. Taylor 1969:278–79.

95. Ibid., 286; Garland to Thomas, June 30, 1854, and Aug. 30, 1854, contained in Message of the President to the . . . Thirty-Third Congress, Report of the Secretary of War, 2:36–37 (see note 90).

96. Col. Dixon Miles to Maj. William Nichols, Dec. 3, 1854, Letters Received, Department of New Mexico, Letters Received by the Office of the Adjutant General, RG 94, M567, R82, NA.

97. Santa Fe *Weekly Gazette*, Mar. 15, 1856.

98. Tiller 1983:76–98.

99. Opler 1971:314; New York *Times*, Sept. 29, 1879.

100. Davis 1996:46.

101. Tiller 1983:231–52.

102. Garland to Lt. Col. Lorenzo Thomas, Apr. 30, 1854, Santa Fe, New Mexico, contained in Message of the President to the . . . Thirty-Third Congress, Report of the Secretary of War, 2:33–34 (see note 90).

103. New York *Times*, May 24, 1854.

104. Skelton 1992:203.

105. Richard N. Grippaldi, "The Best Possible Appointments Should Be Made: The Officers of the U.S. Regiment of Dragoons and Military Professionalism," unpublished manuscript, 2006, Army Heritage Foundation, Carlisle, Pa.

106. For example, in 1851 and 1853, Cooke had written letters to Adj. Gen. Roger Jones complaining that Nathan Boone, a physically ill and badly educated political appointee, rather than himself, had been promoted to the rank of lieutenant colonel of the 2nd Dragoons; Letters Received, Office of the Adjutant General, 1853, RG 478, R3, NA. Nathan Boone resigned his commission in 1853, allowing Cooke, as the senior major in the two Dragoon regiments, to be promoted as lieutenant colonel of the 2nd Dragoons. See "Nathan Boone" and "Philip Cooke" in Heitman 1903:1.230.

107. Bell to Williams, Dec. 27, 1854, Davidson COI.

108. Davidson COI; Winthrop 1920:522. "The law relating to Courts of Inquiry has been—as derived with but slight modification from the provisions of the Articles [of War] of 1786." Winthrop 1920:516.

109. Headquarters, Department of New Mexico General Order no. 1, Feb. 9, 1856, referenced in Davidson, COI, 1.

110. Ball 2001:44–45; Utley 1967:113–15.

111. New York *Daily Times,* Jan. 9, 1854.

112. See note 45, above.

113. Lt. David Bell to Gen. Winfield Scott, Mar. 8. 1856, misc. exhibits, Davidson COI.

114. Gen. Winfield Scott to Lt. David Bell, Mar. 24, 1856, misc. exhibits, Davidson COI.

115. Davis 1982:306; Wetherington 2006:391, 399.

116. General Order no. 14, Sept. 5, 1855, War Department, Adjutant General's Office, Court Martial of Philip R. Thompson, HH 533, NA; Headquarters Department of New Mexico, General Orders no. 6, June 12, 1856, Court Martial of Major George A. H. Blake, convened at Santa Fe, New Mexico Territory, Jan. 21, 1856, Judge Adjutant General's Office, RG 153, HH 660, NA.

117. Testimony of Maj. George A. H. Blake, Davidson COI, 64.

118. Testimony of James Bronson, Davidson COI, 76, 85.

119. Bennett 1996:47, 55–56.

120. Ibid., 79–80.

121. Ball 2001:74.

122. Military historian John Keegan found accounts of battle offered by participants to be confused and inaccurate. This is because

> the soldier is vouchsafed no such well ordered and clear-cut vision [of battle]. Battle for him takes place in a wildly unstable physical and emotional environment; he may spend much of his time in combat as a mildly apprehensive spectator, granted, by some freak of events, a comparatively danger-free grandstand view of others fighting; then he may able to see nothing but the clods on which he has flung himself for safety, there to crouch—he cannot anticipate—for minutes or for hours; he may feel in turn boredom, exultation, panic, anger, sorrow, bewilderment, even that sublime emotion we call courage. (Keegan 1976:46)

123. Peters 1874:427; see also Carson 1966:150.

124. Department of New Mexico, General Order no. 3, Gen. John Garland, commanding, Santa Fe *Gazette*, Mar. 29, 1856.

125. Bennett 1996:xxxiii.

126. Military Service Records, 236, Entry 534, Vol. 53, NA.

127. "Richard Byrnes" in Heitman 1903:1.272; Lowe 1985:20.

128. "George Blake" in Heitman 1903:1.223.

129. "David Magruder" in Heitman 1903:1.528; New York *Times*, Nov. 23, 1910.

130. Santa Fe *Weekly Gazette*, Mar. 25, 1854.

131. Rodenbough 2000:485. "David Bell" in Heitman, 1903:1.207; New York *Times*, Dec. 6, 1860.

132. Rodenbough 2000:177.

133. Scott et al. 2007:1.235; Joseph Ditzler, "Archaeologists Piece Together 1854 Battle," Albuquerque *Journal*, Oct. 26, 2003.

134. Pvt. Hutchinson to Maj. W. A. Nicholson, Asst. Adjt. Genl., July 26, 1854, Letters Received, Department of New Mexico, M1120, R3, NA.

135. Bode 1994:40; Leckie 1967:69.

136. Wilke and Lawton 1976:31.

137. Tate 1999:252; "John W. Davidson" in Heitman 1903:1.355.

138. Johnson 2009; see also Johnson's chapter in this volume. Indeed, in 1851, Col. George McCall found there to be approximately one hundred Jicarilla warriors in the territory. McCall, Report of the Secretary of War, In Compliance with a Resolution of the Senate, Col. McCall's Reports in Relation to New Mexico. Referred to the Committee on Military Affairs, February 1, 1851, ordered to be Printed 1851 (Washington, D.C.), 16.

139. Scott et al. 2007:2.249.

140. Jones 1944:185, 210.

141. Scott et al. 2007:2.434.

The Archaeological Record

David M. Johnson

On the evening of March 29, 1854, sixty men of the 1st Dragoons under the command of Lt. John W. Davidson left Cantonment Burgwin near Taos, New Mexico Territory, to search for a group of Jicarilla Apache known to be in the vicinity of the Embudo Mountains near Picuris Pueblo. Late that night, the dragoons arrived at the small village of Cieneguilla on the banks of the Rio Grande. The next morning, the soldiers left Cieneguilla following the old trail to Embudo. They turned off the trail near the foot of the mountain and found the Jicarillas camped on a small ridge a few miles above the Rio Grande. A fight soon erupted and ended in a serious defeat for the dragoons.

Over the next 150 years, the location of the battle was largely forgotten. Artifacts settled into the ground, vegetation grew, and no obvious signs of the battle remained (figure 2). A few were aware of the general location and had even located artifacts,[1] but the entire site had never been found.

Between the years 2000 and 2005 an interagency team of researchers under the direction of Carson National Forest archaeologists conducted surveys to locate and record the battle site. The initial work was designed to find the site, define the approximate boundaries of the battle, and focus the research on the areas that needed to be examined more closely during a more detailed investigation. This reconnaissance was followed by intensive surveys to map the site and gather detailed information about the battle.

Goals of the research included locating and recording the footprint of the battle and accurately describing the artifacts to provide a description

Figure 2. The Cieneguilla battle site.

of the diagnostic military and Apache artifacts in New Mexico in the mid-nineteenth century.[2] The archaeological results would then be compared with the historical records and written accounts by Lt. Davidson and other soldiers who were in the engagement. Because of the importance of this battle, an accurate description and comparison with the written accounts would provide a detailed look not only at the battle but at the military and Indian battle tactics of the era as well. It would also serve as a final chapter to a court of inquiry that took place in 1856 to examine Davidson's conduct, since the exact location of the battle and the positions of the troops and Apaches could now be investigated.

Another goal was to involve the Jicarilla Apache Nation in the project. The proposal for the research was presented at a tribal council meeting in 2000, where council members and elders expressed their concerns as well as their desire to see this important part of their history investigated. Tribal archaeologists and members of the Jicarilla Apache Culture Committee participated in the project, and several Apache elders and members of the council made visits to the site.

This project was funded in part by the Carson National Forest and a grant from the National Park Service, American Battlefield Protection

Program. Personnel conducting the fieldwork included archaeologists from the Carson National Forest, Lincoln National Forest, Bureau of Land Management, National Park Service, Jicarilla Apache Nation, and University of Michigan; land surveyors from the Carson National Forest; and local volunteers. Much of the fieldwork, research, and analysis was completed by volunteers from these agencies working on weekends and evenings.

Field Methods

Methods for this project involved three stages. First a records search and overview of the topography were used to narrow the search area. It was anticipated that we would be able to reduce the overall area to be examined based on the existing records and focus our attention on a relatively small project location. Next, a preliminary reconnaissance of the area was conducted to examine ridges and canyon bottoms within the area determined to be the likely location of the battle site to identify where the battle took place. Surveyors using metal detectors walked parallel transects to look for metal artifacts indicative of a battle and those indicative of Apache activity. Once the overall distribution of the artifacts had been found, a detailed survey consisting of closely spaced transects with metal detectors resurveyed the artifact scatter to record individual artifacts and artifact distribution patterns precisely.

The term "Apache artifact" as used here includes a variety of artifacts often used by many American Indians groups in the mid-nineteenth century. Indians acquired items such as jewelry, clothing, guns, horses, and utilitarian goods through trade, particularly during the long history of the trade fairs at Taos and Pecos pueblos. When Fort Union was established, post traders brought goods such as kettles, knives, metal points, utensils, and blankets and food staples such as flour, sugar, and tobacco. Raiding Anglo, Mexican, and Comanche settlements, however, was also an important means of obtaining items. As a result of the various methods of acquisition, and the fact that many tribes obtained the same goods, it is difficult to attribute individual artifacts to Apache, Ute, Comanche, Pueblo, Hispanic, or even Anglo use of an area. In our research, therefore, cultural affiliation was largely based on the overall assemblage of

American Indian artifacts, taking into account the documented ancestral use of the area.

For this project, we knew from historical documents that Apaches had occupied the area at that time and were directly involved in the battle. In addition, several key artifact types that have been attributed to Apaches on other sites in New Mexico aided in the interpretation of the archaeological remains.[3] These include metal cone tinklers or jingles, metal arrow points, metal "debitage" (the scraps left from metal point manufacture), and irregular cut and chewed lead balls of a variety of sizes. The chewed balls are typically found on Apache sites. Apaches used whatever lead was available and cut, hammered, or chewed it to fit their firearms. Nevertheless, we considered an artifact assemblage Apache only when found in association with diagnostic Jicarilla Apache micaceous ceramics. Micaceous ceramics are a distinctive type of pottery in which mica temper in the paste or body of the pottery gives the vessel a unique shimmering surface. These ceramics were manufactured by several northern New Mexico groups, but the Jicarilla pots typically were thin with flattened rims and are of distinctive forms.

We expected military artifacts to include uniform components, molded lead balls of a consistent size, percussion caps, as well as military issue horse tack and equipment. These artifacts would be typical of a military encampment or battle, so the predominance of mid-nineteen-century military ammunition and percussion caps associated with arrow points and chewed balls in particular would be an indication that this was the battle site.

In light of the research goals and data needs, it was most appropriate to use a combination of standard pedestrian survey techniques augmented with metal detectors (figure 3). Metal detectors are one of the more important tools historical archaeologists have at their disposal for locating Apache *rancherías* (camps) and battle sites in the American Southwest and were an indispensable part of this research. Historical archaeologists began using metal detectors with success around 1984.[4] Southwestern archaeologists had to some extent ignored this tool, but by the end of the twentieth century the profession had begun to take a serious look at their practicality. If used in a controlled manner by professional archaeologists, they are a cost-effective approach to identifying metal artifacts, and they save countless hours of testing and excavation.[5]

THE ARCHAEOLOGICAL RECORD 47

Figure 3. Surveyors using metal detectors.

Fieldwork

The background research conducted prior to the fieldwork uncovered numerous military letters and accounts of the battle that provided several key pieces of information for locating the site.[6] Some of the more important documents are Davidson's official report on the battle,[7] a letter written by Lieutenant Bell that questioned Davidson's description of the battle and blamed Davidson for the defeat,[8] and a report on a Jicarilla version of the battle recorded by Pliny Goddard in 1909.[9] The records of the court of inquiry were particularly useful.[10] The inquiry was held at the request of Lieutenant Davidson in response to the accusations in Bell's letter, and several soldiers gave their accounts of the battle.

From this research, we knew that the troops found the Apache camped in the mountains three to five miles from Cieneguilla and east of the trail to Embudo. We knew that the dragoons were armed with .69-caliber musketoons and .54-caliber horse pistols, some had .44-caliber Colt Dragoon revolvers, and at least one soldier had a saber. The Indians fired both arrows and firearms and were camped on a ridge, reportedly to manufacture micaceous pottery for trade. We also had a description of the general layout of the battle including the dismount, Apache camp, return to the horses, retreat to a nearby ridge, retreat up a steep ridge, and the final retreat down a narrow ridge at the "point of a hill." And we knew that there was an old trail between Cieneguilla and Picuris that the soldiers likely followed. This information aided in the identification of the characteristics of the terrain and certain diagnostic artifacts that would determine if we had found the location of the engagement.

The initial reconnaissance surveys were conducted between September 2000 and April 2002. Using the written descriptions, a sketch map from the court of inquiry of 1856, and topographic maps of the area, crews averaging four to eight people surveyed the major ridges within an area two miles across in an attempt to find the battle location (figure 4). Most narrow ridges within this area were covered in a single transect with surveyors spaced 3–10 meters apart. When a potential Apache or military artifact was found, the transect interval was reduced to cover the vicinity more intensively to see if other artifacts were present. Artifact locations were recorded using handheld GPS units.

Artifacts from the final retreat route were the first battle-related artifacts located. Initial finds, consisting of .54- and .69-caliber lead balls, military-style percussion caps, metal arrow points, uniform components, and other items, confirmed that we had found part of the arena of battle, and the terrain fit the description of the final retreat route.

The locations of the initial attack and Apache camp were not found until several months later. The first evidence of the Apache camp was the discovery of micaceous ceramics, metal points, metal debitage, percussion caps, lead balls, and a brass military-style spur. An examination of the slope below the camp soon exposed the position where the dragoons had first dismounted and were later pinned down after the Apache attacked the soldiers who were protecting their horses.

Once the general areas of the battle had been identified, the research focused on identifying the full extent of the artifact distribution. The location of the battle site was delineated on a topographic map generated using ArcView 8.1 to provide a base map for recording artifacts found during the intensive survey. Metal rebar datum points were established using a Trimble 4700 series geodetic GPS with RTK capabilities in combination with a total station in areas of dense tree cover, and the entire survey was keyed into a USGS section corner marker. As individual artifacts were found, the

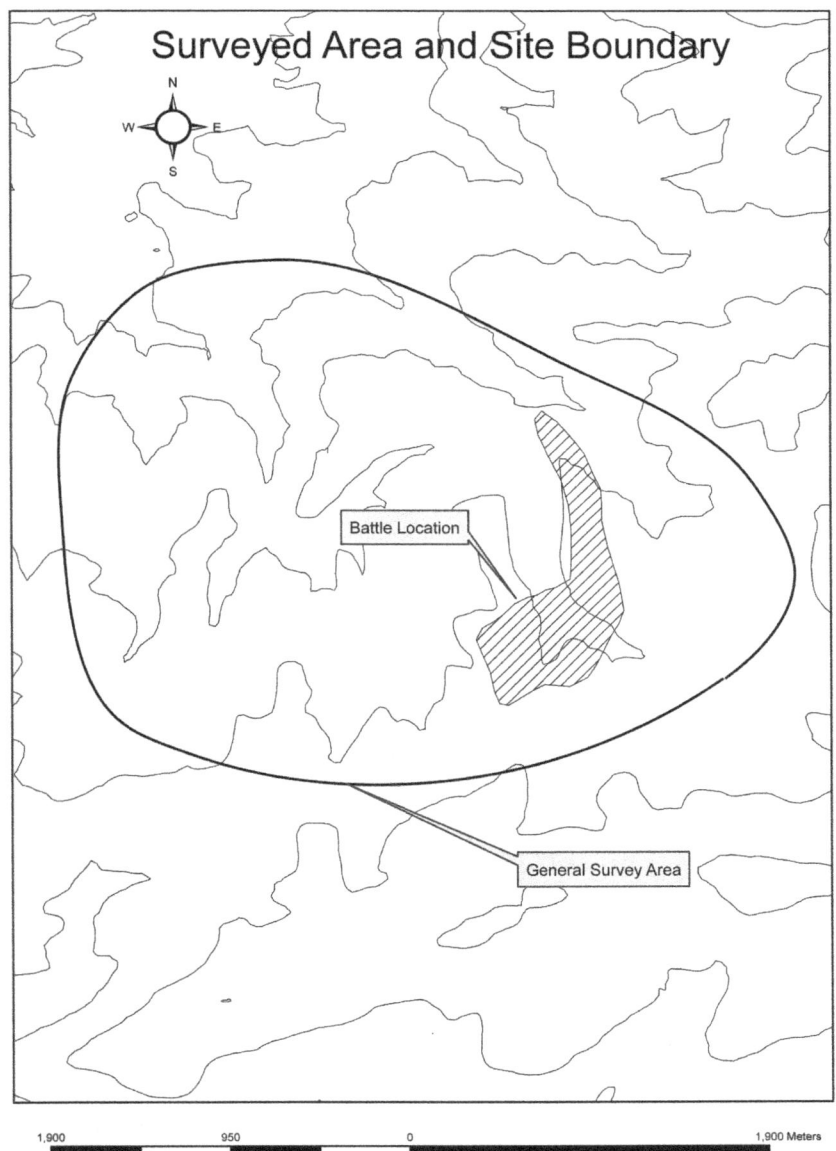

Figure 4. Site boundary.

UTM locations were recorded with handheld GPS units, and the map was updated and expanded daily as the survey progressed.

The intensive survey was completed in two stages. The first field session concentrated on surveying the hilltop stand and retreat route. This area was surveyed in May 2002. The second phase consisted of surveying the Apache camp, the horse position, and all remaining portions of the battle site. This fieldwork was conducted in October 2002. Additional small surveys were conducted between 2003 and 2005 to complete the coverage of the battle area and to check surrounding areas.

For the intensive survey of the battle site, transect lines oriented parallel to the ridgeline were flagged. Surveyors followed closely spaced transects (2–3 meter spacing) across the entire site area. When the surveyor registered a hit with the metal detector, the find was carefully excavated with a hand trowel and marked with a pin flag. A recorder followed the survey crew and examined the artifact, and if it was determined to be a diagnostic artifact or needed for further analysis it was collected and placed in a labeled plastic bag. The location was recorded using a handheld GPS unit so the positions could be plotted at the end of the day. A metal tag with a stamped number was left at the artifact location, the location was covered, and the flag was left in place for the land surveyors who would come in the following week to map the artifacts in place accurately with surveying equipment. The surveyor on the outside of the transect line tied flags in the branches of trees and bushes to mark his route. Surveyors continued along the transect lines until no more artifacts were found or the topography prohibited continuing. On reaching the end of the transect line, the surveyors pivoted and returned in the opposite direction adjacent to the previous transect, following the flag line left by the surveyor on the outside of the previous transect. Overall, approximately 575 acres was surveyed, with approximately 200 acres intensively examined. The site covers approximately 125 acres (see figure 4).

The use of GPS units to map sites has proved to be highly effective and efficient,[11] but in this case tree cover and the deep canyons were problems and accuracy was greatly diminished. The handheld GPS locations of artifacts offered a convenient method of logging in the artifacts and providing a map of the area that could be updated as the fieldwork progressed, but artifact locations were not precise. To record the locations of artifacts more accurately, after each field session land surveyors accompanied by archaeologists mapped each artifact location using a total station. The field map generated from the handheld GPS locations was very useful in relocating the artifacts for the precision mapping with the total station. The individual artifact locations recorded by the handheld GPS units differed from the exact locations shot in with the total station by up to several meters. At a large scale, however, the map of the artifact distributions recorded by the GPS units and those recorded by the total station were very close.

Digital maps were generated in ArcView 8.1 for the initial surveys, and later in ArcGIS 9.1, allowing the data to be sorted and plotted in a variety of ways to allow a closer look at the distributions of and relations among artifact types. These maps proved invaluable during the surveys and in the overall interpretation of the data. The precise artifact locations allowed for the examination of the distribution patterns in detail, as described below. For example, a group of micaceous ceramics associated with metal tinklers, debitage, awls, and other domestic artifacts would be indicative of an Indian camp. Likewise, a group of horseshoes and horseshoe nails, along with military items such as uniform components, dropped ammunition, and fired percussion caps, would indicate a military position.

Survey Results

At the completion of the fieldwork, more than one thousand artifacts had been found.[12] Because of the use of metal detectors, the majority of the artifacts recovered were metal. The primary exception was the numerous micaceous ceramics found in the Apache camp. Although this undoubtedly skews the information from the Apache camp in particular, the results provide an accurate description of the location of the camp and battle site as well as important information concerning the military action.

The artifact types confirm that dragoons fought here. Dragoon coat buttons and other uniform components including trouser buttons, an accoutrement hook, military spurs, and a buckle back plate provide firm evidence. Also, we know that the dragoons were using three types of guns: .69-caliber model 1847 musketoon, .54-caliber horse pistol, and .44-caliber Colt Dragoon revolver. Ammunition for all three of these arms, as well as military-style percussion caps and gun tools and parts designed for the musketoon, were found. The abundance of American Indian artifacts indicative of both camp and battle is also consistent with the written accounts, and all appear to fall into the correct time period. A sample of the artifacts from the battle site is shown in figure 5.

The artifact distribution also confirmed that this was the site of the Cieneguilla fight in question (figure 6). The location and layout of the artifacts closely match written accounts and the sketch map of the battle prepared for the 1856 Cieneguilla court of inquiry (figure 7). The two separate artifact

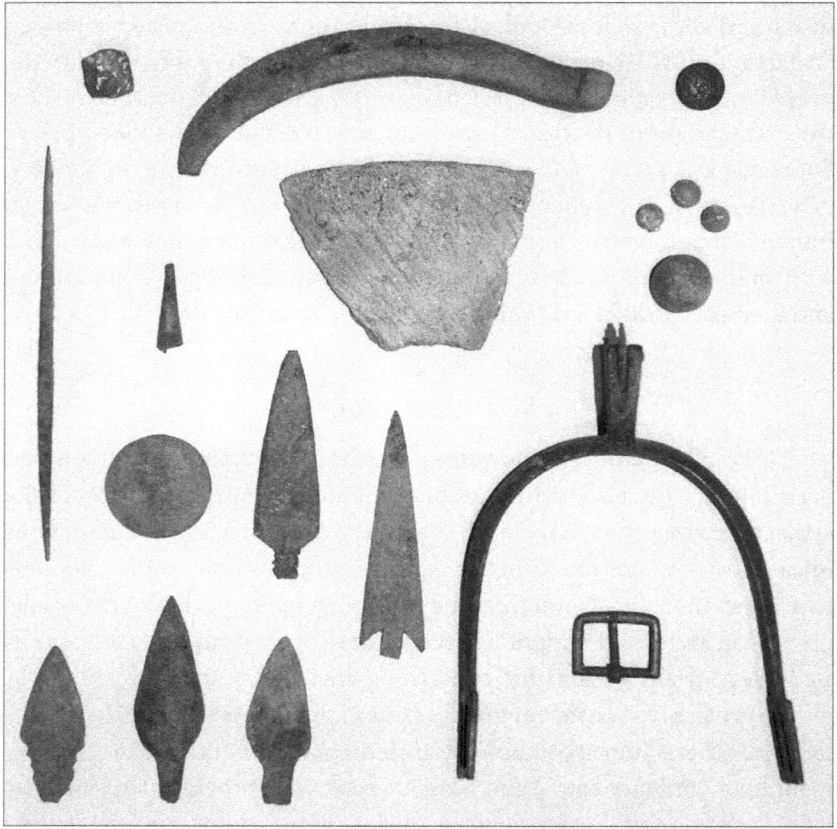

Figure 5. Sample of artifacts.

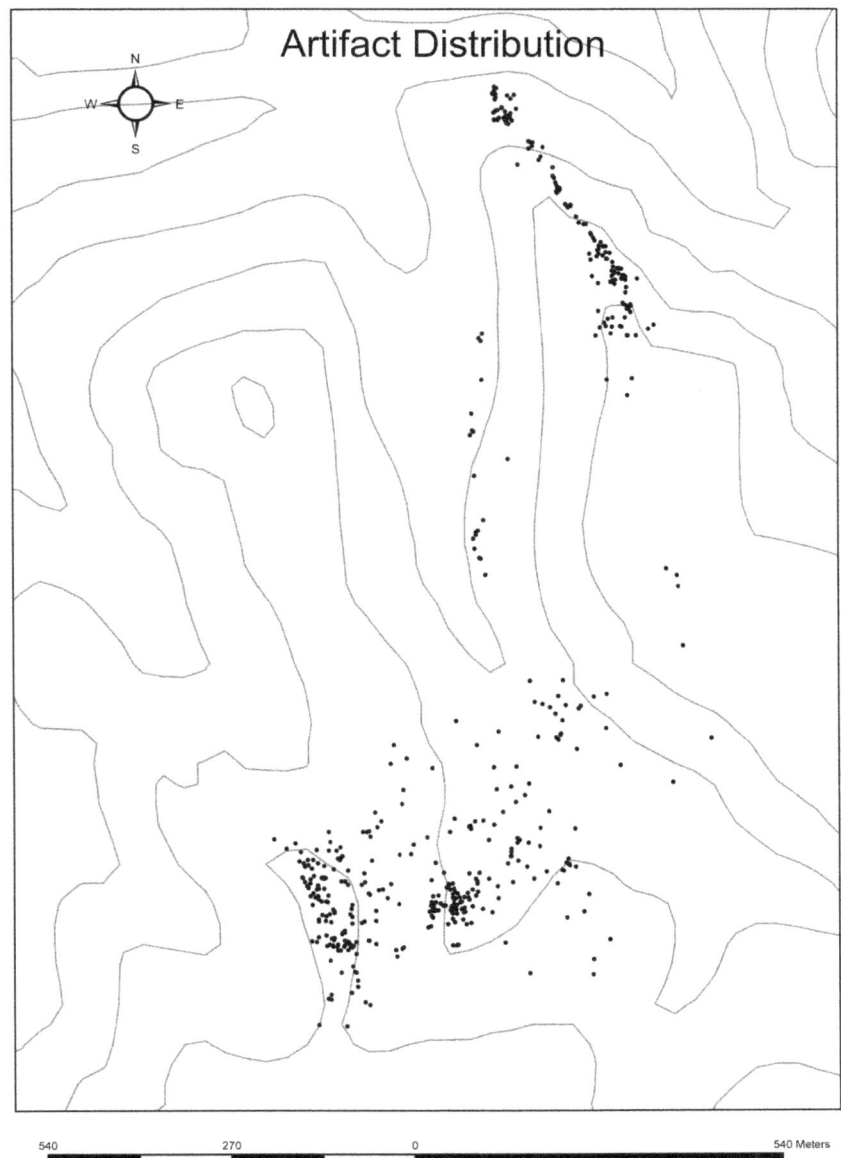

Figure 6. Artifact distribution.

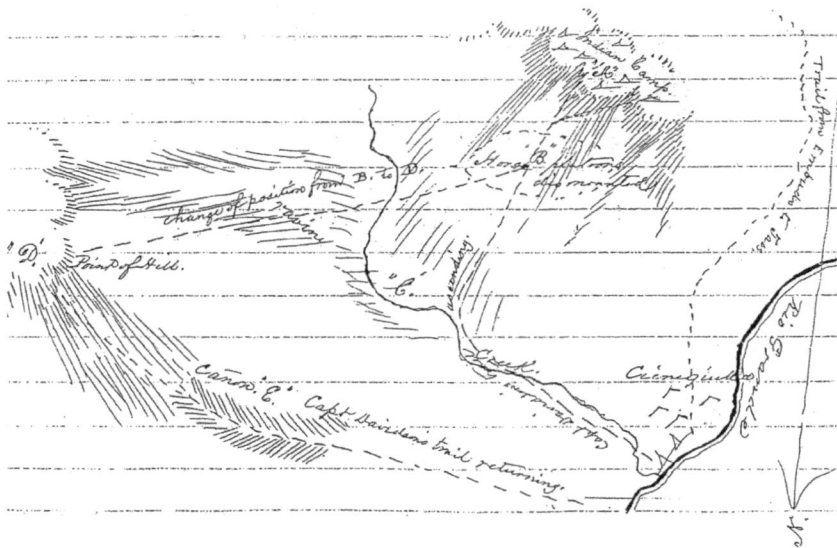

Figure 7. 1856 sketch map of battle. Note that the north arrow points down.

vicinities—one on a ridge where the Apache camp and horse position were located, the other across the canyon on a ridge where the troops fought just prior to their final retreat—are also positively linked, not only by the consistency in types of artifacts found and similarity in layout to the written descriptions of the battle but also by a positive match of the hammer marks on two fired percussion caps, one from the camp and one from the retreat route that confirms that the locations are related.[13]

Interpretation of the Results: The Battle

The distribution, types, and conditions of the artifacts, combined with the sketch map and various accounts of the battle, clarify several questions surrounding this engagement, many of which were raised during the court of inquiry. The following description of the battle draws from the various accounts presented in the court of inquiry documents, augmented by the artifacts that were found at the site and a correlation between the two sets of information.

The dragoons left Cieneguilla early in the morning and headed up the trail to Embudo. Two dragoons and the scout were sent along what is now known as the Apodaca trail to see if the Apaches had crossed the river at Embudo. The remaining dragoons had split off the trail to head east into the mountains. The scouting party soon saw campfires in the distance and sent one of the dragoons back to alert the troops.

The written accounts seem to suggest that the dragoons were going cross-country when they left the Embudo–Santa Fe trail to head up into the mountains, but it is most likely they turned off onto an existing trail that leads from Cieneguilla to Picuris. Although no archaeological evidence was found near the Apodaca trail to confirm that the soldiers had left to follow the Picuris trail, the canyon sides are too steep to have been climbed, and the canyon bottom is blocked by rock outcrops and narrow passages. The trail is the only feasible way to gain access to the Apache camp on horseback from this direction.

The well-established trail to Picuris has been in place for many years. The earliest written reference to this trail is the account of Roque Madrid, who in 1705 left Picuris toward Cieneguilla along a trail through Agua Caliente canyon.[14] This trail, and several others in the immediate vicinity, is shown on an 1876 plat of the Cieneguilla land grant, which encompasses the entire area of the battle. The trail to Embudo is identified on the plat as the old road from Santa Fe to Taos. Several other trails are also shown in the area. In the court of private lands claims in 1895 and 1896, during which the Cieneguilla grant was rejected, testimony by Albino Lopez verifies that there were several trails in the area, including the "Agua Caliente Trail" from Cieneguilla to Picuris.[15] The Agua Caliente Trail is shown on the plat of the grant as the trail to Picuris. On the ground, the footprint of the old trail is now faded, but it is still discernable.

The Agua Caliente Trail climbs the steep slope of a ridge to the southeast, makes one switchback, and then heads up the ridge. From there the trail crosses a saddle and then passes along the western slopes of the ridge adjacent to a deep canyon. The dragoons picked up the Indians' tracks as they neared the Agua Caliente. The Apaches were camped above a small side canyon just ahead. The metal detector survey located numerous nineteenth-century artifacts along the trail that are associated with travel.

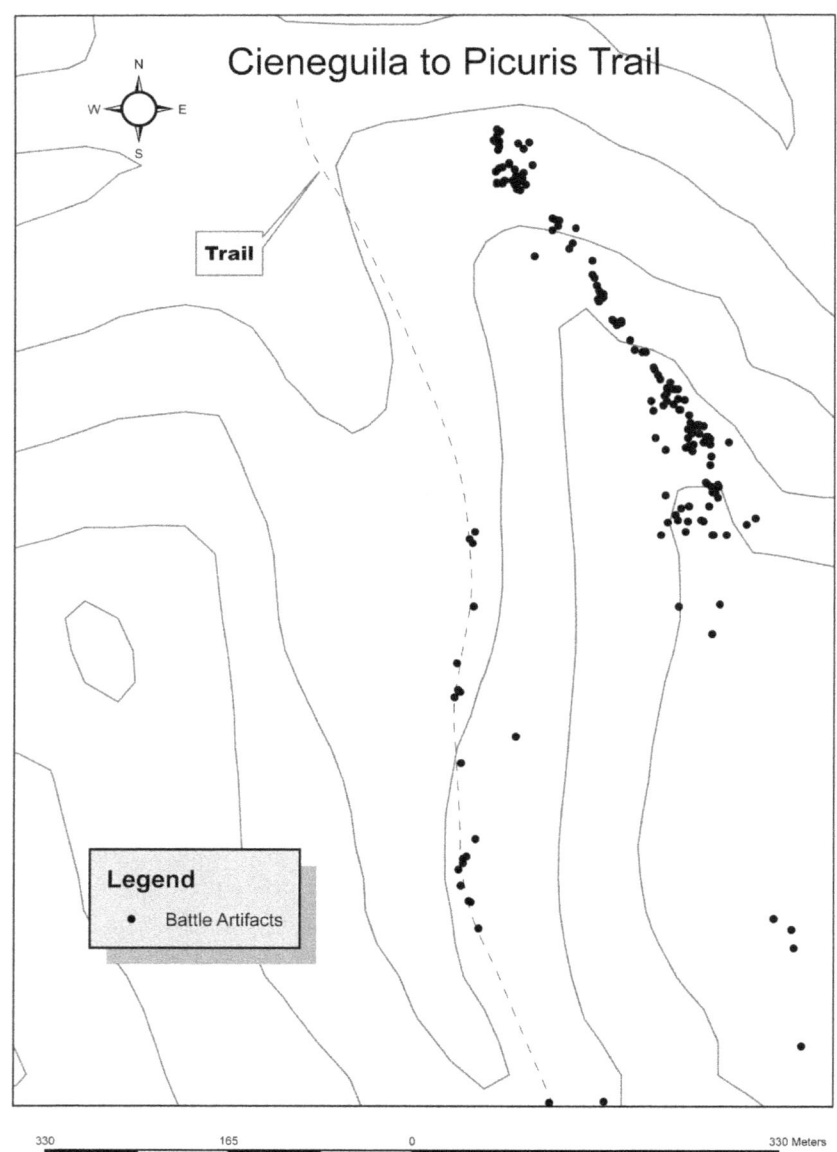

Figure 8. Trail of artifacts.

Though most of these artifacts were not related to the battle, they confirm that this was the historic trail and that it was in use at the approximate time of the battle (figure 8). The artifacts include a silver filigree earring, iron fire striker or *chispa*, thimble, sewing needles, horseshoes, and *coscojos* (metal jingles or tinklers attached to a bridle or bit), all consistent with nineteenth-century use of the trail. A few battle-related items were found, most likely representing overshot bullets and arrow points from the actual battle up the slopes. Following this trail on horseback, it is unlikely that it took the troops much more than an hour and a half to reach the Apache camp from Cieneguilla.[16]

As the dragoons entered a narrow side canyon, they proceeded up the canyon bottom along the Apaches' trail until they reached a small rock outcrop and increasingly steep side slopes that inhibited further progress. They climbed the bank toward their right to a gently sloping area near the base of the ridge just above the canyon bottom and dismounted. During the court of inquiry, Lieutenant Davidson repeatedly denied that he had left his horses in the bottom of a canyon or next to the stream, and he was technically correct. The location where the horses were tethered was clearly defined with a concentration of horseshoes, horseshoe nails, and military artifacts including uniform buttons, percussion caps, and dropped .69- and .54-caliber balls (figure 9). It was evident that, although he was not in the bottom of a small canyon, he clearly had dismounted his troops in low ground, in a difficult position to defend.

The written accounts state that someone from the Apache camp called out to the troops to come ahead if they wanted a fight. The troops reportedly split into two platoons, advanced up the slope, and entered the camp. A small group of soldiers under the command of Dr. Magruder was left with the horses. The archaeological evidence supports such troop movement. Artifacts are sparse, but there is evidence that one platoon went up a small draw just to the north, where fired balls and numerous arrow points with an orientation showing they were fired from the ridge above were found along its course. The other platoon appears to have advanced straight up the slope or slightly to the left, where points, bullets, and percussion caps were found. The dropped balls, caps, and uniform components on the ridge crest support the claim that they had entered the Indian camp.

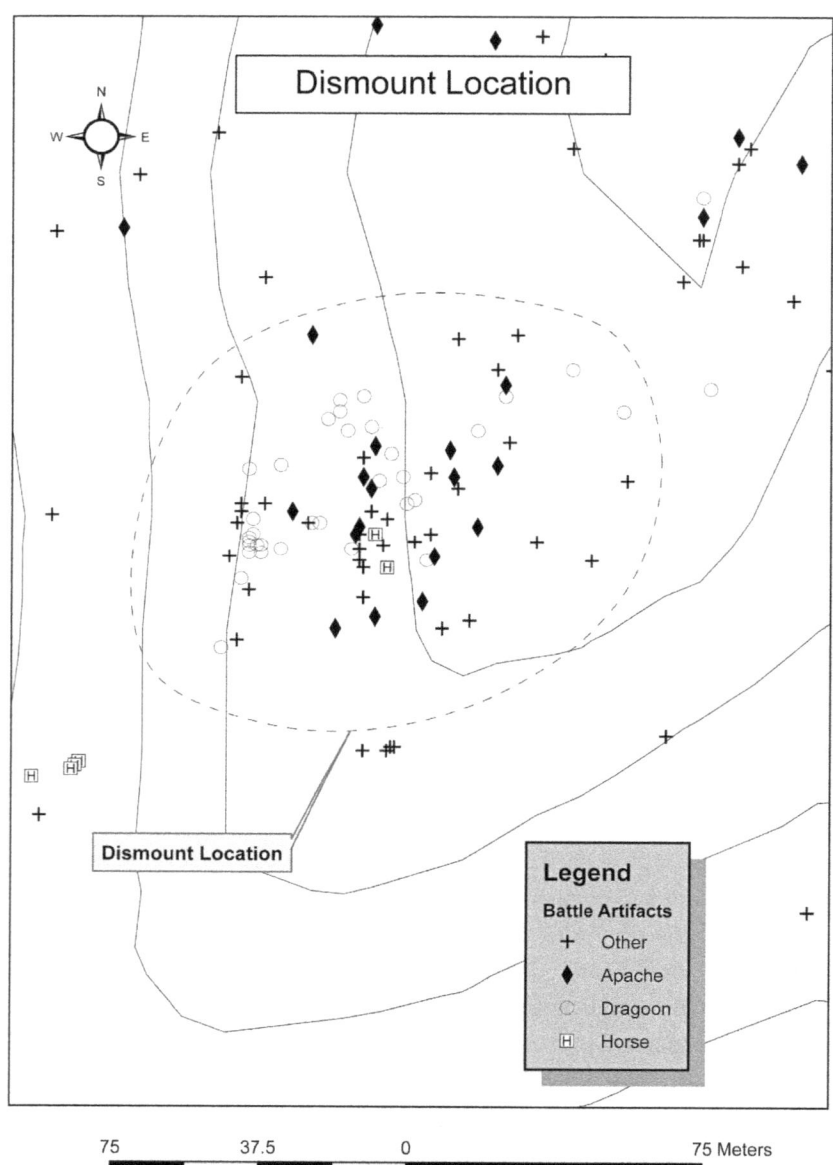

Figure 9. Dismount location.

The Apache camp occupied the top of the narrow ridge, approximately 160 meters above the dismount position. The artifact scatter is approximately 200 meters long and 50 meters wide, not counting a few dispersed artifacts that have moved down the slope (figure 10). Artifacts include micaceous ceramics, brass and tin cone tinklers, metal awls, arrow points, scraps from the manufacture of tinklers and arrow points, brass conchos, dropped lead balls, and other remains of camp activities. The lead balls are of a variety of sizes and generally irregular in shape. Many have been cut with a knife from a larger piece of lead, and some have evidence of tooth marks, indicating that they were chewed to make them round, distinguishing them from the uniformly manufactured military ammunition. No conclusive surface evidence of structures or hearths is present on the site, although that is not surprising for a briefly occupied camp. There are a few cobbles and rocks that are out of character with the shale deposits that cover most of the ground within the camp and were undoubtedly brought into the area. They could be the sparse remains of hearths or possibly even structures, but they were too few and scattered to allow a determination of purpose.

A closer examination of the artifact distribution at the camp reveals an interesting pattern. When only the ceramic artifacts are mapped, there are two distinct clusters, separated by approximately 60 meters.

A visual inspection of a sample of the ceramics from these clusters by Miller, as well as a neutron activation analysis and visual examination by Eiselt, demonstrates that, although the sherds are almost entirely micaceous with Apache characteristics, there are distinct differences between the two concentrations.[17] The northern cluster has predominantly fine self-tempered clays with a high percentage of mica, primarily from one source area but including a few sherds from a second clay source as well. The southern cluster is primarily from the same clay source that is predominate in the northern cluster, but some sherds exhibit a coarse gritty temper, and the paste from a few sherds were found to have been made from a third clay source.

A few of the sherds that were analyzed were large enough to determine vessel shapes, and this too indicated differences between the two concentrations. Large short-necked ollas and small bowls appeared only in the northern concentration. Based on form, the northern concentration contained

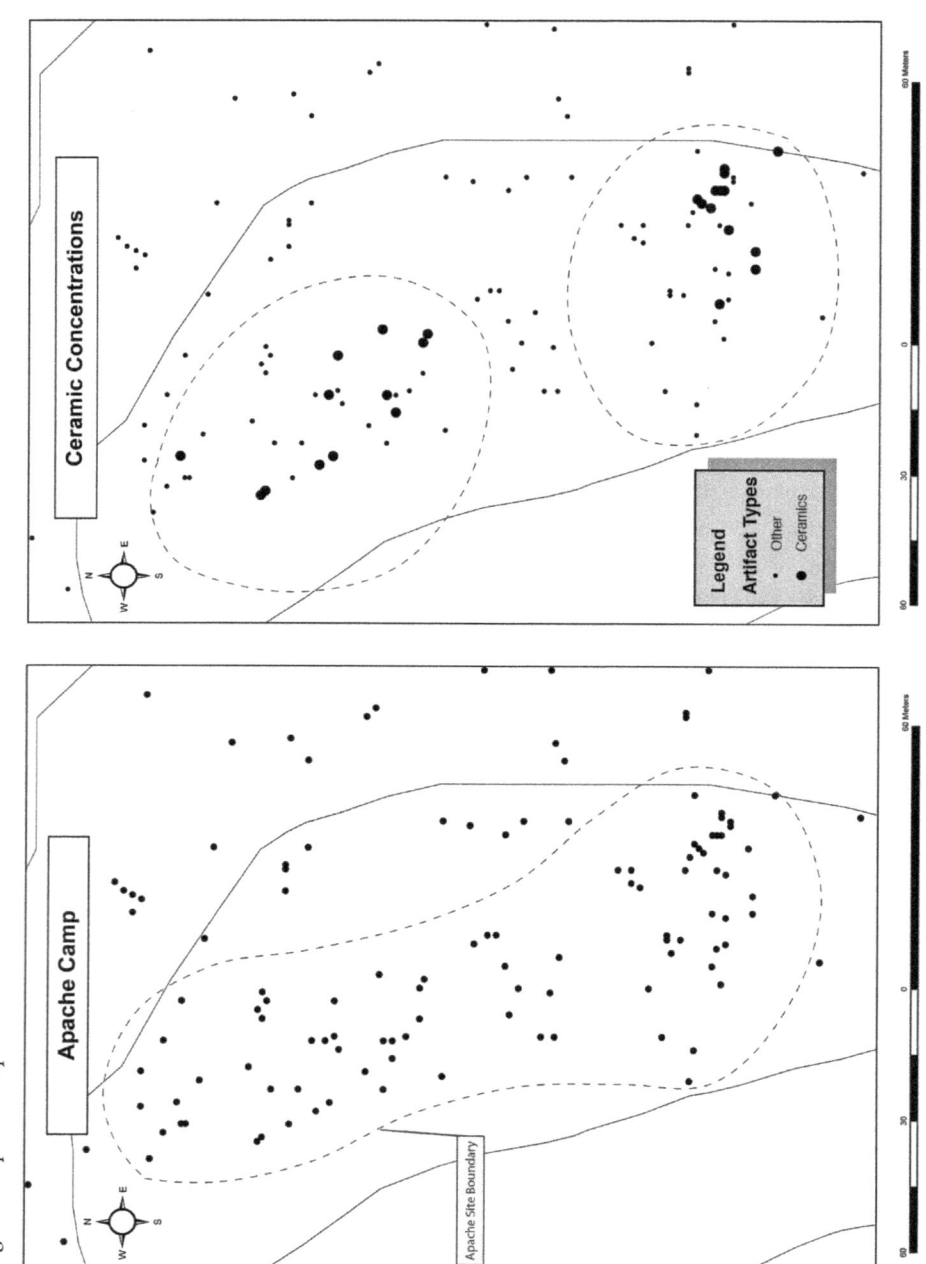

Figure 10. Apache camp

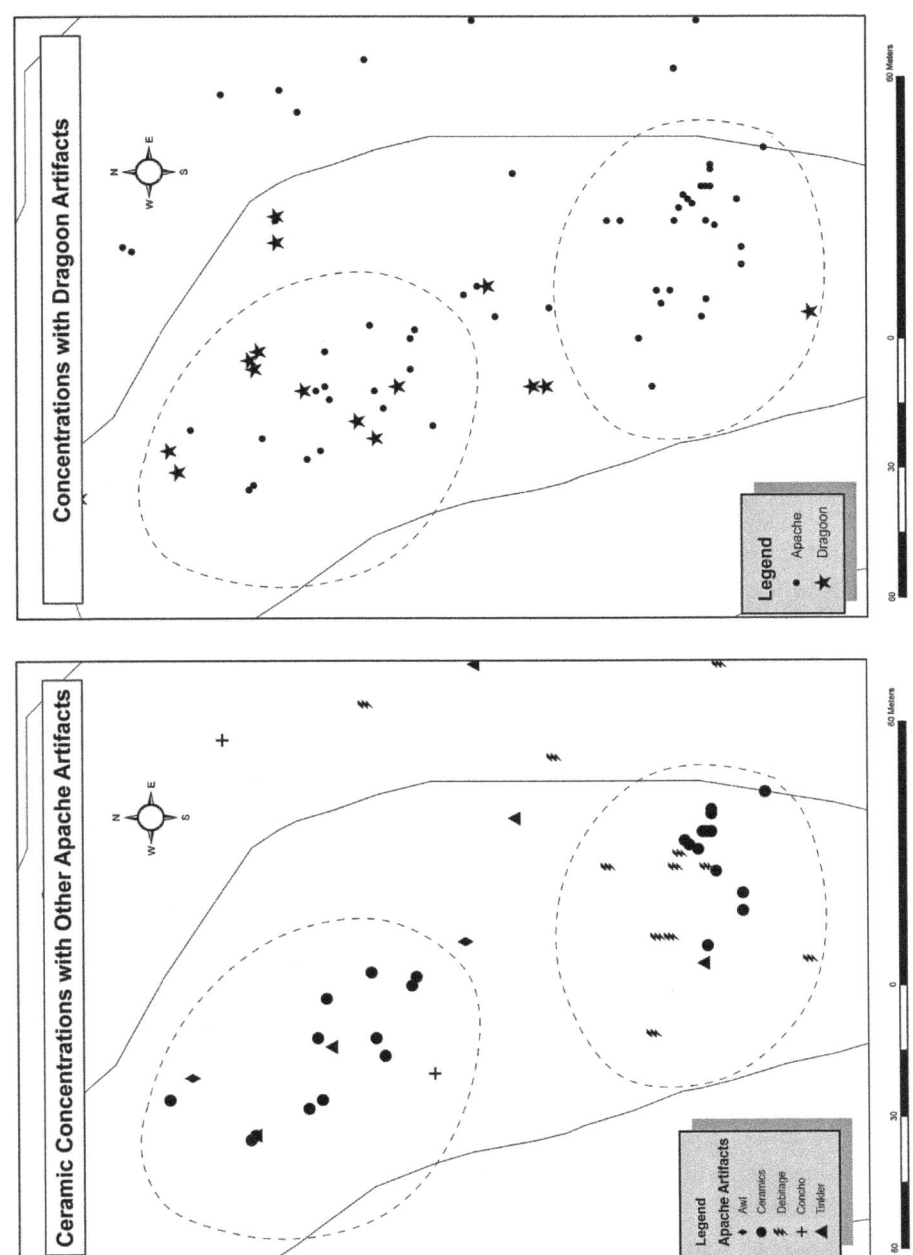

vessels generally associated with both Llanero and Ollero Apache, although most were Llanero. The southern concentration contained only Llanero Apache vessels, although there were San Juan pueblo sherds.

When other Apache artifacts are plotted, the differences are even more apparent. There were metal awls, brass conchos, and brass tinklers at the northern concentration, whereas tin tinklers and scraps of metal debitage from manufacturing points were more common at the southern concentration. There were no conchos or awls in the southern concentration.

When the military artifacts are overlain, the southern artifact concentration seems almost to have been ignored, with activities clustered around the northern group of artifacts. The few military artifacts found in or near the southern concentration are primarily unfired balls and percussion caps, possibly dropped as the troops passed over the area. Initially this was thought to be an indication that the two artifact areas were unrelated and only the northern area occupied at the time of the battle. After an examination of the topography and overall artifact distribution, however, another possibility seems more plausible.

The southern concentration is just below the top of a small hill on the ridge, which is not a particularly defensible position. The northern cluster occupies the high ground. It is quite possible that the two artifact concentrations represent two groups of Apaches who occupied the camp at the same time, and they all moved to the higher ground prior to the dragoons' attack. Several military letters written just before the battle indicate that there was a group of Apaches—two chiefs and about one hundred warriors and their families—moving toward the Rio Grande from Mora. Kit Carson noted that he met with two chiefs whose people were camped near Cieneguilla.[18] This artifact distribution could well be evidence that there were two distinct groups camped at the site, confirming the observations in the historical records. The predominance of Llanero vessel types is also consistent with reports that the Apaches came over from the Mora side of the mountains.

One interesting cluster of military artifacts consisting of buttons, dropped and fired caps, and a brass spur were found in the northern concentration. This may be where one of the soldiers, Sergeant Kent, was reported to have been killed on entering the Apache camp.[19]

THE ARCHAEOLOGICAL RECORD   63

Not long after the soldiers reached the camp, the Apaches withdrew and went around the ridge and attacked the horse position from several directions. The soldiers who had been left to guard the horses called for help. The dragoons had no choice but to leave the Indian camp and moved down the slope to reinforce the troops who were with the horses.

Artifacts from both the Apache camp and dragoons' assault were found scattered down the slope from the camp, ultimately reaching a fairly dense concentration of military, horse, and Apache artifacts that marks the location where the dragoons had originally dismounted and were later pinned down by the warriors (figure 11). Dropped and fired percussion caps, dropped balls, Apache arrow points, and Apache fired balls (irregularly shaped and chewed) were all found here. There are no boulders or large rocks to hide behind, though this was claimed in some of the second-hand accounts of the battle. The troops would have hidden behind trees, bushes, fallen horses, and any dirt breastworks they could have put together. No evidence of breastworks, however, was found.

The dragoons found that they were now situated on low ground, surrounded by the Apaches firing from above and the sides. The archaeological evidence supports this interpretation. Dropped balls, percussion caps, horseshoes, and horseshoe nails pinpoint the horse position, and it appears that soldiers were stationed in and around the horses just above the canyon bottom. There is also a concentration of Apache fired balls and arrows in this locale. Approximately 60 percent of the percussion caps found in this location had been fired, indicating that the soldiers were probably fairly calm under the circumstances. From that position, the ridge they eventually climbed in their retreat is just under a half mile away.

Davidson realized that he had to move his position and led the troops to a small nearby hill that seemed more defensible. Metal points, caps, balls, and two military spurs were found in the canyon bottom and slopes on the adjacent ridge, showing a movement of the troops from where they had been pinned down to the ridge about 175 meters away (figure 12). The limited number of artifacts here suggests that the dragoons were at this location briefly, as described in the written accounts.

The dragoons then left this position and went down to the mouth of the small side canyon. When they reached the trail that they had followed

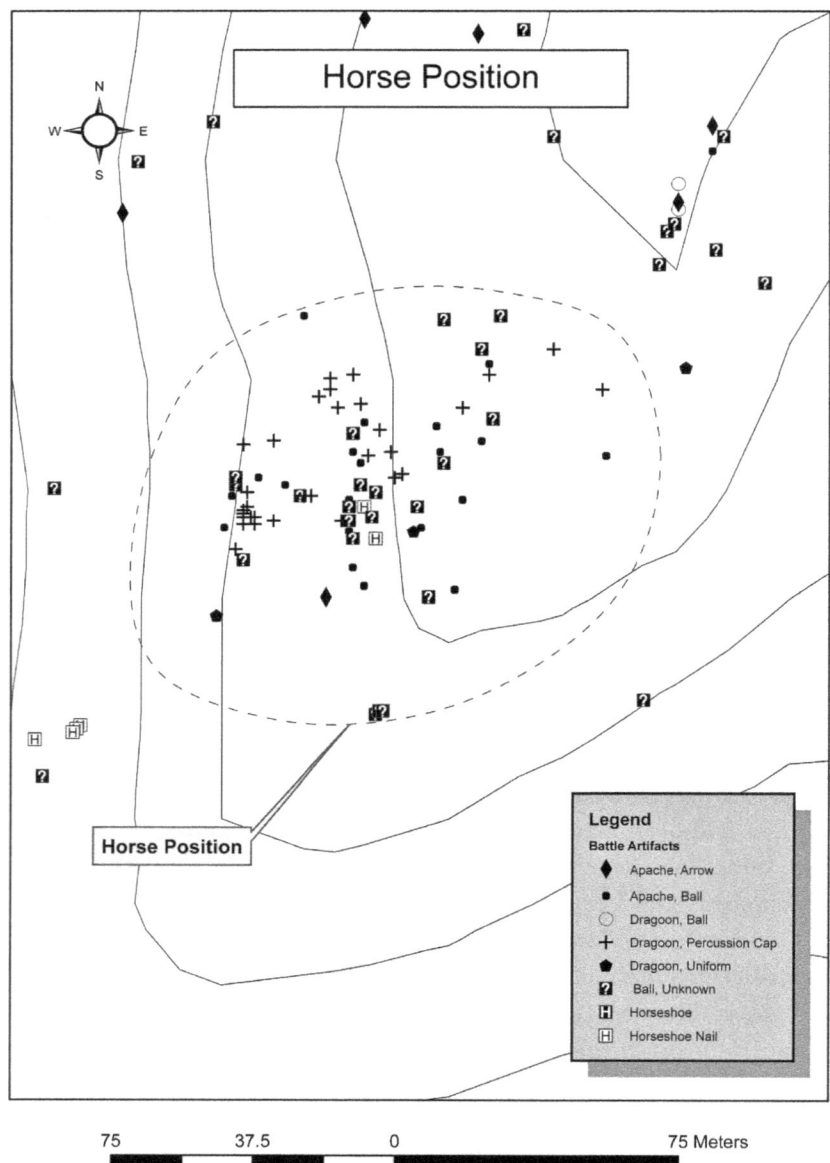

Figure 11. Horse position.

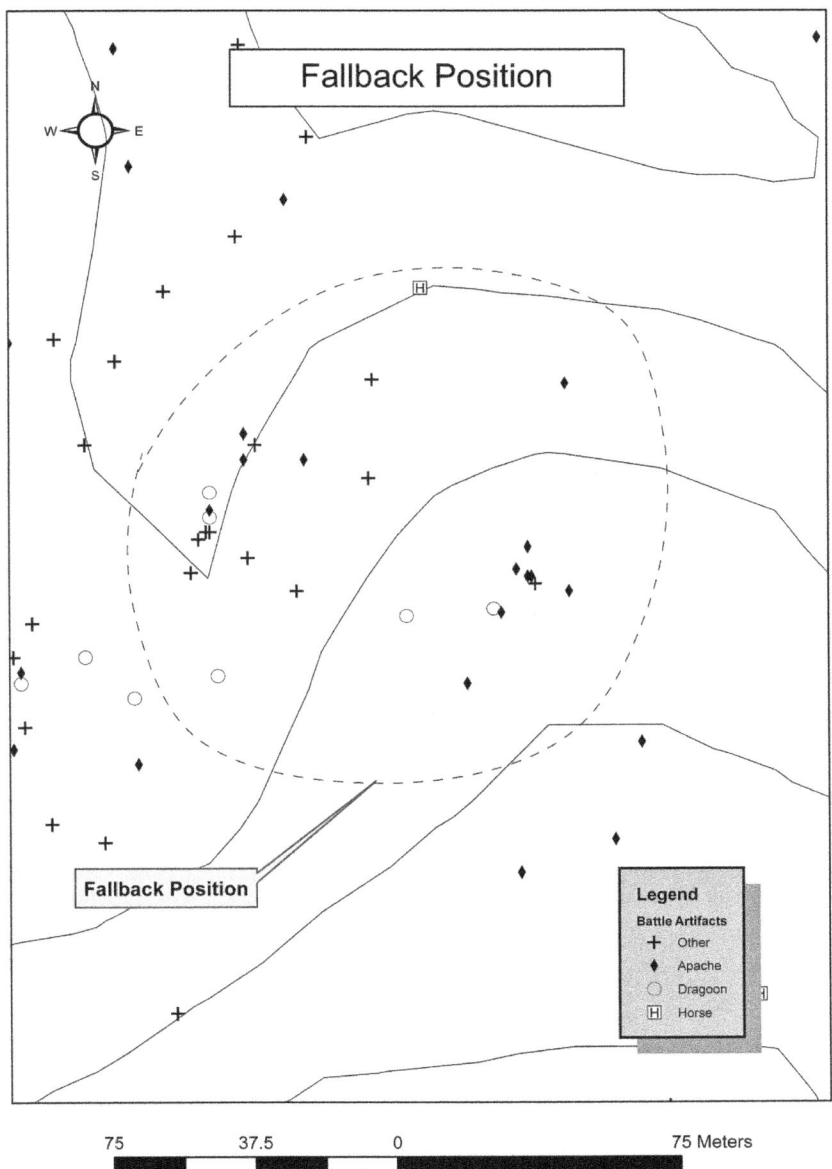

Figure 12. Fallback position.

into the area, either the Apaches blocked their retreat down the trail or the troops did not want to run the risk of an ambush in the narrow canyon. They instead moved across the creek and straight up the steep slope of the large ridge to the north. Though very little was found on the steep slope, there were sufficient artifacts on the lower slope and at the top to identify where the troops had gone up the ridge (figure 13). Boot nails, arrow points, a horseshoe nail, and a few fired balls indicate the probable route. The dragoons would have been fairly spread out to get up the steep ridge without having to wait for those in front to move forward, so there is no single trail. The few military artifacts at the top indicate where they reached the summit.

The dragoons were reported to have met the Indians as soon as they reached the top of the hill. The near lack of artifacts does not support this claim. This may mean that we did not find the point at which the troops reached the summit, or it may that artifact collectors found the locale of this portion of the battle and "cleaned it out." It is, however, unlikely that anyone would have recovered every small piece of lead, every percussion cap, and every boot nail had they plundered the battle site. Certainly artifact collectors would likely not have scoured the steep slopes where the troops ascended the ridge. It seems more plausible, then, that the dragoons did not encounter the warriors until they reached the "point of the hill," as described in the court of inquiry and shown on the sketch map (see figure 7). It is here that the artifacts start to appear.

From the point of the hill, the artifacts are distributed down the narrow ridge crest until the location where the troops angled off down the side slope to the canyon below (figure 14). A close look at the artifact distribution in this area shows several small concentrations spread out along the ridge, perhaps where the troops halted, turned, and fired to repel Apache attacks. Numerous dropped bullets and caps, along with dropped gun tools, fired arrows, fired caps, and Apache bullets confirm that the battle was heavy on this ridge. At the point where the artifacts stop, the location where the troops went down the side of the steep ridge, many additional dropped items were found.

This section of the ridge is where the dragoons lost seventeen men, and the artifacts indicate that the fighting may have been getting desperate.

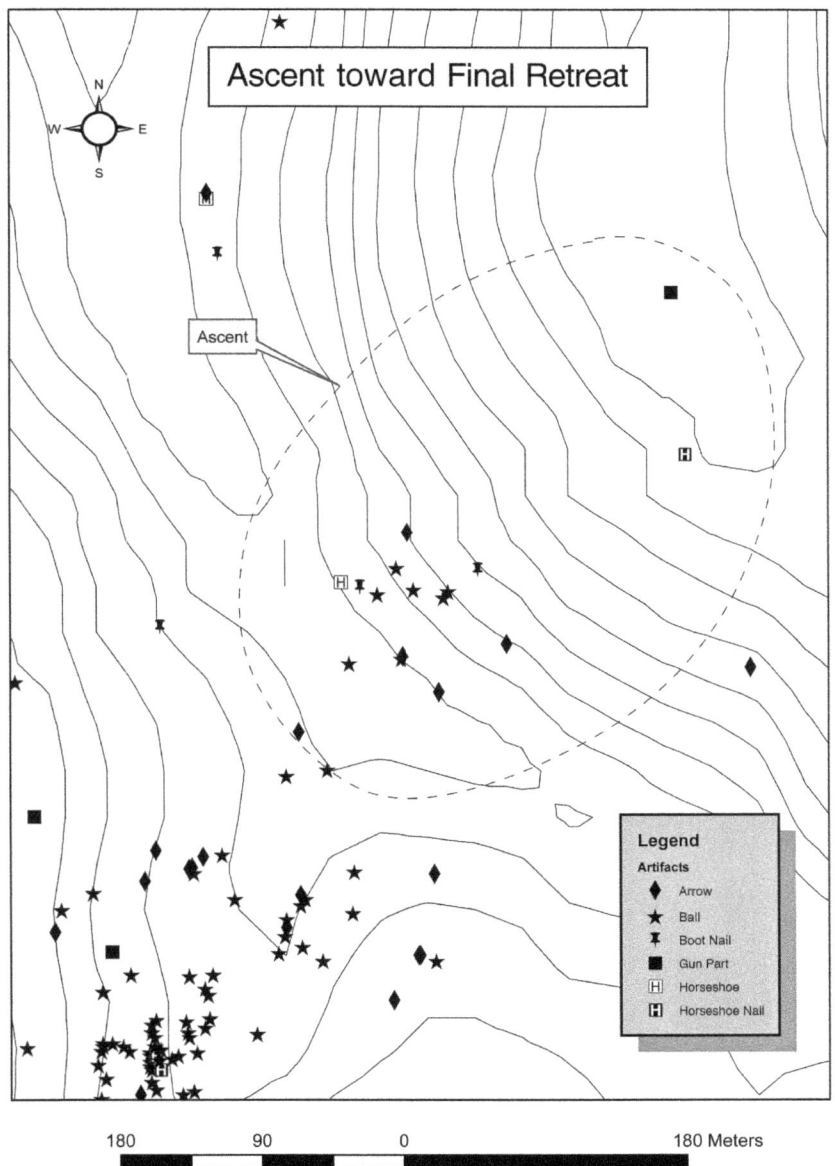

Figure 13. Location of ascent.

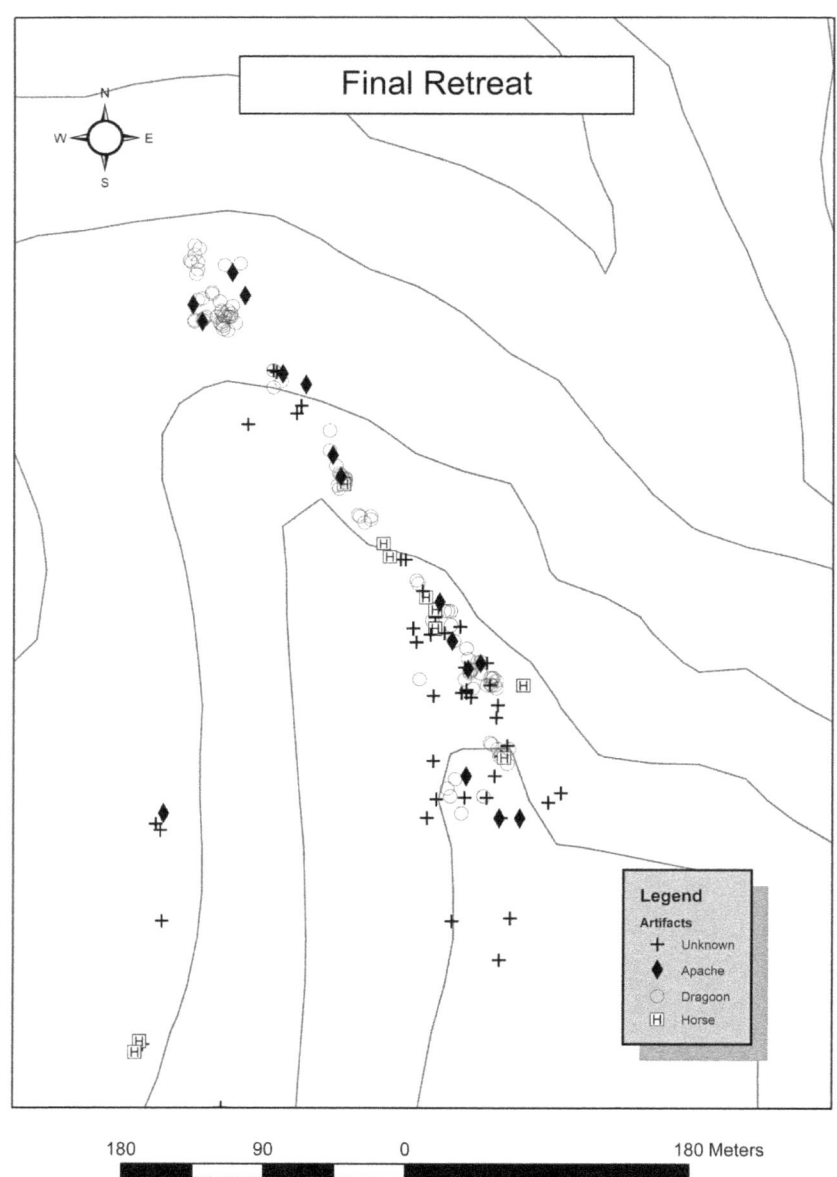

Figure 14. Final retreat.

Seventy percent of the percussion caps found in this area were dropped and had never been fired. The majority of balls were also dropped. This is consistent with the written account of the dragoons being under heavy fire from repeated Apache attacks. A saber belt hook or accoutrement hook found in this area appears to have been shot off someone's belt, and numerous metal arrow points were also found. The dragoons eventually slipped off the ridgetop down the north slope, where they made their final retreat. They were practically in sight of the trail back to Cieneguilla at this point, but they were apparently blocked from this escape route by the Apaches. A single fired cap among dozens of dropped balls, tools, and personal items at this location suggests that the soldiers broke off the fight to flee down the hill toward safety.

Summary and Conclusions

The archaeological evidence confirms that the Cieneguilla battle site has been found and provides us an opportunity to examine the battle in more detail than has been possible for more than 150 years. The battle tactics of both the military and the Apaches are seen in a new light. The research also provides us an opportunity to compare the written accounts with the actual footprint of the battle and in essence reopen the court of inquiry of 1856.

The location of the Indian camp is an indication that the Apaches had defense clearly in mind. The small hill on the ridge where the camp was situated is on the high ground with steep side slopes on either side. Numerous escapes routes are present in the event of an attack. The Apaches could drop off the back side of the ridge to the west, and there were several small washes that would have provided concealed departure to the east. The ridge extends to the north, where it terminates in a steep drop to the canyon bottom. The south end of the ridge abuts Picuris Mountain, allowing for relatively easy access to the southeast along the contours back toward the Rio Pueblo.

Cordero provides a description of late eighteenth-century Apache offensive tactics: "When the time came for attack, they frequently resorted to an ambush in a place favorable to them. This consisted in sending some of their fastest runners or mounted warriors ahead to draw out the enemy. When the latter attacked the swiftly retreating Apache, they suddenly found themselves surrounded by the main body and cut to pieces. After the battle, the Apache retreated with incredible speed, deliberately following a route through rough, mountainous land to discourage pursuers."[20] This is precisely the tactics the Jicarillas used at Cieneguilla.

It is apparent that the dragoons were not prepared for the resistance the Apaches provided and had not realized that the warriors could attack the troops and horses that were left behind. If the written accounts are correct in stating that someone from the camp called out to the dragoons to "come on if you want a fight," it would appear that the Apaches were not at all intimidated by the soldiers. Instead of fleeing from the advancing soldiers or trying to draw them off as the women and children escaped, the Jicarillas seem to have encouraged the troops to attack the village. Then, as the troops approached, they quickly retreated from the camp and dropped around behind the dragoons to attack the horses. This drew the dragoons back down to the canyon bottom, where they were trapped on the low ground below their attackers.

The fact that the Apaches were attacking from different directions suggests that they followed tactics like the dragoons' in that they divided their forces to catch the troops in a crossfire. As the dragoons were pinned down, the Apaches would make sporadic attacks from behind trees in an attempt to capture or kill the horses and as many soldiers as they could. The ratio of bullets to arrow points indicates that for this portion of the fight the Apaches relied heavily on firearms. When the dragoons had enough and retreated to the next ridge, the warriors hurried to the ridge to beat them to the top so they could again claim the better position. Once on the ridge, they caught the troops on a narrow portion of the ridge and sealed them in by closing in behind, then commenced firing on the dragoons from above and below. The written accounts and archaeological evidence support the claim that the fighting was close and fierce. There is a higher ratio of arrow points to fired Apache balls in this portion of the battle, indicating that the Indians may have been running out of ammunition or preferred arrows for close fighting, where they would be more effective.

The archaeological evidence suggests that the dragoons were using one of their standard attacks. They approached the camp in full view and dismounted below the camp. It was typical for dragoons to dismount prior to fighting, but their choice of locations to dismount appears to have been ill advised. It is likely that they did not expect to encounter resistance and therefore were not particularly concerned with where they dismounted or their ability to defend the position if the need should arise.

The troops were reported to have divided into two platoons to advance upon the camp, perhaps thinking that a show of force would intimidate the Apaches. The two platoons entered the camp from different directions in an attempt to catch them in a crossfire. When it was discovered that the majority of the Indians had left the camp, and the call for help went out from the troops down below, they fell back to the horse position and did their best to protect the horses and defend themselves.

This is where the troops changed tactics; instead of being in an offensive mode and controlling the high ground at the Indian camp, they were forced to take the low ground and defend their position. There is little cover in the area of the horses other than trees and brush. The percentages of fired (60 percent) and dropped (40 percent) caps in this area suggest that the troops remained pretty much under control during this time (figure 15). No dropped Dragoon revolver ammunition was found in this location, suggesting that if they were using their revolvers they were not reloading. Instead, they may have been saving their revolvers for close-range fighting.

The claim by Davidson that his troops had dismounted on a slope, entered the Apache camp, and were fighting in the camp is confirmed. However, as noted, Davidson also claimed that he did not leave his horses in the bottom of a canyon or next to the stream before advancing on the camp, but the artifacts reveal that he did leave his horses and a handful of troops *near* the canyon bottom. It would appear that he could have advanced farther up the slope before he dismounted his men, or circled around by going up the adjacent ridge and entering the camp from the south or southeast. Although only five of the twenty-two soldiers were killed in the initial dismounted attack on the camp, this loss combined with being pinned down for a long period undoubtedly affected the soldiers' ability to continue

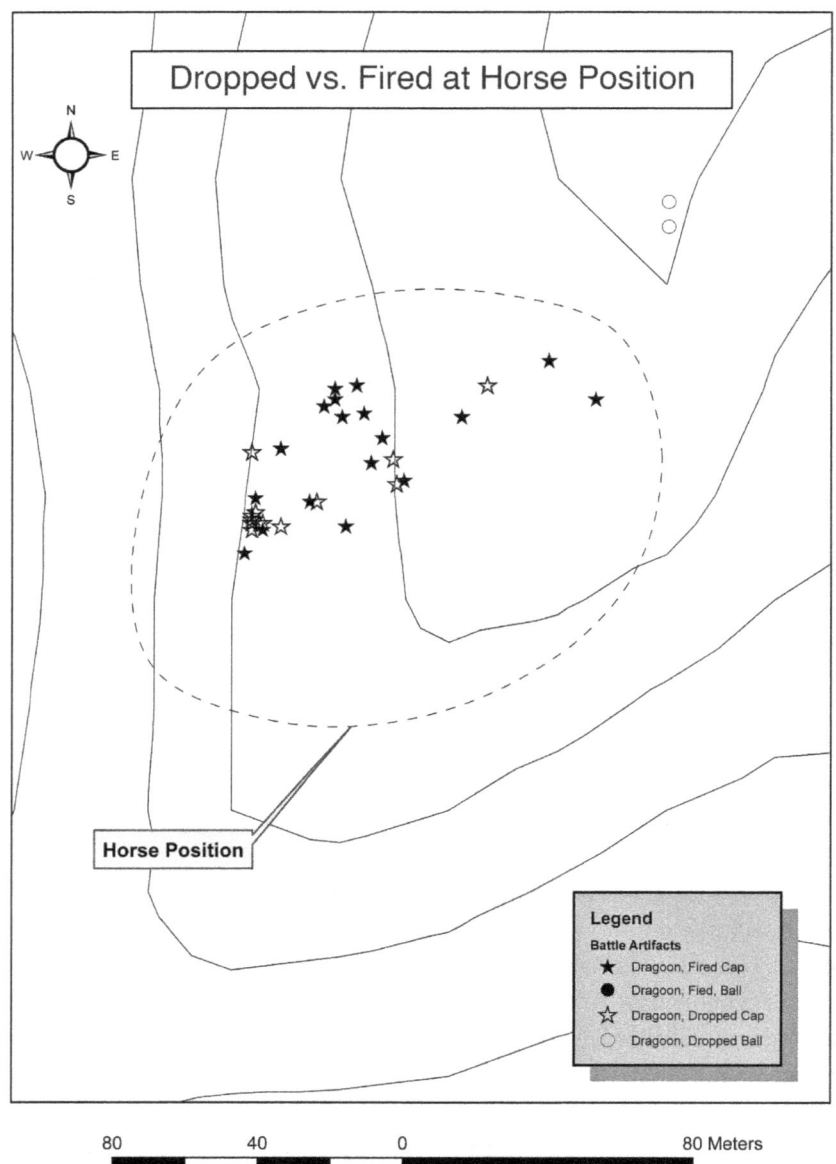

Figure 15. Dropped vs. fired caps at horse position.

the fight effectively. Had the dragoons dismounted in another location on higher ground, they might not have been pinned down at all.

The limited number of artifacts on the steep side slope where Davidson led his men after retreating from the horse position indicates that the battle was in recess during this time. And the near lack of artifacts at the top of the ridge may indicate that the troops rode along the ridge crest some distance before encountering the Apaches at the point of the hill; in other words, they were not confronted as soon as they reached the top, as was presented in several of the testimonies. If this is the case, the dragoons might have been able to retreat down the side of the ridge to the north and avoid the second encounter that left seventeen men dead. It is likely that the dragoons were exhausted from the fight at the horse position and the climb up the steep slope and lulled into a sense of security on reaching the top of the ridge. They chose to move along the ridge back toward the point of the hill in an apparent attempt to reach the trail back to Cieneguilla. They probably felt that they now had the higher ground and would not run into as much trouble as they had when pinned down in the canyon bottom. By the time they reached the narrow ridge where they were to descend to the trail, they found that the Apaches were there first. The warriors then advanced on the soldiers from the rear, trapping them on the narrow ridge. At this point they had nowhere to go and were forced to fight their way to freedom along the narrow ridge.

The tight distribution of artifacts along the ridge seems to confirm that the troops stayed together during their final retreat from the point of the hill. Near the top of the ridge, the ratio of fired to dropped artifacts shows the dragoons were engaged in the battle (figure 16). As they progressed down the ridge toward the saddle, the number of fired artifacts dropped off quickly. Overall, the ratio of dropped to fired bullets and caps indicates that the soldiers were likely weary if not frantic during the push down the narrow ridge.

As the troops fought their way toward the saddle and the trail to Cieneguilla, they soon found they could go no further. Taking advantage of a slightly less steep side slope, they made a final retreat down the side of the ridge to the adjacent canyon. The Apaches apparently did not follow. A dropped percussion cap, one arrow point, and a horseshoe mark the spot

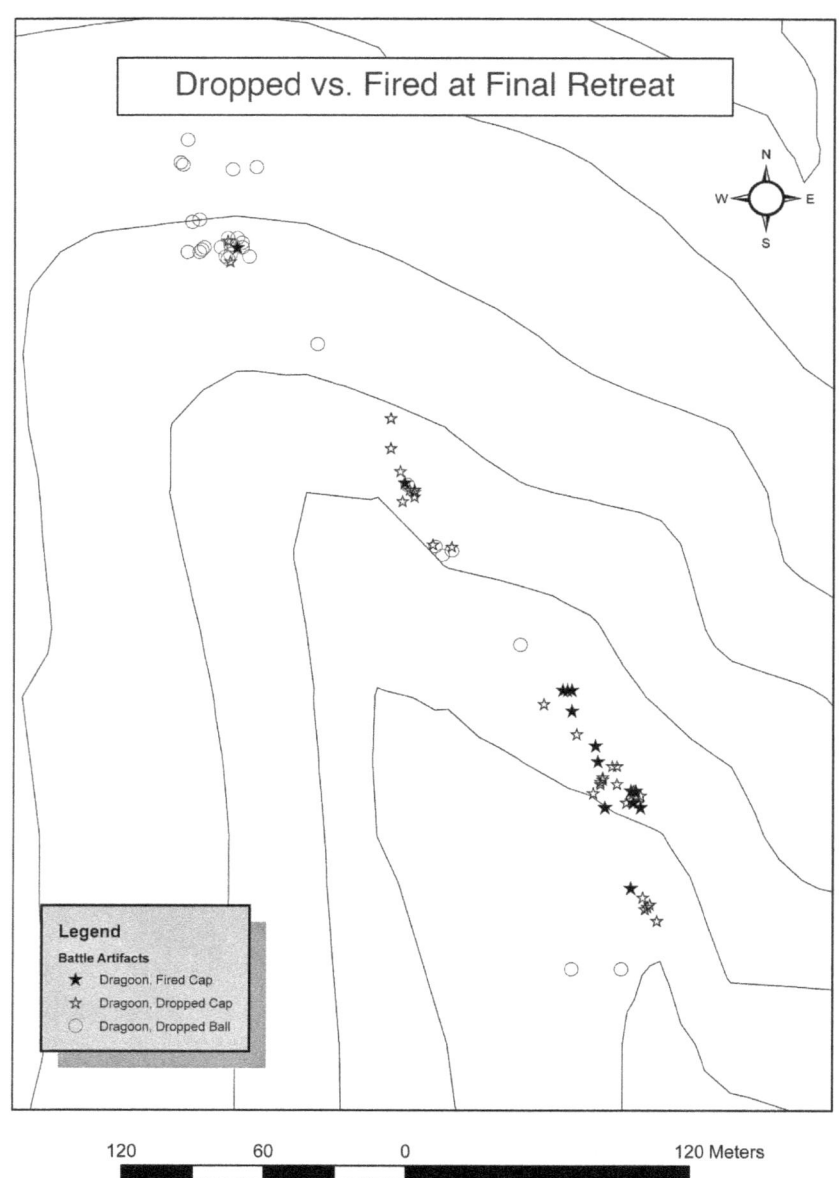

Figure 16. Dropped vs. fired ammunition at final retreat.

where they reached the canyon bottom. The remaining soldiers followed the canyon out of the mountains and returned to Fort Burgwin with their wounded. The final position was littered with dropped balls, percussion caps, tools, and equipment, suggesting that the retreat was not as controlled or as orderly as reported. In the end, twenty-two troops had been killed during the battle, along with an unknown number of Apaches.

The research into this battle site picks up the investigation begun at the court of inquiry that was convened at Lieutenant Davidson's request. At that time, the court declined the invitation to visit the battle site and made their ruling on the basis of soldiers' testimony. In a sense, this site visit has now been concluded. But with today's technology, not only has the footprint of the battle been revealed, but the analysis has provided insights into the battle tactics as well. Perhaps most important, the research has identified differences between the official written record and the evidence found on the ground and has answered many questions that were raised soon after the dragoons' defeat. Research into the battle will undoubtedly continue, allowing others to weigh in on this important event in New Mexico history, but one thing is clear: the archaeological record confirms that the Battle of Cieneguilla has been found and provides firm evidence to make the concluding arguments in the 150-year-old investigation of the fight.

NOTES

1. E.g., Boyer 1965.
2. Johnson et al. 2002.
3. Adams et. al. 2000a, 2000b.
4. Adams et al. 2000a:29–32; Gregory and Rogerson 1984:179; Haecker 1998:9–13; Haecker and Mauck 1997:131; Ludwig and Stute 1993:13–17; Scott et al. 1989:25–30.
5. Adams et al. 1998.
6. Johnson 2003; Johnson and Adams 2005; Johnson et al. 2009; Johnson et al., in press.
7. Davidson to Blake, Apr. 1, 1854, Letters Received, Department of New Mexico, Adjutant General's Office, Record Group [RG] 94, National Archives, Washington, D.C. [hereafter NA].
8. Bell to Williams, Dec. 27, 1854, Letters Received, Department of New Mexico, Adjutant General's Office, RG 94, NA.
9. Goddard 1911. It was in 1909 that Pliny Goddard talked to the Apache elder who told him the story about the battle.

10. Proceedings of a Court of Inquiry Convened at Santa Fe, New Mexico, Feb. 9, 1856, Judge Advocate General's Office, RG 153, NA.

11. Smith et al. 2003.

12. A detailed description of the artifacts can be found in Johnson 2003; Johnson and Adams 2005; and Johnson et al. 2009.

13. Weber and Scott 2003, 2006.

14. Hendricks and Wilson 1996:13, 66.

15. Cieneguilla Grant Case 84, 1895–1896, U.S. Court of Private Land Claims, Santa Fe District, Case Records, in Cieneguilla Grant case records, Thomas B. Catron Papers Collection 1692–1934, Series 301, Box 16, Folder 5, Center for Southwest Research, Zimmerman Library, University of New Mexico, Albuquerque.

16. Hawk 2005.

17. Eiselt 2005; Miller 2003.

18. Carson to Messervy, March 27, 1854, Letters Received, Office of Indian Affairs, New Mexico Superintendency, 1854–1855, RG 75, M234, R547, NA.

19. Proceedings of a Court of Inquiry Convened at Santa Fe, New Mexico, Feb. 9, 1856, Office of the Judge Advocate General, RG 153, NA.

20. Matson and Schroeder 1957:345–46, citing Cordero.

The Battle of Adobe Walls

Commentary

Ronald K. Wetherington

There is, of course, more than one "Battle of Adobe Walls" in the historical record. And although only the second, ten years after the first, earns the credit for precipitating the end of American Indian hegemony in the southern plains, both battles were motivated by the same sentiments. The first, in 1864, pitted Kit Carson and his government contingency of cavalry and Indian scouts, numbering four hundred, against several thousand Kiowa and Comanche warriors at their encampment at the original Adobe Walls trading post of Bent, St. Vrain & Company in the Texas Panhandle. This earlier and far bloodier battle is not the one subject to these comments and the following two essays.

In 1864, U.S. forces, intent on halting the persistent Indian raids on wagon trains crossing the Santa Fe Trail, engaged tribes long resentful of Euro-Americans' profligate killing of buffalo for their hides and the American incursion on traditional lands. The Indians prevailed, despite suffering greater casualties than the troops due to Carson's astute use of field howitzers, and Carson and his troops escaped.[1] The second "Battle of Adobe Walls"—the subject of discussions by J. Brett Cruse and T. Lindsay Baker here—took place ten years later, begun by an attack led by Comanche Quanah Parker and encouraged by Isatai, a Comanche medicine man. In this case, too, the Indians far outnumbered the defenders of the trading post, and their grievances were the same: decimation of their food resources by buffalo hunters. This grievance also, by the way, helped precipitate the Colorado Indian War in the 1860s, leading to the Sand Creek massacre.

As in the other engagements in this volume, there are different perspectives on the battle by the different participants, and as the story was retold through the years there were both contradictory and exaggerated claims. A more thorough archaeological investigation would doubtless clarify the changing positions of both defenders and attackers during this long engagement. The painstaking study of Custer's fight at Little Bighorn reveals the kind of contribution modern archaeological techniques can make.[2] Nevertheless, the research already conducted by Baker and Cruse offers insights into the potential that Adobe Walls holds for the historiography and archaeology of the southern plains.

The two essays are complementary, in part because there appear to be no discrepancies in the historical accounts when filtered through Baker's historiographic sieve to measure reliability, and in part because the archaeological evidence lends credence to some of the more incredulous claims by historical figures—most notably Billy Dixon's "long shot." It is fortunate that later interviews of several of the Indian participants actually present at Adobe Walls not only corroborate historical interpretations but provide some empathy to soften any attempt to demonize the tribes.

It is notable that for the combined tribes the courage of their raid was reinforced by their faith that Isatai's magic would make them immune to the hide men's bullets.[3] After Quanah and others were in fact struck with bullets, they turned their anger on Isatai. They were also dismayed by the unexpected range of the defenders' Sharps rifles, compared with the much shorter range of their own weapons. "Shot kill a mile away," said Quanah, "that pretty hard fight." It was doubtless this dual defeat—the failure of their magic and the long-range accuracy of the defenders—that demoralized the proud attackers and led to their retreat.

The evidence found on the distant hills by the Texas Historical Commission archaeologist testifies to the strong firepower of the hide men, who prevailed despite being so outnumbered. One can only imagine the resignation in the minds of the tribes that this reality had pretty much sealed their fate. Of course it did not, and the Adobe Walls engagement was simply a harbinger of what became known as the Red River War. Here, as in other engagements described in this volume, we see the slow buildup of long-term grievances as they finally reach a point of desperation and, against threatening odds, reach a tipping point of violence. In the Adobe Walls battle, at least, the casualties—three defenders and perhaps two dozen attackers—were substantially fewer than in the others.

NOTES

1. Pettis 1908.
2. Fox 1993; see also Scott and Fox 1987.
3. According to Quanah Parker, as told to Hugh Scott in 1897, "Esati [Isatai] make big talk that time—God tell me we going to kill lots white men—I stop the bullets in gun—bullets not penetrate shirts—we kill them just like old women." Hugh Scott Collection, U.S. Army Field Artillery and Fort Sill Museum, Lawton, Okla.; I thank T. Lindsay Baker for providing a transcript of this document. This strongly parallels the similar medicine claim of the Cheyennes at the battle of Solomon River in 1857; see Chalfant 1989. Because the cavalry used sabers rather than guns, and the medicine was effective only against bullets, the Cheyennes fled the charge.

Historical Perspectives

T. Lindsay Baker

During spring 1874 the commercial buffalo hunt that for three years had centered on southwestern Kansas shifted southward. The systematic killing of thousands of bison had begun in 1871 after tanners in the East developed new methods that could produce usable commercial leather from the otherwise spongy skins. Professional big-game hunters using specialized firearms, together with bands of skinners, decimated the herds on the central Great Plains while steam railways hauled the flat, dry hides eastward to tanneries.

Because the herds had been so thinned, the hunting crews pushed 150 miles southward from their center of operations at Dodge City across the Oklahoma Panhandle into extreme northern Texas. To keep the trade of the hunters, two Kansas trading companies created new branch operations in Texas as well, establishing a trading post on the north bank of the Canadian River at a crossing place called Adobe Walls.[1] The locality took its name from the ruins of a much earlier Bent, St. Vrain & Company post. The Dodge City traders, together with a saloon keeper and a blacksmith, set up a trading center in the Texas Panhandle to sell supplies to the commercial hunters and to purchase their dried hides.

Native people on the southern Great Plains realized very well what was going on. They knew that the hide men were destroying their commissary, taking only skins and leaving the bison carcasses behind to rot. They took the threat so seriously that Comanches, Kiowas, and Southern Cheyennes united for the first time in their histories to drive the hide men away from their traditional hunting grounds, which they felt has been reserved for their use by the 1867 Treaties of Medicine Lodge. What they did not realize was that Texas had retained ownership of its public lands when it entered the United States in 1845, and that the federal negotiators at Medicine Lodge lacked the legal authority to make any commitments regarding hunting in Texas. American Indian leaders did, however, know that they were quickly losing the buffalo on which they depended for their way of life.

Led by two young Comanches named Quanah and Isatai, a medicine man, a combined party of Comanches, Kiowas, and Southern Cheyennes attacked the trading post at Adobe Walls early on the morning of June 27, 1874. The warriors believed that they would club the sleeping white men to death, and that even if they awakened Isatai's medicine would protect them from gunshot injury. Many were shocked to see their friends fall in battle. After several hours the attackers withdrew to the adjacent hills while hunters from surrounding camps made their way to the trading post. The encounter ended as a draw. After a few days the Indians gave up hopes of besting the inmates of the reinforced post, and the hunters and merchants gradually abandoned the place as too dangerous and returned to Kansas. The fight at Adobe Walls was over.[2]

The purpose of this essay is to examine the insights that written historical accounts allow today into the Battle of Adobe Walls. Fortunately both Euro-Americans and native peoples saw the encounter in the Canadian River Valley to have been significant in their histories. Consequently, members of both groups left remembrances that provide the historian with primary data for interpreting the events. There are also important documentary sources that were created at the time of the battle, giving the historian primary evidence.

For decades the site of the events in 1874 lay abandoned, becoming part of a cattle ranch. Whites gathered there for commemorations of the forty-ninth and fiftieth anniversaries of the fight[3] and then in 1929 to rebury one of the hide hunters.[4] In 1941, American Indians gathered at the old battleground to erect and dedicate their own monument to warriors who lost their lives trying to rid the plains of the detested buffalo hunters.[5] Otherwise only occasional visitors made their way via dirt roads to the out-of-the-way location.[6]

Then in 1975 the Panhandle-Plains Historical Museum, which had owned the five acres encompassing the trading post site since 1923,[7] began at Adobe Walls the first-ever systematic archaeological excavation of a place associated with the commercial buffalo hunt. Archaeologist Billy R. Harrison headed the effort, which continued for five summers of fieldwork, each followed by nine months of cleaning and cataloging the artifacts. It was a substantial effort involving dozens of participants. The fact that the site had lain mostly undisturbed for a century meant that the materials found came from an 1874 "time capsule." The archaeological excavations at Adobe Walls were just of the trading post buildings and their immediate environs. There was never a survey or excavation of the battlefield as a whole, and no testing with metal detectors was undertaken on the surrounding privately owned ranch property to determine the extent of land encompassed by the hostilities. Documentary sources describe Indians only as attacking from low hills to the west and using a hill to the east as a lookout point.

Three years into the Adobe Walls project, I joined the effort as a "newly minted" history Ph.D. from Texas Tech University. Though I had worked for several years documenting historic sites and structures, I had no formal background in archaeology. My assignment at the Canyon museum was twofold: to write a thorough academic history of the 1874 Adobe Walls trading post and the fight that took place there, and to undertake research on all artifacts from the site that had discernible makers' marks, such as china sherds, brass buttons, and lamp parts. What more could a young historian want? I had a challenging project and generous institutional support with which to undertake it.

Early in my investigations I came to an important realization. Up to the 1970s most of the historians who had delved into the Adobe Walls story had viewed it as part of Texas history. The events did, after all, take place within the political bounds of the Lone Star State. The participants in the events, however, came predominately from elsewhere. They were hide men or merchants who funneled through Dodge City, or they were warriors who came to the site from the Fort Sill or Darlington Indian agencies. After their engagement in the valley of the Canadian, the great majority of them eventually went back to where they had come from. This meant that Texas had served as the "stage" for "actors" who had come mostly from Kansas and Oklahoma. With the exception of 1920s and 1930s interviews undertaken by historians based in Texas, the major primary sources for the Adobe Walls events were preserved in other states where the participants had gone.

Repositories in Texas mainly offered transcripts of interviews undertaken seventy to ninety years earlier by such historians as J. Evetts Haley and Lester F. Sheffy. Both of them had connections to the Panhandle-Plains Historical Museum, and the majority of their interview transcripts went either to the museum in Canyon or to the Haley Memorial Library in Midland, Texas. No previous scholars had used these interviews thoroughly in investigating the events at Adobe Walls, and some of them provided insights unavailable elsewhere.[8] Some printed works prepared in Texas also shed valuable light on the Adobe Walls story, notably the book-length memoir that buffalo hunter William Dixon dictated to his wife before his death in 1913, published the subsequent year.[9]

Having found the important but limited documentary sources on the Adobe Walls story that were available in Texas, I next went farther afield. Kansas beckoned, and libraries and archives in the Sunflower State proved to be brimming with primary accounts of events in the Texas Panhandle during 1874. The files compiled in the 1930s by Merritt W. Beeson for his private museum in Dodge City that had been transferred to the Boot Hill Museum proved to be especially rich. There I found goodly numbers of manuscript and published accounts of events at Adobe Walls from several actual white participants.[10] Beeson's old files also contained otherwise unavailable biographical materials on many Euro-American participants in the fight.[11] Here I also found a nineteenth-century transcription from the diary of U.S. Army officer Frank D. Baldwin describing the Adobe Walls post at the time of his visit there after the battle in August 1874.[12] Kansas newspapers provided invaluable contemporary reports on the establishment and operations of the stores at Adobe Walls as well as on the fight and its aftermath.[13]

The Kansas State Historical Society in Topeka likewise contributed significant materials on the history of the events at Adobe Walls. Particularly helpful were materials gathered in the 1920s from white participants in the fight, including remembrances, sketch plans, and drawings of the trading post.[14] The society had artifacts recovered from Euro-American graves at the site and even the actual blacksmith-made sod-cutting plow that was used in spring 1874 in constructing the saloon and one of the stores.[15]

Other Euro-American documentary sources found their way to more far-flung repositories. Discovery of the Frank D. Baldwin diary extracts from 1874 in Kansas led me to his personal papers in the Colorado Historical Society in Denver.[16] By far the most important of the more distant evidence on the Adobe Walls fight, however, came from the National Archives in Washington. There I was able to locate the U.S. Court of Claims Indian depredation suits filed by buffalo hide men for their losses at the time of the Adobe Walls encounter; these documents included contemporary sworn testimony about events at the post and in the outlying camps.[17] The National Archives also holds the copious manuscript records on the 1874–75 Red River War, which the Adobe Walls fight precipitated.[18]

The Euro-Americans from Adobe Walls went back mostly to Kansas; the American Indians returned to present-day Oklahoma. It was here that I found perhaps the most abundant and important documentary evidence on the events at Adobe Walls. My first stop was at Lawton, adjacent to Fort Sill, location of the former Comanche and Kiowa Agency. There a treasure trove awaited me at the U.S. Army Field Artillery and Fort Sill Museum. Among the important materials there were the 1940s research files compiled by Wilbur Sturtevant Nye, author of important books dealing with native peoples and their interactions with the U.S. Army on the southern Great Plains. Seventy years ago Nye interviewed numerous individuals who either fought the whites at Adobe Walls or had family members who did, including Co-hay-yah, Poafebitty, Frank Yellow Fish, and Botalye.[19] Not only did Nye's interview notes survive, but the Fort Sill Museum also had the multiple large ledger books in which post commander Hugh Scott in the 1890s made notes on Comanche and Kiowa life. Among these materials is his 1897 interview with Quanah about the encounter, four oversize pages in Ledger Book One with the title "Told in English & Signs & Comanche: Quanah Parker's Account of Adobe Walls Fight."[20]

More unexpected materials surfaced after my research shifted from Lawton to the state historical society in Oklahoma City. There, for example, were the contemporary reports from the white Indian agents at the Darlington and Fort Sill reservations, chronicling the deteriorating lives of the Southern Cheyennes, Comanches, and Kiowas in the years following their signing of the 1867 Medicine Lodge Treaties, not to mention their response at Adobe Walls to the decimation of the bison.[21] The Indian-Pioneer Papers, a massive oral history project undertaken in Depression-era Oklahoma, contained multiple 1930s interviews with both American Indians and Euro-Americans with connections to Adobe Walls.[22] Perhaps the most unexpected surprise in Oklahoma City, however, was discovery of the bulk of the original 1913 typescript for Olive K. Dixon's *Life and Adventures of "Billy" Dixon*, complete with the blue fountain-pen-ink changes introduced by editor Frederick S. Barde on the eve of World War I.[23]

Having worked hand-in-hand with archaeologist Billy R. Harrison, both in the field at Adobe Walls and in the laboratory, I was able to draw from his insights as I prepared the "history half" of the Adobe Walls book. As a result of his careful excavation and recording, we knew for the first time the actual size, configurations, and relative positions of the buildings at the site. Based on the locations of window glass sherds, for example, we learned the arrangement of fenestration and understood how this affected the abilities of the people inside to fight. Similarly for the first time we learned the locations of doorways, corral fences, and defense bastions. This is not to mention our having the opportunity to correlate historical documentary sources with archaeological evidence relating to the daily lives of the merchants, hunters, and skinners. Always I had access to Mr. Harrison and his ever-sharp mind so that we could discuss fine points of interpretation.

As study and research progressed, I concluded that as usual in historical research the sources that were closest in time to the actual events tended to be the most reliable. Generally I favored those sources that came from actual participants in the events of 1874. Among the documented Euro-American participants in the fight, I weighted accounts on the basis of where the person was at the time of the specific event (in this case, which building they were in). If an informant was inside the Rath and Company store at the time of the fight, I considered his account of events in that building as more reliable than that of a person who was dozens of yards away in the Myers and Leonard Store and unable to see what was happening at the other end of the trading post. Generally I considered accounts that were closer in time to the events to have been the least corrupted by faulty memory or erroneous later published accounts. Finally, I attempted to corroborate all documentary evidence with other records or archaeological evidence. Every piece of evidence had to be evaluated individually and on its own merits. These standards of objectivity apply in any historical investigation, whether it is battlefield history or settlement history.

With the passage of time, subsequent retellings of the stories strayed farther and farther from reality. In chronicling the number of Indians engaged in the fight, for example, a report from one of the store managers at Adobe Walls four days after the engagement noted about two hundred warriors, a figure reported by others in 1874, and it most likely is as close to an accurate accounting as we are likely ever to know. As time passed, the number of attackers seemingly increased with the telling of the tale, with the number growing to between five and eight hundred by about 1900 and an astronomical six thousand in a popular account published in the 1960s.[24]

At times the Euro-American and American Indian sources observed the same events and interestingly corroborated each other. In describing the first exchanges of gunfire in the fight, Olive K. Dixon in her edited memoir of hide man Billy Dixon penned, in her husband's words, "One of Hanrahan's men had gone after the horses some two or three hundred yards. Presently he came running back and I heard the Indians yell and they came rushing up with our horses in front of them. I grabbed my gun and fired one shot [before] I retreated into Hanrahan's."[25] Comanche Frank Yellow Fish, excited by his first attack as a warrior, later vividly remembered seeing the bright flash of just one hide man's gun in the first assault in semidarkness, and one can only imagine that the shot was Dixon's.

In most historical studies one must grapple with conflicting evidence. The Adobe Walls study was no different from any others in this regard. The most obvious disagreement in the evidence revolves around the question of whether the Euro-Americans at Adobe Walls had received any warnings of impending Indian attacks. From the 1870s to the 1930s, known published accounts indicate that the hunters and traders had received no specific warnings. These versions generally asserted that the hunters were awakened early on the morning of the attack by the cracking of the ridgepole that supported a sod roof on the saloon building, where several of them were sleeping. As early as 1927, Josiah Wright Mooar, a hunter who departed Adobe Walls just prior to the fight, asserted that he disagreed with most of the versions of the story, in particular the one presented by Olive K. Dixon in her biography of her husband. According to Mooar, "The ridgepole on the house did not crack that night, as is claimed in his book, and some time I am going to tell about that."[26] He waited half a dozen years but eventually told his version of the story to the Reverend James Winford Hunt, who edited his memoirs in 1932 for a series of articles in *Holland's magazine*. He then elaborated on the story in a 1939 interview.[27]

According to Mooar, the ridgepole breaking was only a ruse by saloon keeper Jim Hanrahan to awaken the hunters because he had received a secret warning of the imminent Indian attack. The old hunter declared that he and his brother learned of the warning and left Adobe Walls in advance of the battle. Most accounts of the battle support the premise that the ridgepole did indeed break, but some support the Mooar thesis. After the fight, for example, Billy Dixon and others examined the ridgepole and could find nothing wrong with it. The original typescript for Olive K. Dixon's biography of her husband contains the statement, "It has been told that the ridge pole broke. As a matter of fact, when the ridge pole was examined afterwards, it was sound and firm."[28] On account of their contradicting the rest of the story, editor Frederick S. Barde in 1913 struck the two sentences and they never reached print. The questions of the saloon ridgepole remain, and we may never be able to reconcile the conflicting evidence on what actually happened there early on the morning of the battle. I left the decision about what happened to my readers.

In preparing *Adobe Walls: The History and Archeology of the 1874 Trading Post*, I had the satisfaction of employing documentary sources from both Euro-American and American Indian sources combined with archaeological evidence that corroborated written evidence and at times provided new insights not before available. It would be difficult for a historian to ask for a happier situation.

NOTES

1. The commercial buffalo hunt was distinct from the much older trade of American Indians in tanned buffalo robes, which were furs; see Baker 1987.

2. For an overview of events at Adobe Walls in 1874, see Baker and Harrison 1986.

3. "Adobe Walls Celebration Plans Advancing Rapidly as June 27 Approaches," *Amarillo (Tex.) Daily News*, June 8, 1924, Western Weekly Supplement, 10; "Adobe Walls Celebration Plans Continue; Hope to Get Funds for Monument," *Amarillo*

Daily News, May 20, 1923, 2:6; "Big Celebration Is to Mark Fiftieth Anniversary of Big Indian Battle of Adobe Walls," *Amarillo Daily News*, June 22, 1924, 10; "Thousands Participate in Fiftieth Anniversary of the Famous Adobe Walls Fight," *Amarillo Daily News*, June 29, 1934, 1, 10.

4. "Adobe Walls Celebration on Thursday: Re-burial of Colonel Billy Dixon to Be Feature of Historic Event," *Amarillo Daily News*, June 26, 1929, 1; "Adobe Walls Ceremony Plans June 27 Completed," *Miami (Tex.) Chief*, June 13, 1929, 1; "Billy Dixon Rites to Feature Adobe Walls Celebration, *Amarillo (Tex.) Globe*, June 27, 1929, 1, 2; "Col. Billy Dixon Gets Last Wish: Buried at Site of Adobe Walls," *Amarillo Daily News*, June 28, 1929, 1, 15.

5. "Adobe Walls Pageantry of Yester-year Re-enacted: Borger Jammed for Gala Event," *Amarillo Daily News*, Oct. 18, 1941, 10; "Borger Takes on a Gala Appearance as Intensive Preparations Get Under Way for Big Indian Celebration Next Week," *Borger (Tex.) Daily Herald*, Oct. 10, 1941, 1; "Chief Baldwin Parker, Son of Quanah Parker, Will Bring His Family to Borger Celebration," *Borger Daily Herald*, Oct. 10, 1941, 2; "Gala Ceremonies at Borger Today," *Amarillo (Tex.) Sunday News-Globe*, Oct. 19, 1941, 1:1; "Indian Ceremonials End Stamped Definite Success," *Borger Daily Herald*, Oct. 20, 1941, 1, 2.

6. "Dodge Citizens Find Grave at Adobe Walls: History of Old Plains Battle Recalled by Comrades after Finding Bones," *Miami Chief*, Jan. 18, 1923, [8]; "Indian Survivors of Dobe Walls to Visit Old Scene," *Dodge City (Kans.) Daily Globe*, Jan. 20, 1931, 1; Roy Riddle, "Indian Survivors of Adobe Walls Visit Site 65 Years after Fight," *Amarillo Daily News*, Apr. 26, 1939, 1, 13; Joe Sargent, "War-Paint Off: Comanches Return to Scene of Second Battle of Adobe Walls," *Hutchinson County (Stinnett, Tex.) Herald*, Apr. 29, 1939, 1, 3.

7. Hutchinson County, Texas, Deed Records, 26 332, Office of County Clerk, Hutchinson County Courthouse, Stinnett, Tex.

8. For a list of interviews employed in the research, see Baker and Harrison 1986:360–62.

9. Dixon 1914.

10. For representative examples of these accounts from white sources, see Merritt L. Beeson, "Adobe Walls Fight, June 27, 1874," manuscript, Andrew Johnson Papers; and "Dodge Citian Recounts Battle of Adobe Walls," unidentified newspaper clipping, ca. June 1923, Scrapbook no. 1768, 36, both in Historical Files, Boot Hill Museum, Dodge City, Kans.

11. For representative examples of these biographical materials, see "Came to Dodge from Sweden," unidentified newspaper clipping, Scrapbook no. 1782, 23; Andrew Johnson, "Andrew Johnson," typescript, Mar. 19, 1913, 7 lvs., Andrew Johnson Papers; "The Story of 'Dutch Henry' Borne," typescript, [1941], 8 lvs., and "Dutch Henry Borne" vertical file, all in Historical Files, Boot Hill Museum, Dodge City, Kans.

12. Frank D. Baldwin, diary transcript for Aug. 9–20, 1874, manuscript, ca. Feb. 20, 1890, 5 lvs., "Adobe Walls" vertical file, Historical Files, Boot Hill Museum, Dodge City, Kans.

13. For examples of the contemporary press coverage, see *Atchison (Kans.) Daily Champion,* July 7, 1874, 2; *Commonwealth (Topeka, Kans.),* Aug. 8, 1874, 2; *Dodge City (Kans.) Messenger,* June 25, 1874, 2; and *Leavenworth (Kans.) Daily Commercial,* July 26, 1874, 2.

14. George W. Baird Papers, microfilm; William E. Connelley, "In Relation to the Visit of Tom Stauth of Dodge City, Kansas, to the Site of the Battle of Adobe Walls, on the Canadian in the Panhandle of Texas," typescript, ca. Mar. 10, 1923, "History—Adobe Walls" file, Manuscript Department; Tom Stauth, Dodge City, Kansas, to W. E. Connell[e]y, Topeka, Kans[as], Oct. 17, 1921, manuscript, Artifact Documentation File 21-45, Office of Museum Registrar; and untitled drawing of corral gate at 1874 Adobe Walls Trading Post and untitled plan of 1874 Adobe Walls Trading Post, "History—Adobe Walls" File, Manuscript Department, all in Kansas State Historical Society, Topeka, Kans.

15. Artifact Documentation Files 21.45 and 23.6, Office of Museum Registrar, Kansas State Historical Society.

16. Frank Dwight Baldwin Collection, manuscript, Stephen H. Hart Library, Colorado Historical Society, Denver, Colo.

17. U.S., Court of Claims, Indian Depredation Case Files, Cases 711, 1167, 4593, 4601, 10102, 10316, and 4593, National Archives, Washington, D.C.

18. U.S., Department of War, Army, Office of the Adjutant General, Letters Received Relating to "Campaign against Hostile Indians in the Indian Territory," Consolidated File 2815-1874," manuscript, National Archives, Washington, D.C.

19. W. S. Nye, "H. L. Scott Material" spiral notebook, "Bad Medicine and Good" correspondence file, and W. S. Nye, "Carbine and Lance" research materials, W. S. Nye Collection, U.S. Army Field Artillery and Fort Sill Museum, Fort Sill, Okla.

20. Quanah, "Told in English & Signs & Comanche: Quanah Parker's Account of Adobe Walls Fight," Ledger Book 1:14-17, Hugh Scott Collection, Fort Sill Archives, Lawton, Okla.

21. U.S., Department of the Interior, Office of Indian Affairs, Microfilm Roll CAA 24 (Cheyenne and Arapaho Agency—Depredations 1878-1927), "Cheyenne and Arapahoe Agency: Military Relations and Affairs, 1869-1932"; and U.S., Department of the Interior, Office of Indian Affairs, Letters Received from the Kiowa Agency, National Archives, microfilm, both in Oklahoma Historical Society, Oklahoma City, Okla.

22. Herman Asanap to R. B. Thomas, Interview at Indiahoma, Oklahoma, Oct. 30, 1937, Interview no. 9041, typescript, 99:232-37; and J. L. Puckett to James R. Carselowey, Interview at Vinita, Oklahoma, [ca. 1937], Interview no. 7120, typescript, 70:376-92, both in Indian Pioneer Papers, Oklahoma Historical Society, Oklahoma City, Okla.

23. [Olive K. Dixon,] "Life and Adventures of William ("Billy") Dixon of Adobe Walls, Texas Panhandle," 1913, Battle of Adobe Walls File, Frederick S. Barde Collection, Oklahoma Historical Society, Oklahoma City, Okla.

24. *Atchison (Kans.) Daily Champion,* July 10, 1874, 2; Dolores Stark, "Terror at Adobe Walls!" *Gasser* (Colorado Springs, Colo.) 20 (Oct. 1963):7-10.

25. Dixon, "Life and Adventures," 203–206; Frank Yellow Fish interview cited in Joe Sargent, "War-Paint Off," *Hutchinson County Herald,* Apr. 29, 1939, 1, 3.

26. J. Wright Mooar to J. Evetts Haley, interviews at Snyder, Texas, Nov. 25, 1927 and Jan. 4, 1928, 9, J. Evetts Haley Papers, Research Center, Panhandle-Plains Historical Museum, Canyon, Tex.

27. J. Wright Mooar to Earl Vandale, J. Evetts Haley, and Hervey Chesley at Snyder, Tex., Mar. 2, 3, and 4, 1939, Earl Vandale Collection, Center for American History, University of Texas at Austin, Austin, Tex.; Mooar 1932.

28. Dixon, "Life and Adventures," 165.

Archaeology at Adobe Walls

J. Brett Cruse

The attack on the Adobe Walls compound on June 27, 1874, was the primary catalyst that prompted the U.S. Army to wage all-out war against the southern Plains tribes and force them onto reservations established in the western Oklahoma Indian Territory. The primary objective of the army's Indian campaign of 1874—known by historians as the Red River War—was the removal of the Indian groups from the southern plains, thereby opening the region to Anglo-American settlement.[1]

The Battle of Adobe Walls is perhaps one of the best-known engagements of the frontier west. The contingent of defenders of the compound, twenty-eight men and one woman, were able to hold off a much larger force of Indians and suffered only three casualties. Although many historical accounts of the battle exist, including some by those who were there, and American Indian oral histories of the battle have been recorded, little archaeological investigation of the battle site as a whole has been conducted. Even though the building remains within the Adobe Walls compound have been subjected to a substantial amount of archaeological investigation, the larger battle site including the locations where many of the Indian attackers took cover and fired from long range at the Adobe Walls defenders has been neither investigated nor defined.[2]

Because the larger battle site has not been examined archaeologically, it is difficult to achieve a complete understanding of the events of the battle and what tactics the Indian warriors used during the battle. Questions remain concerning the battle to which additional archaeological investigations at the site might provide answers. One of the lingering questions has been how the twenty-eight men and one woman inside the buildings were able to repel an attack by some two hundred warriors. Were the Anglos better armed than the Indians? What types of weapons did the attackers have? What were the Indians' tactics and how did they utilize the topography surrounding the site? Before we assess how additional archaeological investigations at the site might provide information to answer these questions, it is useful to review what we know historically about the site. It is also useful to examine the results of the previous archaeological work at the Adobe Walls compound and to compare the Adobe Walls battle site to the other Indian Wars battle sites that have been investigated in the region.

What Is Known about the Battle

Most of what we know about the Adobe Walls battle comes from historical accounts. The accounts generally agree that the Indian attackers approached the compound from the east, up the north side of the Canadian River. Around 4:30 A.M., before dawn yet light enough to illuminate their way, the warriors launched their attack—expecting to overpower the sleeping occupants of the compound easily. However, many of the Adobe Walls dwellers, perhaps as many as half, were already awake. Just two hours before the strike, the ridgepole in the saloon purportedly cracked, which gave way to shouts to get out of the way. The commotion awakened everyone sleeping in the saloon and nearby. Repairs were made to the ridgepole, and sod was shoveled off the roof to lighten the weight.

In the meantime, outside the saloon, Billy Dixon was rising from sleep near his wagon in preparation for hitching up his horses to begin another buffalo hunt. Dixon, with Billy Ogg, had started east to gather the animals grazing a half mile away along East Adobe Creek when they observed motion in the distance. The warriors charged down on the settlement, but both Dixon and Ogg were able to return safely to the saloon and give warning. The initial attack from the warriors came right at the center of the compound where the saloon and blacksmith shop were located. Intense firepower from the saloon occupants, however, had the effect of splitting the charge and providing the occupants of the other two buildings time to prepare a defense.³

Because of the swiftness of the assault, the Adobe Walls defenders possessed little organization, with the battle being waged in three independent actions. The numerically strongest force of eleven men occupied the Myers and Leonard store. At Hanrahan's saloon there were nine defenders. The weakest stronghold was in the Rath and Company store, defended by only seven people, including Mr. and Mrs. Olds. Ike and Shorty Shadler, along with their dog, were killed in the initial stages of the battle while sleeping in their wagon outside the Myers and Leonard corral.

During the initial attack, the warriors rode right up to the buildings, even striking the doors with their gun butts. Mounted warriors circled the buildings, hurling lances and shooting arrows and lead bullets at the defenders. The livestock and wagons were plundered. Some warriors, including Quanah Parker, climbed onto the roofs in unsuccessful attempts to breech the structures. The medicine man, Isatai, naked, his body painted yellow, had assured the warriors the white men's bullets would not harm them. He watched the proceedings from a distant hill. Quanah led the Comanches, Lone Wolf the Kiowas. Stone Calf, White Shield, and Old Whirlwind were principal leaders of the Cheyennes.

Despite the onslaught of the Indian attack, the defenders held out, finally forcing their assailants to seek refuge away from the structures and out of range of the hunters' big buffalo guns. The buffalo hunters, armed with big-bore Sharps rifles and a plentiful supply of ammunition, inflicted heavy casualties on the warriors. After the first half hour, the warriors pulled back, leaving about a dozen dead or wounded within range of the hide hunters' guns. Early in the fighting, Quanah Parker's horse was shot from under him a quarter of a mile from the structures. Taking cover behind the carcass of a buffalo, the Comanche warrior recoiled from a stinging blow from a bullet that smashed into his shoulder and neck region. Stunned and unable to continue the fight, the Comanche war leader reached a plum thicket where a fellow tribesman rescued him.⁴

Meanwhile, the Indian attacks on the buildings fell off to sporadic assaults and taunts. Some warriors positioned themselves under the protective cover of the corral fences. Billy Tyler, one of the occupants of the Myers and Leonard store, foolishly entered the corral to protect the livestock. There, an Indian bullet slammed into his chest, perforating his lung. News of Tyler's mortal wounding was shouted over to Hanrahan's saloon. Bat Masterson, a close friend of Tyler, hastily abandoned his post in the saloon and made his way to the dying Tyler. Suffering intensely, Tyler requested water. The store contained no water, but there was a well in the corral. William Keeler grabbed the bucket from Masterson's hand and darted out the back door. Under a volley of Indian fire, he miraculously retrieved the water and returned to the store unharmed. The agonizing Tyler received his water, then shortly afterward died.[5]

The large quantities of ammunition among the Adobe Walls contingent of hide men was not evenly distributed. The reserve supply of cartridges was in the Rath and Company store. About noon, the defenders in the saloon had depleted most of their ammunition. Dixon and Hanrahan volunteered to go after more. The two men exited through one of the saloon's windows and ran the gauntlet of long-range Indian fire to reach the store safely. The defenders in the store pleaded for the two men to stay, citing their small numbers and having the added burden of defending Mrs. Olds. Hanrahan declined and returned to his saloon to resupply his party with cartridges, but Dixon stayed.[6]

Around 2 P.M., the Indians began to withdraw from Adobe Walls, although they kept firing. The warriors reportedly occupied the high hills east and west of the structures. For two more hours they maintained intermittent fire. Occasionally, in an act of bravery, individual warriors attempted to make a run at the compound, which cost the Indians a few more casualties from the long-range weapons of the defenders. By now, Isatai's vision of an easy victory was in ruins. The hide hunters had not been overrun, and fifteen to thirty warriors had been killed or wounded. Overlooking the settlement from a ridge, Isatai deliberated with other Indian leaders. While he was mounted, a bullet from one of the Adobe Walls defenders struck and killed his horse.[7]

Near 4 P.M., the Indians disengaged the Adobe Walls defenders. Cautiously, the frontiersmen ventured forth to collect trinkets from the Indian corpses and to assess the situation. Dead horses, oxen, and mules littered the landscape. The bodies of thirteen Indians stained the ground around the buildings with blood. The hide men cut off the heads of the dead and stuck them on the gateposts.[8] For the next few days, the defenders spent an uneasy time, unsure the warriors would not return. Indeed warriors did reappear, but only at long range. On one occasion, June 29, about fifteen mounted warriors were seen on the high ridge east of Adobe Walls. Billy Dixon reportedly accepted the challenge and coaxing of his comrades and took a shot at the mounted warriors, who supposedly were more than 1,500 yards away. Seconds later the defenders watched in amazement as one of the distant figures tumbled from his horse in what has been heralded in folklore and legend as the most famous shot in the West, though Dixon never actually claimed to have made the shot.[9]

Within weeks most of the defenders of Adobe Walls, especially the merchants, departed for Dodge City. With the abandonment of Adobe Walls, the Indians returned to loot what remained and to burn the buildings to the ground. This battle at Adobe Walls precipitated military intervention in 1874. The encounter placed the military and civilian populations on alert that the southern Plains tribes would not return to the reservations without a fight. It also had a humiliating effect on the warriors. Stung by their inability to destroy a small contingent, the Indians expanded their raids deep into Texas. Just twenty-three days after the attack on Adobe Walls, Gen. William T. Sherman granted official ratification to a state of war, which was to be known as the Red River War. Although not a military action, Adobe Walls can be classified as the first major conflict of the Red River campaign, which ultimately aided in drawing the military and the tribes into a confrontation for final control and supremacy of the southern plains.[10]

Archaeological Investigations at Adobe Walls

Beginning in 1975 and continuing systematically over the next five years, the Panhandle-Plains Historical Museum in Canyon, Texas, conducted archaeological investigations at the site of the Adobe Walls compound. Under the supervision of the late Billy R. Harrison, then curator of archaeology at the museum, a team of archaeologists spent a total of fourteen months in the field excavating the remains of the compound buildings. The focus of these investigations was on the interior of the building foundations, with only limited excavations occurring outside the buildings. Before the start of the excavations, the remains of the larger structures were seen to be outlined by low rounded ridges forming rectangular patterns with central depressions. Only a conical pit marked the location of the blacksmith shop, whereas the privy was marked by a low mound.[11]

The excavations resulted in the delineation of the walls of the buildings and internal features, and they provided a clearer picture of how the buildings were constructed. The Myers and Leonard store building, for example, was found to contain trenches in which its picket walls stood. A circular trench measuring 10 feet in diameter at the northeast corner of the store supported pickets that formed a defense bastion. Excavations at the Rath and Company store revealed that the walls of the building were of sod construction, and the exterior dimensions of the building measured approximately 22.5 by 59 feet. Another defense bastion, measuring 13 feet north-to-south by 12 feet east-to-west and constructed of sod, was added at the southeast corner of the store at some date after the original construction. The building undoubtedly had an earthen roof, as shown by a thick bed of red clay in the excavations.

The saloon building was also built of sod, and excavations there revealed a building measuring 17 feet north-to-south by 36 feet east-to-west. The three-foot thick walls of the building gave it an outside dimension of approximately 23 by 42 feet. Finally, the excavations revealed that even though Tom O'Keefe erected a picket building to house his blacksmith shop, it differed from the picket structures that Myers and Leonard had built in that it had no trench to support its walls. Instead, O'Keefe set substantial wooden posts in the ground at each of the corners and on either side of the entries. Split-log top and bottom plates were then attached to the posts, and the space between the posts was then filled with small vertical pickets that were held in position by the plates.[12]

The excavations yielded an array of building fragments including such materials as mud daubing, door hardware, and window glass. In addition to the building remains, the excavations also recovered a substantial number of other artifacts that included pieces of furniture (two charred tabletops and a chair) and elements of lighting devices (candleholders and kerosene lamps). Tools and equipment of various kinds were one of the largest artifact categories from the site. Items in this category include horse, mule, and ox shoes; firearms and other weapons; firearm accessories; ammunition of various calibers; faunal remains from different animals consumed by the building inhabitants; dishes, plates, utensils, cans, bottles, and food preparation items; clothing, buttons, and personal items; axes and adzes; and numerous items related to wagons and transportation.

Of particular interest are the weapons and firearms-related artifacts from the site. Weapons from both Indians and whites were found during the excavations. Three iron arrow points were recovered within buildings at the site, indicating that at least some of the warriors were still using bows and arrows in warfare, although most historical accounts of the battle mention only the use of firearms and lances by the warriors. Several pieces of firearms, including barrels, butt plates, a rifle hammer, and trigger guards, were also recovered. The barrels include fragments from Spencer carbines and a muzzle-loading rifle.[13]

A total of 465 cartridges, cases, bullets, and balls found at the site represent ammunition for at least two dozen different firearms. Twenty-six musket balls represent four different muzzle-loading firearms, in calibers of .38, .40, .45, and .56. The 140 lead bullets recovered range in caliber from .38 to .56 and include both solid-base and hollow-base types as well as patched and grooved forms. The majority of the bullets are .50-caliber from Spencer cartridges. The bullets were found both inside and outside of the buildings, which makes it difficult to determine if they were shot by Indians or dropped by the hide men. However, many of them are mushroomed, which suggests that Indians fired them into the buildings during their attack. The recovered bullets suggest that the primary firearms of the Indian warriors were .44-caliber Henrys or Winchesters and Spencer carbines. A surprising number of musket balls were recovered, and these indicate that, in contrast to the modern repeater rifles, a significant number of the Indians were using old and obsolete muzzle-loaders at the battle.[14]

The 244 cartridge cases recovered during the excavations represent at least twenty different types or sizes of cases. Presumably, the Adobe Walls defenders dropped the majority of the cases during the battle. Calibers of the recovered rifle or carbine cartridge cases include .32, .44, .45, .50, and

.56. Pistol cases in .44-, .45-, and .50-caliber were also recovered. In addition to the cartridge cases, fifty-five unfired cartridges, in sizes representing eleven types of firearms, were recovered: .44 Henry, .44 Smith & Wesson, .44-77, .44-90, .45 Colt, .45 U.S. Government, .50 Remington pistol, .50-70 U.S. Government, .50-90, .50-70 or 90, and .56-56 Spencer carbine. Thirty of the fifty-five unfired cartridges are .50-70 U.S. Government rounds found in a single pile or cache within the bastion at the Myers and Leonard store. Based on the cartridges, cases, and identifiable bullets recovered from the site, .50-caliber firearms were preferred by the hide men at Adobe Walls.[15]

Methods

The historical records offer valuable insights into the order of events of the Adobe Walls battle and details pertaining to the positions of the defenders within the compound, but they provide only general information concerning the positions of the Indian attackers after the initial charge failed. To determine how the warriors attacked and fought the Adobe Walls defenders, it is helpful to understand the topography and landscape that surrounds the Adobe Walls compound. This understanding is also useful for developing methods for any future archaeological investigation that might occur at the battle site.

The Adobe Walls post was built on a broad meadow on the north side of the Canadian River between Adobe and Bent creeks (figure 17). Extending southward from the site, the floodplains of Adobe and Bent creeks merge with the broader floodplain bordering the north side of the Canadian River. Only tree-lined stream channels and a gravel-topped low mound break this level floodplain. Adobe Creek, about 600 yards east of the site, is bordered along its east bank by erosional remnants that rise steeply to approximately 100 feet in elevation and are topped by broad mesas. A low, sand-covered projection that forms the divide between Adobe and Bent creeks is dotted on its north and east slopes by seep springs that create a broad marsh area between the Adobe Walls compound and the divide. Immediately to the north of the springs is a small gravel-topped ridge. To the west of the compound, at 800–1,000 yards, are additional steep and broad mesas and erosional remnants. Since the time of the battle, only minor alterations to

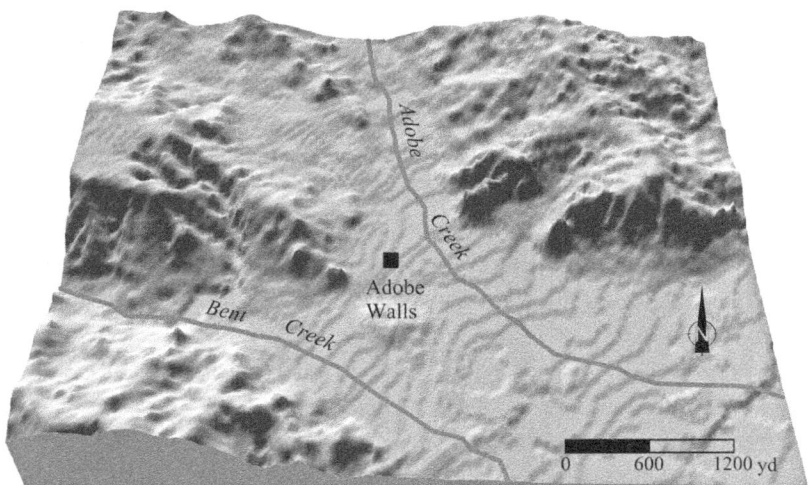

Figure 17. Topography of the Adobe Walls site.

the topography and terrain surrounding the battle site have occurred. An unpaved, county-maintained dirt road leads down to the remote location of the site. In addition, and more recently, several oil and gas wells have been installed around the Adobe Walls site.

Though to little success, the Indian warriors tried to utilize the topography to their advantage both during the initial assault on the compound and later as they laid siege to the Adobe Walls defenders. Their initial charge came from the east across the broad meadow and from the timberline along Adobe Creek. Their apparent intent was to move swiftly across the open meadow and catch the defenders by surprise. At this initial stage of the battle, the Indians were not concerned with finding cover to conceal their attack or to protect themselves, but rather to get to the compound as quickly as possible. They were probably not firing their weapons during the charge, since they wanted to surprise the buildings' occupants. Thus, there are probably few battle-related artifacts associated with the charge across the broad meadow east of the compound.

After the warriors' unsuccessful attempts to gain entry to the buildings, they apparently began circling the compound, firing from the backs of their horses and taking cover behind any small rise, wagon, or buffalo hide pile they could find. Hence, all of the area from 200 to 300 yards in every direction around the Adobe Walls complex is likely to contain artifacts associated with the Indian warriors and their attack on the compound. Such objects might include fired and unfired cartridge cases, horse equipment, and items of personal adornment. After the warriors broke off the attack and retreated from the compound, several of the defenders went out to pick up Indian artifacts as souvenirs. Reportedly, they stripped the dead bodies that lay close to the stores and retrieved weapons, shields, quirts, bridles, and other items from the area around the compound.[16] Still other artifacts that might be expected in this area are bullets fired by the Adobe Walls defenders toward the attacking warriors, as well as items related to the hide hunters' daily activities around the site prior to the battle.

After the failure of the assault on the compound, many of the warriors sought refuge on the distant hilltops away from the compound. The hide men, however, were accustomed to shooting targets and game from long distances, and they were using firearms especially designed for this purpose. It was common for the hide hunters to kill buffalo that were several hundred to a thousand yards away. Numerous accounts report the hide men's shooting at distant groups of Indians on the hilltops where they had retreated after the failure of their initial assault on the compound, including the story of Billy Dixon's famous long shot.[17]

To ascertain the validity of these accounts, archaeological investigations of the surrounding distant hilltops might provide evidence of warrior-associated cartridges or bullets fired by the hide men. In fact, some battle-associated artifacts have been found on at least one of the mesa tops east of the Adobe Walls compound. In 2005 avocational archaeologist Alvin Lynn, while using a metal detector, found twenty-two fired cartridge cases, six bullets, and a hat or hairpin on the crest of one of the mesas northeast of Adobe Walls (figure 18). The top of this particular mesa is approximately 720 yards from the Adobe Walls compound. Sixteen Spencer and six .44-caliber Henry cartridge cases were recovered.

Douglas D. Scott of the Midwest Archeological Center subjected the cartridge cases and bullets to microscopic firearms analysis.[18] Firearm characteristics on cartridge cases are firing pin and extractor marks; on bullets, they are land-and-groove marks. These characteristics allow determination

ARCHAEOLOGY

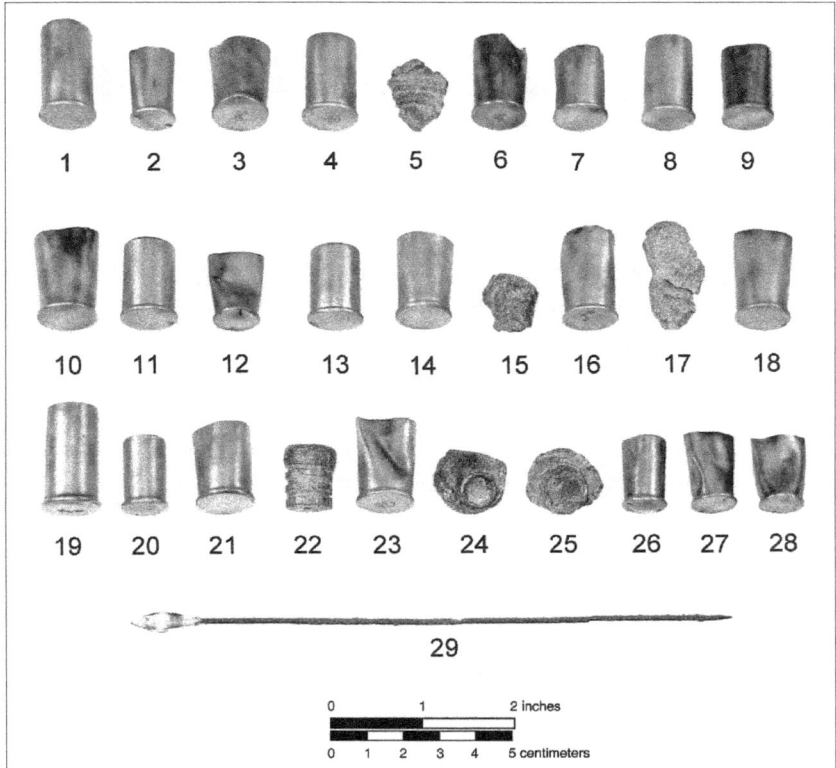

Figure 18. Cartridge cases, bullets, and hairpin recovered from the Adobe Walls site. Spencer cartridge cases: 1, 3–4, 6–11, 13–14, 16, 18–19, 21, 23; .44-caliber Henry cartridge cases: 2, 12, 20, 24, 26–28; .44-or .45-caliber bullet: 24; .50-caliber bullets: 22, 25; bullet fragments: 5, 15, 17; hairpin, 29.

of the type of firearm (model or brand) in which a given case or bullet was fired. This then allows determination of the number of different types of firearms in use at a particular battle. Further, individual weapons can be identified by comparing the unique firearm identification characteristics.

According to Scott, three of the .44-caliber cases are Henry Long cartridges that were fired in a Henry or Model 1866 Winchester. These cases are all headstamped with an "H," indicating manufacture by Winchester. The other three .44-caliber cases are non-headstamped Henry Long cases that were also fired in Henrys or Model 1866 Winchesters. The analysis of the cartridges further indicates that four individual weapons fired the cartridge cases, with cases 2 and 28 fired in the same weapon, cases 12 and 27 in another weapon, and cases 20 and 26 fired in different Henrys or Model 1866 Winchesters.

The sixteen Spencer cases were all fired in .56-56-caliber Spencers, although a few of the cases (1, 16, 18, and 19) are .56-50-caliber. There are three different manufacturers represented in the collection: Frankford Arsenal (cases 1 and 10), Winchester (cases 3, 4, 6, 7, 8, 14, and 23 with an "H" headstamp), and Sage Ammunition Works (cases 16 and 19 with "SAW" headstamp). The remaining five cartridge cases do not have a headstamp or any tool point marks indicative of their source of manufacture.

From the microscopic comparisons, six Spencers are represented. Cases 1, 9, and 19 were fired from one carbine; cases 3, 4, 7, 8, and 23 were fired from the second carbine; cases 6, 10, and 11 from the third; case 13 from the fourth; cases 14 and 16 from the fifth; and cases 18 and 21 from the sixth Spencer carbine.

The six bullets recovered include three that are so fragmented that their caliber could not be determined. The remaining three are two .50-caliber and a .44- or .45-caliber. One of the .50-caliber bullets is a three-lubricating groove 450-grain bullet. It was fired in a Sharps, based on the type of six land-and-groove marks on the bullet body. Another bullet is a .50-caliber 450-grain bullet with a raised solid base. It is typical of a government-made bullet for the .50-70. There are six land-and-groove rifling impressions on the bullet that indicate it was fired in a Sharps. The final bullet is a .44- or .45-caliber bullet with a solid but slightly recessed base. It is mushroomed from impact, but the bullet does retain enough of the land-and-groove rifling impressions to indicate that it, like the other identified bullets, was fired in a Sharps. It seems likely that the bullets were fired from rifles belonging to the Adobe Walls defenders.

The hair- or hatpin (see figure 18) was found in three pieces. Laid end-to-end, the pieces are approximately 6.5 inches long. On one end of the pin is a gold-plated, metal finial. One of the Indian warriors most likely lost the pin.

The assemblage of bullets and cartridge cases on the mesa top are undoubtedly associated with the Adobe Walls fight. The cartridge cases are of the same types that appear to be associated with the Indian warriors at the Adobe Walls compound. Their presence on the mesa at a distance of more than 700 yards would seem to corroborate the claims made by the hide men that they shot at groups of Indians on the distant hilltops around Adobe Walls. The three bullets that were fired from Sharps rifles and recovered from the same location as the warrior-associated cartridges suggest that the hide men were firing at the Indian group on the mesa top.

The recovery of these artifacts indicates a high likelihood that similar artifacts would be found on the other mesa tops that surround the Adobe Walls site. The best way to investigate these areas would be with a team of archaeologists trained in the use of metal detectors to search the areas carefully and to record and map the locations of any artifacts found. Additionally, other locations at the site should also be searched in an effort to record and document the presence of other battle-related artifacts. The battle-related artifacts recovered to date from the Adobe Walls battle site suggest that at least some of the defenders were using long-range, large-caliber Sharps rifles, while the Indian warriors were relying on shorter-range and smaller-caliber rifles such as the Spencer, Henry, and Winchester. Additionally, some of the Indian warriors were apparently using bows and arrows, lances, old trade guns, and muzzle-loaders. For the smaller-caliber Indian rifles, the effective firing range would have been 100–300 yards. The effective range for the large-caliber firearms used by the Adobe Walls defenders would be 500 yards or more.

Adobe Walls and the Red River War

If the weapon types reviewed above are typical of the weapons the battle participants used, then is it the case that the firepower of the numerically inferior defenders was so much greater than that of the numerically superior Indian attackers? To examine this question, it is helpful to compare the Adobe Walls artifact assemblage to those recovered from other Indian War battle sites in the region, namely, battle sites of the Red River War.

After the attack on Adobe Walls, generals Philip Sheridan and William T. Sherman laid the basis for an offensive campaign against the Indians in early July 1874, and Secretary of War William Belknap approved it on

July 20. This new policy by the army called for enrollment and protection of innocent and friendly Indians at their reservations and pursuit and destruction of hostile Indians without regard for reservation or departmental boundaries.

Over the course of the next ten months, the army, with some three thousand soldiers and scouts participating in the campaign, would engage the Indians in battles and skirmishes across the Texas Panhandle. The Indians could claim victories in only a few of the encounters. For the most part, they were simply outnumbered and overpowered by the well-armed and well-supplied U.S. Army. Many of the Indian warriors who participated in the Adobe Walls battle were also participants in some of the Red River War battles.

Several Red River War battle site locations have been identified and archaeologically investigated by the Texas Historical Commission. Between May 1998 and May 2003, the Commission conducted archaeological investigations at six battle sites during their Red River War Battle Sites Project. The sites, all of which at that time were on private property, are the Battle of Red River (also known as the First Battle of Palo Duro Canyon), the Battle of Lyman's Wagon Train (also referred to as the Battle of the Upper Washita), the Battle of Buffalo Wallow, the Battle of Palo Duro Canyon (also known as the Second Battle of Palo Duro Canyon and now on property owned by the State of Texas), the Battle of Sweetwater Creek (Major Price's Engagement), and the Battle of Round Timber Creek (Lt. Farnsworth's Engagement).[19]

At each of the battle sites, archaeologists using metal detectors scanned the ground surface searching for battle-related metallic artifacts. When an artifact was found with the metal detector, it was excavated, identified, and its location marked with a pin flag. The recording crew then mapped each artifact location using a GPS data collector and receiver and collected the artifact. The GPS data were then used to create artifact distribution maps for each battle site. More than three thousand battle-related artifacts were recovered during the project. Douglas Scott conducted a detailed firearms identification analysis of the recovered cartridge cases and bullets from each site.

One of the primary objectives for the Red River War Battle Sites Project was to determine the types and quantities of armaments that the Indians used at the battles. Several of the army documents refer to the Indians' use of firearms, but few documents provide specific details regarding type or quantity. By utilizing modern firearms identification procedures, Scott was able to determine the minimum number of firearms per weapon type that were used at each of the battle sites. The identified weapon types that were not associated with the army based on official army records and ordnance returns were assumed to be from Indian firearms.

The firearm identification analysis for the artifacts from the Red River War battle sites identified thirty firearm types used at the battles by both the army and the Indians. The number of individual firearms identified by the analysis is a conservative estimate in that only those cartridges and bullets that could be sorted and identified with certainty were counted. In addition, some cartridge cases were too oxidized to be analyzed. The figures obtained from the firearms analysis represent only the minimum number of firearms that could be identified from the archaeological evidence. There is little doubt that many more firearms were used by the combatants. Nonetheless, of the firearm types identified, the Indian combatants used at least twenty-six types, the army combatants nine.

The twenty-six Indian-associated types represent an impressively diverse array of firearms. These include obsolete muzzle-loaders and trade guns, single-shot carbines, revolvers, and repeater rifles or carbines such as the Henry or Winchester and the Spencer. Despite the diversity of the Indian firearms, the analysis suggests that the Indians were not very well armed. Generally, it was found that only 30–50 percent of the Indian combatants at any battle had firearms of any kind. The Spencer carbine was the most common firearm represented among the Indian guns, followed by Henry or Winchester Model 1866 and 1873 rifles. Together, these repeater models account for about 53 percent of the Indian firearms overall. Approximately 36 percent of the Indian firearms were single-shot rifles or carbines of various models and calibers, 8 percent were old trade guns and muzzle-loaders, and 3 percent were revolvers. The trade guns and muzzle-loaders are probably underrepresented because groups of rifle balls, such as the .44-, .50-, and .54-caliber, were counted as representing only one gun in each type.[20]

Because many of the Indian warriors at the Adobe Walls battle also participated in the Red River War battles, it can be assumed that the same types and quantities of Indian firearms were used at all of the battles. Thus it is probable that only 30–50 percent of the Indian attackers (60–100 warriors) at Adobe Walls had firearms of any kind. Most of these would have been repeater rifles. Approximately 36 percent of the Indian rifles would have been single-shot rifles or carbines, and at least 8 percent or so (and probably more) obsolete muzzle-loaders. A smaller number of warriors probably had pistols. These numbers suggest that perhaps as many as 100–140 of the Indian attackers at Adobe Walls were using only traditional bows and arrows and lances. If this was the case, then the warriors were not as well armed as previously believed, and even though the hide men at Adobe Walls were greatly outnumbered they possessed much greater firepower and more abundant ammunition than did the Indian warriors.

The psychological impact that the long-range weapons of the defenders had on the attackers must have been significant. For the defenders to be able to shoot effectively at the warriors at such great distances clearly worked to their advantage and allowed the defenders the ability to prevent the compound from being overrun. The archaeological evidence shows that the defenders were able to fire into a group of Indians on a mesa that was more than 700 yards away. The group of Indians that were with Isatai when his horse was shot out from under him must have believed they were out of the range of the defenders guns. How demoralizing it must have been to the Indians when Isatai's horse went down.

In the end, the Indians simply could not match the firepower of the Adobe Walls occupants. Because the Adobe Walls defenders had such greater firepower in their long-range and large-caliber weapons, they were able to hold off the warriors and prevent the compound from being overrun by the far greater number of Indian attackers.

NOTES

1. *Army and Navy Journal* 12 (July 25, 1874): 790; Leckie 1963:198–99; *New York Herald*, July 22, 1874.
2. Baker and Harrison 1986.
3. Dixon 1914:203–206; Grinnell 1955:312–13; Roy Riddle, "Indian Survivors of Adobe Walls Visit Site 65 Years after Fight," *Amarillo Daily News*, Apr. 26, 1939, 1, 13.
4. Baker and Harrison 1986:53, 63; Dixon 1914:239–40; Hyde 1968:360.
5. Dixon 1914:212; Little 1958:79.

6. Baker and Harrison 1986:65; Dixon 1914:216–17; Little 1958:82.
7. Coyle 1911:65; Little 1958:81.
8. Baker and Harrison 1986:97–98; Miles 1896:163.
9. Dixon 1902:4; Dixon 1914:227–28, 232–33; Van Sickel 1890:18.
10. Among the accounts of the Red River War are Crane 1925; Crimmins 1947; Cruse 2008; Haley 1976; Leckie 1956, 1963; and Utley 2007.
11. Baker and Harrison 1986:130.
12. Ibid., 142–65.
13. Ibid., 186–89.
14. Ibid., 192–93.
15. Ibid., 191–92, 193–96.
16. Dixon 1914:221–24.
17. Little 1958:81; Rye 1909:324.
18. Doug Scott to Alvin Lynn, Apr. 26, 2005. Copy on file with the author.
19. Cruse 2008.
20. Ibid., 144–45.

The Sand Creek Massacre

Commentary

Frances Levine

Sand Creek and Wounded Knee arguably are among the most widely known of the western American battlefields. And their significance has likely been the most mutable, depending on the era, the context, and the telling of their lessons. The Sand Creek encounter took place during the Civil War when the nation was rent internally. At the same time, the Great Plains Indian Wars erupted in escalating battles as settlers expanded into the traditional hunting grounds of tribes that would be forced from the widening American frontier. Sand Creek, fought on November 29, 1864, was a massacre, but that was not immediately told. For the commander of the Colorado volunteers, Col. John M. Chivington, it was a hard-won victory that he must have thought would surely be a credit to those who took part and to his congressional aspirations. But what happened on that early wintery morning and exactly where the battles and killings took place are still open to interpretation.

In his essay, Ari Kelman traces the historiography of Sand Creek, starting with the initial reporting by Chivington and conflicting reports by Silas Soule, who refused to commit his troops to what he considered atrocities committed by the Colorado regiments. From these 1864 reports, through the conflicting reinterpretations of events in the 1880s, the early twentieth-century revisions, and finally the more recent public and private commemorations of the battlefield, Kelman finds that context and meaning of the events are often derived from the point of view of the reporter. What matters in characterizing or commemorating the conflicting accounts is whether Sand

Creek is seen against the background of the evolving westward expansion or through the eyes of reformers or Native American descendants.

Archaeological study, which the National Park Service had hoped would define the limits of the battlefield, seems to have rekindled debates over the best way to memorialize Sand Creek. Douglas Scott used archaeological techniques to analyze the campsite and the battlefield—but not just the usual sort of archaeological survey or excavation strategies. He examined both archaeologically controlled collections made on National Park Service land and a large collection made by a neighboring private landowner that was not as systematically collected. These latter data, which others might have dismissed as unprovenienced and therefore meaningless, provided a useful comparative data set that allowed Scott to define the limits of the campsite, the routes of retreat, and the sand pits where some Cheyennes and Arapahos took futile shelter from the mob actions of the soldiers.

The actual location of the battlefield was imprecisely defined before Scott's analysis. Cheyenne and Arapaho descendants and National Park Service historians and archaeologists claim one stretch of the creek; local landowners and relic hunters claim a different area. Here, Scott compares the archaeological assemblages, artifacts, and locations where they were recorded on several stretches of the creek to make a case for the location of the battle and to reconstruct the action of the battle and routes of escape. The distribution patterns not only identify the fury of shots fired into the village, they also show the long but largely ineffective range of shots fired at fleeing women, children, and the elderly.

The mangled condition of the artifacts found in the campsite makes the case that the Cheyennes and Arapahos were not prepared to defend themselves, not only because this was supposedly a campsite protected by Black Kettle's truce but also because few men were in camp at the time of the attack. The household items recovered on the site show wanton destruction, another indication that the Chivington's men were intent on annihilating the Indian people. In many ways the most disturbing evidence recovered in the archaeological assemblage is the cannonball fragments. The location and condition of these fragments show that they were used as a kind of grenade, meant to explode on contact. In this case, they were lobbed into pits where Indians sought refuge from the battle.

The distribution and breakage of the artifacts clearly indicate that this was not simply a battlefield. Sand Creek was a killing field. Murder on a large scale was committed at Sand Creek. It was a crime scene, and one that still weighs heavily on our national conscience. The intensity of this battle makes it a touchstone of American nation building set within the context of the violence that was so long a part of characterizing the western American frontier. As Joe Watkins discusses in the final essay of this volume, it also points toward a new empathy for the Cheyenne and Arapaho desire to preserve the larger Sand Creek drainage as a memorial to the struggles, the losses, and the oral traditions of their own history.

What's in a Name? The Fight to Call Sand Creek a Battle or a Massacre

Ari Kelman

To name something is a kind of power: to categorize that thing, often to place it in a broader context, to begin to define how it will be understood by other observers. Perhaps never has this truism been more clearly borne out than in the wake of the bloodshed at Sand Creek on November 29, 1864, which, for the century and a half since, has been subject to struggles over nomenclature. This essay explores the fight over naming Sand Creek, focusing especially on the question of whether the violence would be labeled and recalled as a massacre or a battle. To be clear, the deeper question has long since been definitively answered. Sand Creek was, as federal investigators determined in its aftermath and as most scholars have since agreed, a massacre. The argument here, then, focuses on the politics of memory surrounding Sand Creek, suggesting that disputes emerged out of a number of nettlesome issues: What caused the bloodshed? Who should have been held accountable? And, more broadly, did labeling the violence a massacre risk undermining the perceived righteousness of westward expansion and the wars—the Civil and the Indian—spawned by that process?[1]

The essay opens with an exploration of two incommensurable narratives of the massacre: one offered by an enthusiastic perpetrator, John Chivington, the other by a reluctant witness, Silas Soule. Chivington, the colonel who led the 3rd Colorado Voluntary Regiment of Cavalry and part of the

1st Colorado Voluntary Cavalry at Sand Creek, believed that the bloodshed was a glorious battle, a mile marker on the road to civilizing the American West. Soule, who refused to commit troops under him to the fight, believed that Sand Creek was a tragedy, a massacre of peaceful Indians.[2]

The next section examines the war of words fought between the renowned author and Indian reformer Helen Hunt Jackson and William N. Byers, the editor of the Denver *Rocky Mountain News*, which took place in the late 1870s and early 1880s. Jackson picked up where Soule left off, arguing that Sand Creek had been a massacre and suggesting that the violence, along with other similar tragedies, demonstrated that federal Indian policy needed to be placed in civilian rather than military hands. Byers took issue with Jackson's characterization of the slaughter at Sand Creek and, as he had in the immediate aftermath of the bloodshed, mounted a spirited defense of Colonel Chivington and his troops.[3]

From there, we examine George Bent's memory work at the turn of the twentieth century, focusing on a series of essays he published in a Colorado Springs periodical, *The Frontier*, with the help of a historian named George Hyde. Bent's articles were the first instances of an American Indian describing Sand Creek in print as a massacre. But, more than that, Bent argued that the bloodshed had been a predictable outgrowth of westward expansion and misguided public policy. One of Chivington's surviving subordinates, Maj. Jacob Downing, at the time a proud member of Denver's elite society, faced off with Bent in print. Downing published a rebuttal in the *Rocky Mountain News* and insisted that Sand Creek had been a battle. He then helped sponsor the casting of a Civil War memorial on the Colorado capitol steps, one that included Sand Creek in a list of Civil War "battles" in which Colorado troops fought.[4]

Turning to the mid-twentieth century, I discuss two monuments placed outside Eads, Colorado, near the massacre site in 1950. One of those markers, still standing today, reads, "Sand Creek Battle Ground." The other, now gone, included a more ambiguous inscription: "Sand Creek: Battle or Massacre." Finally, a brief conclusion examines recent efforts to create the Sand Creek National Historic Site, detailing the ways in which longstanding contests over the massacre's meaning shaped the National Park Service's effort to memorialize this tragedy.[5]

◉◉◉◉

Focusing on two issues, John Chivington depicted Sand Creek as a battle and a pivotal chapter in the story of westward expansion: first, because the vanquished tribes there had been hostile, he said; and second, because the bloodshed had taken place in the context of the Civil War, with the fate of the nation, including its western territories, uncertain. Chivington initially advanced these arguments on November 29, 1864, as broken bodies cooled on the banks of Sand Creek. He wrote to his superior, Gen. Samuel Curtis, noting that "at daylight this morning" his men had "attacked [a] Cheyenne village of 130 lodges, from 900 to 1,000 warriors strong." After bragging that his troops had killed several chiefs and hundreds of their followers, Chivington justified the attack by pointing to depredations ostensibly committed by the fallen Cheyennes and Arapahos. "Found a white man's scalp, not more than three days' old, in one of the lodges," he noted. Later that day, Chivington wrote another note, this time to editors at Denver's newspapers. Grander in the second telling than the first, what had been an "engagement" became "one of the most bloody battles ever fought on these plains." But he concluded, as in his note to Curtis, by referring to the fallen enemy's barbaric acts: "I was shown by [my] chief surgeon the scalp of a white man taken from the lodge of one of the chiefs." The scalp of a lone victim represented to Chivington just one among several pieces of gory evidence of the hostility and depravity of the Indians at Sand Creek.[6]

On December 16, Chivington wrote a more complete report to General Curtis. He explained that a month earlier he had ordered the 3rd Colorado Volunteers to hunt "hostile Indians" on the plains east of Denver. On November 24 he had taken "command in person of the expedition," which had added men from the 1st Colorado Volunteers. The column left Fort Lyon four days later and marched overnight before "at daylight on 29th November striking Sand Creek." "Here was discovered an Indian village of 130 lodges, comprised of Black Kettle's band of Cheyennes and eight lodges of Arapahos with Left Hand," he noted. The native people, though stunned by the onslaught, rallied and "stubbornly contest[ed] every inch of ground." As evening fell, Black Kettle's and Left Hand's people "finally abandoned all resistance." Chivington again justified the attack by pointing to his victims' mutilation of white bodies, this time multiplying the proof recovered at Sand

Creek. Not just one scalp, as previously, but "several," hacked from "white men and women," were "found in their lodges." Based on these remains, he concluded, "the evidence was clear that no lick was struck amiss." In this view, Chivington's men, agents of an ascendant civilization sweeping across the plains, had battled hostile savages, the Cheyennes and Arapahos, guilty of terrible crimes against white settlers.[7]

Early in the New Year, after some of Chivington's subordinates, including Silas Soule, began publicly questioning the veracity of their commander's accounts of Sand Creek, suggesting that the violence had been a massacre rather than a battle, Congress and the Department of War launched their own investigations. In April 1865, Chivington submitted written testimony on his own behalf to one of these inquiries. Responding to allegations suggesting that Black Kettle's people had been peaceful, he demurred: "Many of the Indians were armed with rifles and many with revolvers." More damning still, the Cheyennes and Arapahos had prepared for battle by fortifying their camp in the preceding days: "They had excavated trenches under the bank of Sand Creek. The Indians took shelter in these trenches as soon as the attack was made," he huffed, "and from thence resisted the advance of my troops." He concluded by mentioning still more evidence discovered at Sand Creek of atrocities committed against whites. This time, nearly half a year after the fact, the single scalp that he had originally reported had multiplied into "the scalps of nineteen (19) white persons" as well as a horrifying case of "a child captured at the camp ornamented with six white women's scalps."[8]

After investigators offered Chivington a chance to add exculpatory material into the record, he waved the bloody shirt by painting Sand Creek against the backdrop of the Civil War. "Rebel emissaries," he noted, "were long since sent among the Indians to incite them against the whites." With the Cherokees already allied with the Confederacy, westerners had to guard against more Indian trouble on the frontier, he suggested. In Colorado, Chivington continued, George Bent (misidentified as "Gerry Bent"), son of William Bent, a borderlands trade tycoon, and Owl Woman, his Cheyenne wife, had served as agents of the South. Bent had promised the Cheyennes that with "the Great Father at Washington having all he could do to fight his children at the south, they could now regain their country." In this way,

Chivington made the native people killed at Sand Creek enemies not just of whites in Colorado Territory but of the Union more broadly, the bloodshed not just a triumph in the Indian Wars but of the Civil War.⁹

For the rest of his life, Chivington defended his actions in the same way. In 1883, for instance, the Pike's Peak Pioneers of '58, a Colorado heritage organization devoted to celebrating the first generation of white settlers in the Rocky Mountain region, invited him to speak at their annual banquet. As he had two decades earlier, the aging colonel began by reminding his audience that Sand Creek had taken place as the Civil War raged, with U.S. Army regulars busy fighting Confederate troops back east. Chivington then asked the tough question: "Was Sand Creek a massacre?" In answer, he suggested, "If it was, we had massacres almost without number during the late rebellion." From the horrors visited on African American troops at Fort Pillow to William Sherman's ruthless tactics at war's end, the conflict had been brutal and bloody, he suggested. Given that, yes, Chivington allowed of Sand Creek, "there may have been some excesses committed on the field." But, he then wondered, "was there ever a battle fought in which no excesses were committed?" Chivington then concluded, as ever, with his clearest justification for the attack: mutilated settler bodies, whose numbers, in this grisly telling, had increased yet again. From a single scalp in his first report, Chivington now raged about "scalps of white men, women, and children, several of which they had not had time to dry and tan since taken" and an "Indian blanket ... fringed with white women's scalps." These remains, he said, "and more were taken from ... the *battle-field* of Sand Creek." Having recovered the damning evidence, the original question answered itself: "Peaceable!" he cried out, in high dudgeon, "I stand by Sand Creek!"¹⁰

Silas Soule did not. Inverting Chivington's claims—Sand Creek, Soule said, had undercut the process of settling the West, and American Indian rather than white bodies had been desecrated there—he insisted it had been a massacre. On December 14, Soule wrote to his former commander, Ned Wynkoop, recalling that after Chivington arrived at Fort Lyon he had "declared [his] intention to massacre the friendly Indians camped on Sand Creek." Soule warned other officers that "any man who would take part in the murder, knowing the circumstances as we did"—he thought the Indians at Sand Creek were peaceful and being protected by Fort Lyon's men—"was a low lived cowardly son of a bitch." Nevertheless, after being reassured that Chivington planned to target "fighting Indians," Soule had joined the campaign. He noted, "We arrived at Black Kettle's and Left Hand's Camp, at day light." After Chivington ordered the attack, an interpreter and a soldier from the 1st Colorado trading in the camp "ran out with white flags," signaling that the Cheyennes and Arapahos were peaceful. The troops "paid no attention." Soule remembered that "hundreds of women and children were coming towards us . . . getting on their knees for mercy." Maj. Scott Anthony responded by shouting, "Kill the sons of bitches." Soule, though, "refused to fire." Then, "when the Indians found that there was no hope for them they went for the Creek, and buried themselves in Sand and got under the banks." Here, Soule offered a different view of the fortifications that Chivington often cited as proof that he had attacked hostile Indians primed for a fight.[11]

Depicting a world turned upside-down, in which native people were civilized and whites savage, Soule cataloged the terrible cruelties that Chivington's men inflicted on their victims. In one case, a woman and her two children "were on their knees, begging for their lives, of a dozen soldiers, within ten feet of them all firing." Finally, the woman "took a knife and cut the throats" of her family and then herself. In another instance, a "woman was cut open, and a child taken out of her, and scalped." In still another case, "squaws' snatches were cut out for trophies" by the soldiers. Among the desecrated bodies were those of chiefs White Antelope and War Bonnet, who both "had Ears and Privates cut off." In the end, Soule wondered about the attack's lingering implications for the project of settling the plains: "It was hard to see little children on their knees . . . having their brains beat out by men professing to be civilized." He wrote, "You would think it impossible for white men to butcher and mutilate human beings as they did there, but every word I have told you is the truth, which they do not deny."[12]

Four days after sending his letter off to Wynkoop, Soule wrote to his mother. He first admitted that he had been "present at a Massacre of three hundred Indians mostly women and Children." But then he reassured her that he had "not let [his] Company fire." Soule recounted the event's gruesome details, mourning the "little Children on their knees begging for their lives" who had "their brains beat out like dogs." When he wrote to his mother again, early in 1865, Soule, who had recently been detailed by his commanding officer to comb through the moldering corpses still lying on the killing field near Sand Creek, noted that the remains mocked Chivington's grandiose claims of five hundred or more dead. "There were not as many [killed] as reported," he explained, "not more than one hundred and thirty killed." Soule also revealed that the dead were mostly "women and children and all of them scalped." He concluded with his hope that "authorities in Washington will investigate the killing of these Indians." If they did, Soule remained confident that his actions would be vindicated.[13]

When he got his wish and Congress and the War Department looked into the attack, Soule offered testimony that neatly rebutted Chivington's Sand Creek stories. In summer 1864, he noted, Ned Wynkoop had recovered some white captives from a large group of Cheyennes camped along the Smoky Hill River. When "Wynkoop asked them to give up the white prisoners," he recalled, the Indians replied, "They were desirous of making peace with the whites." Wynkoop "pledged himself to protect them from Denver and back" so they could parlay with Gov. John Evans. At that meeting, "the Indians . . . seemed very anxious to make peace." Evans, though, insisted that he did not have the authority "make peace with them," that they must "look to military power for protection." Soule remembered Chivington next telling "them that he left the matter with Major Wynkoop; if they wanted peace they must come into the post and subject themselves to military law." "Major Wynkoop," for his part, "told them to bring the Indians of their tribe who were anxious for peace to Fort Lyon, and camp near the post." Wynkoop then sent word to General Curtis, asking if he could forge such a peace. The Cheyennes and Arapahos, meanwhile, "complied with Wynkoop's orders, and camped near the post." Soule explained that no word from Curtis had arrived back by late November. In sum, white officials had repeatedly assured Black Kettle's bands that, pending further instructions from higher authorities, they would be safe. Their fears allayed, the tribes had waited near Fort Lyon for word of their fate.[14]

Soule then recounted the details of the massacre. He explained that the evening before the violence he had explained to Chivington that the Indians camped near Sand Creek were "considered as prisoners" by the officers in Fort Lyon. But Chivington ordered his men to attack anyway, and all manner of horrors ensued. After investigators called for a brief recess, Chivington cross-examined Soule, asking if he personally had witnessed any barbaric acts committed by the Colorado volunteers. Soule admitted, speaking of the Indians at Sand Creek, that he could not say for certain "how they were mutilated." He "saw soldiers with children's scalps during the day, but did not see them cut off." The next day, Soule underscored his sense that Black Kettle's people had believed at the time of the assault that the troops at Fort Lyon would protect them: "I heard Wynkoop tell some of the chiefs, I think Black Kettle and Left-Hand, that—in case he got word from Curtis not to make peace with them, that he would let them know, so that they could remove out of the way and get to their tribe." Again, that word never came from Curtis. And a month later Chivington's men had fallen on the Sand Creek camp. With that, Soule finished relating his massacre story for the last time.[15]

Just a few weeks later, on April 23, 1865, a soldier from the 2nd Colorado Cavalry killed Silas Soule as he walked home through the streets of Denver after nightfall with his young wife. Because President Lincoln had been assassinated only nine days earlier, and because Soule's killer ultimately escaped justice and disappeared from Colorado Territory, the murder spawned a vast array of conspiracy theories suggesting that Colonel Chivington had orchestrated the violence to silence Soule. Soule thus became a martyr for many observers in Denver, including one federal official looking into Sand Creek who noted, "The barbarism of slavery culminated in the assassination of Mr. Lincoln, the barbarism of Sand Creek has culminated in the assassination of Capt. Soule." Regardless, even with Soule unavailable to provide further testimony, each of the federal investigations determined that Sand Creek had been a massacre. But John Chivington and many other westerners refused to accept those findings, maintaining that the violence had been a battle, that the soldiers there had fought bravely and well, and that their actions had pacified tribes hostile to the inevitable settlement and civilization of the region. The fight over naming Sand Creek would continue into the future.[16]

In 1879, for instance, noted author Helen Hunt Jackson attended a lecture by Chief Standing Bear of the Ponca tribe. To that point in her life, Jackson had mostly remained ignorant of the plight of American Indians, but

Standing Bear's tales of his people's forcible resettlement in Indian Territory (present-day Oklahoma) moved her to turn her literary talents to the cause of Indian reform. She wrote a series of letters to major newspapers excoriating Secretary of the Interior Carl Schurz for his role in shaping Indian affairs. She then turned her attention closer to home, to Colorado, focusing on the cases of the Ute uprising and Sand Creek. In a letter to the New York *Tribune*, Jackson argued that Sand Creek had been an unwarranted and depraved bloodletting. She insisted that the slaughtered Cheyennes and Arapahos had been guaranteed "perfect safety" by authorities in Colorado Territory; that Black Kettle had flown both the American and a white flag over his lodge on the day of the attack, signaling his peaceful intentions; that Chivington's troops had committed atrocities; and that they had nonetheless returned to Denver as heroes, where the press had celebrated those brave "Colorado soldiers" who had "covered themselves with glory."[17]

Such charges rankled William Byers, who, as editor of the *Rocky Mountain News* in 1864, had dismissed claims that Chivington had perpetrated a massacre. Byers replied to Jackson by echoing Chivington's Sand Creek stories, noting that the Colorado troops had found evidence of the Indians' hostility in their camp: "scalps of white men" which "had not yet dried"; "an Indian saddle-blanket entirely fringed around the edges with white women's scalps"; and the skin of a white woman stretched over the pommel of a saddle. He also insisted that the Native Americans killed at Sand Creek had not been under the protection of Fort Lyon and that the investigations into the violence had been corrupt. Finally, he explained that Sand Creek had "saved Colorado, and taught the Indians the most salutary lessen they had ever learned." Jackson, a newcomer to Colorado born and raised in Massachusetts, could not understand this, he contended, because she possessed effete eastern sensibilities out of place in the rough-and-tumble West. Jackson rebutted Byers's regional prejudices with her own nationalism, arguing that fighting the Indian Wars that grew out of Sand Creek required "no less than 8,000 troops . . . withdrawn from the effective forces engaged with the Rebellion." Sand Creek had not only been a massacre, she said, but it had also detracted from the Union war effort.[18]

As Jackson sparred with Byers, she worked on a book examining the federal government's longstanding mistreatment of American Indians.

Century of Dishonor, bound in red and embossed with a quote from Ben Franklin—"Look upon your hands! They are stained with the blood of your relations."—was published in 1881. A relentless exposé, the book details the shattered agreements between federal authorities and native peoples: "The history of the United States Government's repeated violations of faith with the Indians," Jackson writes, "convicts us, as a nation, not only of having outraged the principles of justice . . . but of having made ourselves liable to all punishments which follow upon such sins." Only by overhauling their treatment of Indian peoples could Americans repent of those sins. With the Modoc War, the Red River War, and the Great Sioux War, including the Battle of the Little Bighorn, having just taken place, many officials in the Department of the Interior were coming around to the idea that federal Indian policy had largely failed. Some of them were even ready for reform. But even with the climate surrounding federal-tribal relations shifting, Chivington's perspective still had many adherents, often westerners touched by the ongoing Indian Wars, including editors at the *Gunnison Democrat* who, around the time that Jackson published *Century of Dishonor*, called for "another Sand Creek" to quiet the region's tribes.[19]

Aware of such retrograde sentiments, George Bent weighed in on Sand Creek's collective memory around the turn of the twentieth century. Bent was shot in the hip at the massacre and survived, but officials inquiring into the violence never sought his testimony. Still, despite intense pressure to forget—federal programs in the 1880s and 1890s, the Era of Assimilation, included reprisals for preserving tribal practices and histories—Bent fought to keep memories of Sand Creek alive. At the time, Frederick Jackson Turner fretted over what he called the closing of the frontier; conservationists warned about the impending extinction of the bison and the tribes that depended on those animals; and readers consumed piles of dime novels about cowboys and Indians. The West stood at the center of debates about the nation's future, and Bent worried that native people had no voice in such discussions. He began relating tribal lore to James Mooney, a Smithsonian ethnographer, George Bird Grinnell, a founder of the field of professional anthropology, and George Hyde, a relatively obscure historian.[20]

Bent ultimately soured on Mooney and Grinnell, but he collaborated with Hyde for more than a decade. In 1905–1906 they placed a series of articles in *The Frontier*, a magazine published out of Colorado Springs. In those essays, Bent publicly labeled Sand Creek a "massacre" and rejected Chivington's history of the violence. In letters to Hyde, Bent recalled that after the Camp Weld meeting in Denver Wynkoop "told Black Kettle and other chiefs that they could move to Fort Lyon and they would be protected." Bent remembered, "This was the reason the Cheyennes moved toward Fort Lyon that winter." Turning to the massacre, Bent explained that he "saw that Black Kettle had a flag up on a long pole, to show the troops that the camp was friendly." The Colorado volunteers, though, ignored the signal and "opened fire from all sides." Running for his life, Bent discovered "the main body of Indians, who had dug pits under the high banks of the creek." These "holes" were the trenches that Chivington later claimed proved that the Cheyennes and Arapahos had prepared in advance for combat. Finally, Bent emphasized the desecration of bodies at the massacre, suggesting, as Soule had before him, that the only savages present at Sand Creek had been Chivington's men.[21]

Bent's essays infuriated Chivington's surviving troops. Their colonel had died a decade earlier, and Bent's characterization of Sand Creek struck them as impertinent and a threat to their reputations and his memory. Writing in the Denver *Times*, Maj. Jacob Downing labeled Bent a "cut-throat, and a thief, a liar and a scoundrel, but worst of all, a halfbreed" and insisted that Sand Creek should be celebrated as a noble part of civilizing Colorado and winning the Civil War in the West. He then tried to embed Chivington's perspective on Sand Creek in a glorious Civil War narrative being constructed at the time by heritage groups nationwide—work that culminated in Colorado with the unveiling of a memorial in 1909. In that year, the Colorado Pioneers Association placed a statue on the state capitol steps in Denver. The monument (a Union cavalryman, on foot and gazing west, cast in bronze) featured a plaque affixed to its base that catalogued the "battles" in which Coloradans had fought during the Civil War. Sand Creek was among them. This was significant because of the memorial's placement near the capitol, suggesting that it represented a state-sponsored memory of the bloodshed at Sand Creek.[22]

The Civil War memorial fit within a generational commemorative impulse. With most Civil War veterans, including members of the 1st and

3rd Colorado Volunteers, nearing the end of their lives or already dead, an effort to shape how future generations would remember the war swept the nation. But for stewards of the Civil War's memory in Colorado, an event like Sand Creek proved somewhat complicated. A heroic narrative of the conflict in which both North and South had fought hard and well predominated at the time. The war's root rather than proximate causes—slavery and the repercussions of westward expansion—could be forgotten in service of amicable reunion. If Sand Creek were to be part of this emerging narrative, it would have to be as a "battle." And so, when on July 24, 1909, the Pioneers Association unveiled its new memorial, Sen. Thomas Patterson remarked, "We are all Americans today, and we all glory in one flag and in one country." Ignoring Sand Creek's impact on the Cheyenne and Arapaho peoples, Gen. Irving Hale then suggested that the "Civil War . . . made freedom universal." The Pioneers Association had smoothed away the massacre's rough edges and cast John Chivington's Sand Creek story into bronze. The massacre was just one among twenty-two Civil War "battles" in which Coloradans had participated.[23]

Less than half a century later, Coloradans reversed themselves and began trying to segregate Sand Creek from memories of the Civil War, associating the engagement exclusively with the process of westward expansion and the Indian Wars. On August 6, 1950, Kiowa County, Colorado, unveiled two Sand Creek historic markers. One sat on a hill overlooking a bend in the creek, believed at the time and since confirmed (see Douglas Scott's chapter in this volume) to have been part of the massacre site, a few miles north of State Highway 96. That monument hewed closely to important elements of John Chivington's Sand Creek story. An ochre marble slab, the marker featured an image described at the time as a "lifelike Indian" wearing a "full war headdress" above the words "Sand Creek Battle Ground." The hilltop marker paired with the second monument, an obelisk located just off Highway 96 sponsored by the Colorado State Historical Society. A bronze plaque thereon included the mixed message "Sand Creek: 'Battle' or 'Massacre,'" suggesting that by 1950 the monument was part of a shifting political landscape. Still, the Historical Society relied on the passive voice to obscure culpability for the violence and avoided mentioning atrocities or the number of people killed. The text finished by calling Sand Creek "one of the regrettable tragedies of the conquest of the West"—an ambiguous message, to be sure, whispering of the need to maintain the status quo among Historical Society donors and local people.[24]

Leroy Hafen, Colorado's chief historian at the time, oversaw the dedication ceremonies at both monuments. Hafen's private notes from the period indicate that he struggled with the implications of the wording on the Historical Society's roadside marker, especially with the question of whether the bloodshed should be depicted as a battle or a massacre. In a short essay published in the *Lamar Daily News* four days before the monuments' unveiling, Hafen tried to explain to his readers how it came to pass that Colorado troops had perpetrated such a heinous crime. He described Sand Creek as "perhaps the most controversial subject in Colorado history," noting that "some have called it a 'battle' in which the Indians got what they deserved, while others have labeled it an 'unjustifiable massacre.'" In his view, the "tragic engagement" grew out of "contact" between the "incompatible cultures of the red man and the white man." Sand Creek, then, had emerged out of westward expansion. After contextualizing the violence in that way, Hafen concluded: "As is common in human relations, there are various points of view, and right is not all on one side."[25] Looking back, Hafen's essay reads like moral equivocation, but at the time it represented a relatively nuanced treatment.

One thing Hafen did not mention was the relationship between Sand Creek and the Civil War. Divorcing the massacre from that context, as opposed to linking the violence to the Civil War as at the memorial erected on the state capitol steps in 1909, made sense in 1950. Following the run-up to World War I, continuing during the era of World War II, and through the start of the cold war, federal authorities drummed up support for involving the nation in overseas conflicts by encouraging Americans to recall the Civil War as a virtuous war, emblematic of the nation's commitment to fighting against tyranny and for freedom. President Lincoln's standing as a great liberator as well as that of citizen soldiers soared in these years. Sand Creek, increasingly perceived in an ambiguous light, did not fit with this vision of the Civil War as a good war. It might have been a massacre, but then it was best remembered as distinct from the Civil War. The 1950-vintage memorials reflected these priorities, as did

Hafen's speech and essay, which placed Sand Creek against the bloody background of the Indian Wars only.[26]

On April 28, 2007, it seemed that the National Park Service might finally have answered the enduring question of what to call Sand Creek. On that day, the Sand Creek Massacre National Historic Site, the first unit of the National Parks system to label American soldiers explicitly as perpetrators rather than heroes, opened its gates. But even then, the tortuous process of memorializing Sand Creek suggested that many observers were not yet satisfied that the age-old controversy had been resolved. Although the Park Service never considered labeling Sand Creek a battle—Sen. Ben Nighthorse Campbell's original enabling legislation, signed into law by President Clinton in 1998, made it clear that the violence would be called a massacre—critics quibbled with that decision. A vocal minority in Kiowa County wondered if having a federally designated massacre site in their backyard would reflect badly on their community. At the same time, the members of some heritage groups, especially the Order of the Indian Wars, suggested that the historic site's name smacked of politically correct pandering to American Indians. Meanwhile, the stakeholders in the Sand Creek memorialization project—tribal descendants, Park Service employees, Colorado officials, and local landowners—tried to make sense of the competing accounts of the violence.[27]

Over the course of nearly a decade, these heritage groups struggled with the question of how best to commemorate Sand Creek. But first they had to find the massacre's location. It turned out that in 1998, after Senator Campbell's legislation passed, nobody could prove to the Park Service's satisfaction where the violence had taken place. A massive search for the site ensued. But even that process proved contentious, as a series of disagreements about method pivoted on disparate readings of the historical record. American Indian descendants of Sand Creek's victims typically based their understanding of the episode's history and geography on Silas Soule's and George Bent's massacre stories, on traditional tribal methods, and on ethnographies collected during the memorialization process. The Park Service team, by contrast, tried to solve the mystery of the killing field's location by looking to other sources, especially records produced by soldiers in the U.S. Army and archaeological findings. Many of the descendants were outraged when the Park Service placed greater emphasis on sources produced by Sand Creek's perpetrators rather than its victims, especially George Bent. The Park Service, caught off guard by the controversy, eventually floated a compromise: a historic site with boundaries capacious enough to encompass several different interpretations.[28]

Even then, controversy persisted. In 2002, after the site had been located but before it opened to the public, the Order of the Indian Wars arrived in Colorado for its annual conference, focused on Sand Creek. On September 4, a group of independent scholars gave papers that recalled John Chivington's perceptions of the violence. Jerry Russell, the Order's founder, warned that "Ben Nighthorse Campbell will make sure the site only deals with the Indian side. And that's just wrong." He continued, "For years the Battle of Little Bighorn was called the Custer Massacre. But . . . they don't say 'massacre' anymore because it's pejorative, divisive. And yet the Park Service will call Sand Creek a massacre even though the monument down there says battleground." Mike Koury, a local author, gave a paper titled "I Stand By Sand Creek: A Defense of Colonel Chivington and the Third Colorado." Koury explained that he would "not infuse the [Sand Creek] battlefield with a modern meaning untrue to the past" nor "bend it artificially to serve contemporary needs." He then concluded: "The 3rd Colorado did their job. Now some of them were overly zealous, and they did more than their job. But that's not to condemn the regiment, the entire group."[29]

Sand Creek remains a "history front" in an ongoing "culture war," as contested perceptions of the past reveal fault lines in the present. Each new fight over American memory highlights the difficulty of agreeing on a single historical narrative within the confines of a pluralistic society, but the case of Sand Creek seems unusually complicated. For federal authorities to encourage collective remembrance of an event that resists placement within the narratives of redemption and steady progress that are so common at most national historic sites is a risky proposition. Recalling Sand Creek, in other words, is likely to tear scabs from old wounds as to provide the healing that so many memorials, including the Murrah Building in Oklahoma City and the National September 11 Memorial located at Ground Zero in Lower Manhattan, promise supplicants who arrive to worship at these shrines. Nevertheless, the Sand Creek Massacre National Historic

Site has opened its gates, and heritage tourists are now welcomed there to contemplate the culpability of the federal government in the commission of a massacre. What visitors will make of the experience, including the site's name, is an open question.[30]

NOTES

1. Aldrich 1955; Barr 2011; Bourdieu 1989; Felstiner et al. 1980–81; Gengenbach 2000; LaDuke 2005:132–50; Méndez-Gastelumendi 2001; Min 2006; Sellars 1962; Thornton 1997; Tuan 1991; Weyeneth 2001; Wiener 1963.

2. The clearest expression of John Chivington's views on Sand Creek can be found in "Massacre of Cheyenne Indians," in *Report of the Joint Committee on the Conduct of the War, at the Second Session, Thirty-Eighth Congress* (Washington, D.C.: Government Printing Office, 1865), 104–108. The most concise iteration of Silas Soule's perspective on Sand Creek can be found in Roberts and Halaas 2001; and "Report of the Secretary of War," 39th Cong., 2nd Sess., S. Ex. Doc. 26, 8–29.

3. The Byers-Jackson exchange can be found in Jackson 1881:343–58.

4. Bent and Hyde 1905–1906; Halaas and Masich 2005:327–48; Roberts 1984:676.

5. *Lamar Daily News*, July 22, 24, and 26, August 2, 1950; *Kiowa County Press*, July 28, 1950; Greene and Scott 2004:30–33.

6. Col. John Chivington to Maj. Gen. Samuel Curtis, Nov. 29, 1864, *Official Records of the War of the Rebellion*, Series I, XLI, Pt. 1, 948; Col. John Chivington to Messrs. Beyers and Dailey, Editors News, Nov. 29, 1864, *Official Records of the War of the Rebellion*, Series I, XLI, Pt. 1, 950–51.

7. Chivington to Curtis, Dec. 16, 1864, *Official Records of the War of the Rebellion*, Series I, XLI, Pt. 1, 948–50.

8. "Massacre of Cheyenne Indians," in *Report of the Joint Committee . . . Second Session, Thirty-Eighth Congress*, 101–104 (see note 2).

9. Ibid., 106.

10. Thayer 1887:241–46, emphasis added.

11. Roberts and Halaas 2001:25.

12. Ibid., 25–26.

13. Silas Soule to Mother, Dec. 18, 1864, Carey Collection, Box 5, Folder 13; Silas Soule to Mother, Jan. 8, 1865, Carey Collection, Box 5, Folder 13, both in University of Denver Special Collections, Penrose Library. See also *Official Records of the War of the Rebellion*, Series I, XLI, Pt. 4, 948.

14. "Report of the Secretary of War," 39th Cong., 2nd Sess., S. Ex. Doc. 26, 8–10.

15. Ibid., 16–29.

16. Roberts 1984:492. See also *Rocky Mountain News*, Apr. 24, 25, and 27, 1865. Two of the three inquiries have been collected in Carroll 1985.

17. Jackson 1881:343–45; exchange between Jackson and Schurz, 359–74. See also Byers 1969:143–48, 1975–76:331–46; Gonzalez 2004:437–65; Marsden 1979:109–12;

Mathes 1989:42–53, 1997:21–26; Mathes and Lowitt 2003:9–104; Senier 2003:11, 14–18, 23–26.

18. The Byers-Jackson exchange, including the quoted material, can be found in its entirety in Jackson 1881:343–58.

19. Mathes, 1997:36; Jackson 1881:27, 29; *Gunnison Democrat*, Oct. 20, 1880. See also Berthrong 1979; Hoxie 2001:3–29, 36–40, 87–104, 130–36, 159–81, 239–44; Prucha 1984.

20. Halaas and Masich 2005:xii–xiv, 23–25, 39, 59–72, 86–89; Hoxie 2001:41–81; Hyde 1968:vii–xiii; Moses 2002:7–31, 71–86, 130–40; Punke 2007:177–204.

21. George Bent to George Hyde, May 14, 1913, and Apr. 30, 1906, Coe Collection, Beinecke Library, Yale University, New Haven, Conn.; Bent and Hyde 1905:3–5 (Oct.). See also Bent to Hyde, Oct. 15, 1914, Letter 10, George Bent Manuscript Collection no. 54, Colorado Historical Society, Denver, Colo.; and Bent to Hyde, Jan. 19, 1905, Jan. 23, 1905, Mar. 15, 1905, Dec. 21, 1905, Feb. 28, 1906, Apr. 14, 1906, Apr. 25, 1906, Apr. 30, 1906, June 4, 1909, Feb. 22, 1912, Nov. 29, 1912, Feb. 19, 1913, Jan. 17, 1914, and Oct. 17, 1916, Coe Collection.

22. Roberts 1984:676. See also "Soldier Monument to Be Unveiled at Capitol," *Denver Daily News*, July 24, 1909, 1; "Shaft for Hero Dead of State," *Rocky Mountain News*, Nov. 10, 1905; *Colorado Transcript*, Oct. 10, 1894; *New York Times*, Oct. 14, 1894; *Denver Republican*, Oct. 5, 1894; Grinnell 1955:103–201, 1972:1.21, 158 and 2.271–73; Halaas and Masich 2005:327–48; Hyde 1968:v–xvi.

23. Quotes from "Shaft to Civil War Martyrs of State Unveiled with Pomp," *Denver Daily News*, July 25, 1909. See also "Hosts Gather to Show Honor to Fallen Heroes," *Denver Post*, July 24, 1909; "Soldier Monument to Be Unveiled at Capitol," *Denver Daily News*, July 24, 1909; Blight 2001:1–5; Foster 1988:4–8, 23–67; Hobsbawm, "Inventing Traditions," in Hobsbawm and Ranger 1992:1–14; Kammen 1993:101–39.

24. File 287, "Sand Creek Massacre," in Colorado Historical Society, Denver, Colo.; *Lamar Daily News*, Aug. 2, 1950. In an interview conducted in 2005, Modupe Lobode, the Colorado Historical Society's chief historian, described notes made by Leroy Hafen, chief historian in 1950, accompanying the Historical Society's plans for the obelisk. Hafen alluded to the politics impinging on the memorialization process. Lobode regretted that the notes had been lost. Interview by author, June 3, 2005, Denver, Colo., tape recording, in author's possession. See also *Kiowa County Press*, July 28, Aug. 11, 1950; *Lamar Daily News*, July 22, 24, and 26, Aug. 6–7, 1950.

25. *Lamar Daily News*, Aug. 2, 1950.

26. Blight 2001:381, 2011:3–6; Bodnar 2010:113; Peterson 1995:198; Schwartz 2000:224–55, 2009:59–90.

27. Public Law 105-243, "An Act to authorize the Secretary of the Interior to study the suitability and feasibility of designating the Sand Creek Massacre National Historic Site in the State of Colorado as a unit of the National Park System, and for other purposes"; Deborah Frazier, "Massacre Mystery," *Denver Post*, Sept. 21, 1998, B-6; Michael Romano, "Massacre Remembered," *Rocky Mountain News*, Oct. 7,

1998, 7-A; Michael Romano, "Save Site of Massacre, Indians Say," *Rocky Mountain News*, Mar. 25, 1998, 8-A; Elliot Zaret, "House OKs Bill for Massacre Site," *Denver Post*, Sept. 19, 1998, 6-B.

28. Greene and Scott 2004:30–53.

29. Quotes from author's notes, Annual Assembly of the Order of the Indian Wars, Colorado Springs, Colo., Sept. 4, 2003.

30. Kammen 1993:687; Linenthal 1995:52; Sheehan 1981;Wilkinson 2005:249.

Reassessing the Meaning of Artifact Patterning

Douglas D. Scott

Oral histories, written records and documents that historical archaeologists utilize, especially firsthand accounts of historical events, are often thought to be tantamount to eyewitness testimony. They provide material for generating hypotheses that can be tested in the archaeological record. They also furnish the basis by which archaeologically observed patterns can be assigned historically meaningful identities. The archaeological record contains clues in the form of physical remains, specifically artifacts, and their in situ contextual relationships. These relationships include distributions and spatial associations of various types of artifacts and can reveal a great deal about the activities that were carried out at a site.

The Sand Creek Massacre of 1864 involving the Colorado volunteer cavalry attack of a Cheyenne and Arapaho camp is sacred to the descendents of the native peoples who fought and died there. That sacredness manifests itself in several ways. First and foremost is the overriding desire to see the site as a memorial to past injustices. There is little conflict among those interested in the site regarding such an interpretation of the past. However, interpretations of the precise location where events occurred are a continuing source of conflict among constituent groups. In particular, large numbers of relic finds on private land immediately north and west of the Sand

Creek National Historic Site boundary now allow for a reinterpretation of newly found relic and artifact patterning relative to Cheyenne and Arapaho participant accounts.[1]

Historical Background

The Sand Creek massacre is one of the most significant and tragic events in American history.[2] On November 29, 1864, Col. John M. Chivington led a group of approximately 700 soldiers of the 1st and 3rd Colorado Volunteer Cavalry regiments from old Fort Lyon (near present-day Lamar, Colorado) to an Indian village of more than one hundred lodges on Sand Creek, which was then also known as the "Big Sandy."[3] Approximately 650 Cheyenne and Arapaho Indians were camped at this village, believing they were under U.S. Army protection. As instructed by Colorado governor John Evans, the Indians had earlier presented themselves to the army at Fort Lyon, at which time they were told to remain at their Sand Creek camp. The Indian camp was at the edge of the Cheyenne and Arapaho reservation that had been established by the 1861 Treaty of Fort Wise. Nevertheless, volunteer troops led by Colonel Chivington launched a surprise attack on the village. The strike began at dawn, when the soldiers charged at the village firing with small arms. After the ground assault began, an artillery battery section fired perhaps one salvo about the time the soldiers reached the north end of the largely evacuated village. Many villagers fled to the north, upstream. Approximately one mile above the village, according to most accounts of the massacre, the Indians sheltered themselves in hastily dug trenches along the banks of the creek. This area, known as the "sandpits," was one of the areas of highest casualties. The army troops brought at least four 12-pounder mountain howitzers to the sandpits area and employed them with deadly effect.

By day's end, at least 150–200 Indians—mainly women, children, and elderly people—had been killed. On the army's side, ten soldiers died and thirty-eight were wounded. Although Chivington's troops returned to a heroes' welcome in Denver, the Sand Creek massacre was soon recognized for what it was—a national disgrace—and investigated and condemned by two congressional committees and a military commission.

Sand Creek remains to this day an important sacred site to the Cheyenne and Arapaho peoples. The site embodies disenfranchisement and the loss of life they suffered because of U.S. government policy toward them in the nineteenth century.

Physical Evidence: The Formal Archaeological Investigations

Archaeological reconnaissance investigations were undertaken in 1997 and again in May 1999 in concert with historical research and oral histories in order to identify the Sand Creek village and massacre site. The artifacts, their distribution on the landscape, and the context in which they were recovered indicated that the main campsite was identified. Artifacts of the 1864 period were found scattered all along the Sand Creek drainage, beginning at the traditional location of the village site at what is now known as the Dawson South Bend of Sand Creek and continuing northwesterly for several miles along the creek (figure 19).

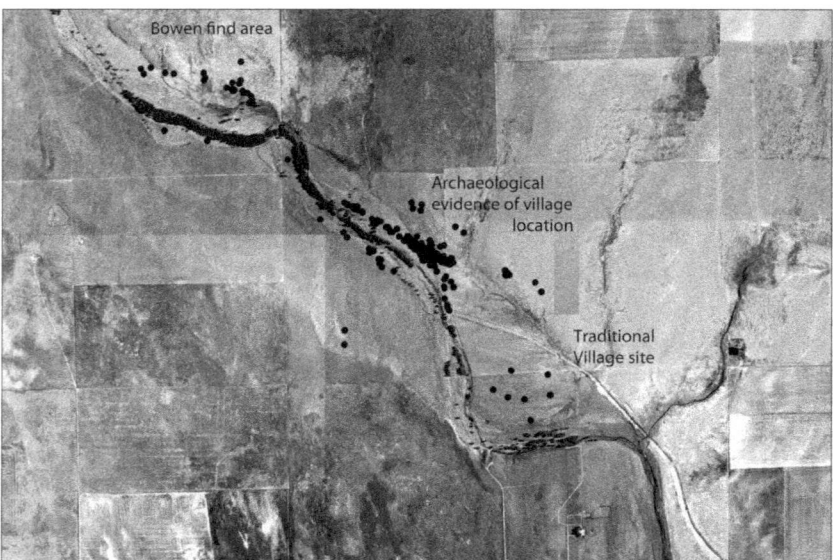

Figure 19. Aerial photograph of Sand Creek site. North is at the top. Circles represent artifact distribution.

The largest concentration of 1864 era artifacts (about 400) was found on the eastern side of Sand Creek about one mile north of the site location where the battle is generally thought to have taken place. The artifact concentration, situated on an eastern terrace above Sand Creek, is about 450 meters long, trending southeast-northwest and about 160 meters wide. The artifacts found in the concentration include tin cups, tin cans, horseshoes, horseshoe nails, plates, bowls, knives, forks, spoons, barrel hoops, a coffee grinder, a coffee pot, iron arrowheads, bullets, and cannonball fragments.

Figure 20. Altered iron objects. Iron scraper on left, possible arrow shaft scrapers made from scrap tools in center, and triangular file on right.

The concentration includes artifacts that are usually considered unique to American Indian sites of the nineteenth century. Besides the arrowheads, some of which are unfinished, are a variety of iron objects modified for American Indian uses (figure 20). These artifacts include knives altered to awls, iron wire altered to awls, fleshers or hide scrapers, strap iron altered by filed serrations as hide preparation devices, and several iron objects altered by filing possibly to serve as arrow shaft fabrication tools.

Cheyenne and Arapaho annuity requests, annuity lists, and other correspondence provide a set of comparative data for what constituted items that would be found in a camp.[4] The annuity lists, requests, and correspondence were researched and clearly demonstrate that most of the artifact types found at Sand Creek are the same types as listed for the Cheyenne and Arapaho tribes. Tin cups, bowls, plates, coffee grinders, coffee pots, kettles, pans, knives, forks, spoons, fleshers, axes, butcher knives, horse tack, guns, lead, and bullets are consistently listed. These are the durable goods, the ones that can be expected to survive in the archaeological record, and indeed they were found during the field investigations. There are many more items of a perishable nature, such as flour, sugar, salt, and dresses, that would leave only minor or no traces in the archaeological record.

Present in the village were two lines of evidence that this village was attacked and destroyed. First is the evidence of arms and munitions. The village site yielded bullets for various calibers and types of firearms. Among the ammunition components are bullets for the .52 Sharps rifle or carbine, .54 Starr carbine, .54-caliber musket, .58-caliber musket, .36-caliber revolver, and .44-caliber revolver. These weapon types and calibers were used during the American Civil War and can be readily dated and identified. Lists of ordnance used by the 1st and 3rd Colorado Volunteer Cavalry units during late 1864 exist. The concordance of the archaeological munitions finds and the lists of weapons in the volunteers' hands is quite remarkable inasmuch as archaeological battlefield firearms identification often demonstrates a far wider range of firearms employed than is reported in historical documents. In addition, there has been some limited archaeological investigation of one of the Colorado Volunteer campsites in eastern Colorado at Russellville.[5] Among the artifacts recovered at that site are numerous bullets of the types known to fit the handguns and shoulder arms of the 1st and 3rd Regiments.

The Russellville archaeological collection and the Sand Creek collection also show a very high degree of concordance.

Perhaps the single most important artifact type that can definitively identify this village as being attacked are cannonball fragments. The Colorado Volunteers employed two 12-pounder mountain howitzers during their attack on the village. The cannonball fragments are nearly unequivocal evidence in their own right that this is the site of the Sand Creek massacre.

The firearms artifact distribution also adds to the story. There were two concentrations of firearms artifacts and several widely dispersed bullets.[6] One concentration consists of bullets found in the village site. These bullets are both fired and unfired items. Almost all calibers associated with the Colorado Volunteer units are present. A 12-pounder howitzer case shot fragment was also found in the village. It provides mute testimony to the fact that the camp was shelled by the artillery. But with only two case shot fragments recovered, the data suggest that artillery fire was limited, which is consistent with the historical narrative indicating that only one salvo, perhaps one shot from each of the two guns put into action, was fired on the village.

The second concentration of firearms artifacts was found on the west side of Sand Creek and about 1,000 feet directly opposite the village. The artifacts were found along a line about 1,000 feet long. Sharps and Starr bullets were found, as were three 12-pounder case shot fragments. These bullets and cannonball fragments probably represent rounds that were fired at the horse herd, or they may be overshots of their intended targets in the camp or simply ricochets from the firing on the camp. Another possibility is that the bullets and cannonball fragments represent rounds fired at Cheyennes and Arapahos as they fled. However, the narrow linear distribution more likely reflects overshot or ricochet rounds falling to earth once their maximum range was reached. This artifact distribution probably reflects firing along nearly the entire length of the camp and thus is another strong indicator that the camp was attacked and fired on.

Other widely dispersed firearms artifacts were found east of the camp, ranging in distance from 300 to 600 meters and north of the camp ranging from a few tens of meters to well over 2.5 miles. Among the bullets closest to the camp are also mingled bits of village items that may reflect attempts to salvage a treasured item at the time the Cheyennes and Arapahos were fleeing the attack on the camp. The distribution of these fired bullets and privately collected cannonball fragments clearly shows the line of the flight for survival by the fleeing villagers and the pursuit by the Colorado troops.

The firearms data are particularly striking in one respect: the absence of bullets or other weaponry evidence of resistance in the camp itself. Bullets representing weapon types that can be reasonably associated with the Cheyennes and Arapahos are singularly absent from the artifact collection from the campsite. The absence of definitive artifacts of resistance supports the American Indian oral tradition that the attack came as a complete surprise. Other evidence of combat or armed resistance is not great, but more compelling, as seen in the firearms artifacts found along the route of flight.

The final bit of evidence that identifies this site as Black Kettle's village is the condition of the artifacts found in the camp. Every spoon, the fork, all tin cups, plates, bowls, and containers (buckets, pots, and kettles) have all been crushed and flattened. Even the tin cans are crushed. The cast iron pieces—kettles, pots, and skillet—are broken. The patterns of crushing and breakage point to the intentional destruction of the camp equipage so as to make it unserviceable to its owners.

The more northerly areas of Sand Creek, the privately collected lands, have yielded hundreds of artifacts of the 1864 era as well. That evidence was found in the form of bullets and spherical shell and case shot fragments. These combat-related materials were found along either side of the creek and were widely scattered, but concentrations of relics were found along a stretch of Sand Creek with highly eroded banks, according to the landowners Chuck and Sherri Bowen and a map of finds they had made.

Physical Evidence in Private Collections

Relic collecting began on the field of battle almost as soon as the air cleared of gun smoke. Lt. Gen. William T. Sherman even had a collection made at the site during a visit in 1868. Relic collection or attempts to find and collect the site continued sporadically throughout the late nineteenth century and through the twentieth. Among the first to find unequivocal evidence of

Sand Creek were adjacent landowners, who found mid-nineteenth-century bullets and 12-pounder cannonball fuse ring fragments. The cannonball as fired in the mountain howitzer was a hollow sphere with a hole in the top. The sphere's interior was filled with black powder, and a fuse graduated in seconds was screwed into the opening. At the distance prescribed by the fuse length, the shell would burst into fragments (shrapnel). A second type of hollow sphere, somewhat thinner in wall thickness, was filled with lead balls and a black powder bursting charge and likewise when fused and fired would burst into fragments, sending the lead balls outward as projectiles. This round is known as case shot.

All of these finds broadly delineate the western portion of the camp. Significantly, several defined clusters contain high counts of artifacts typically found on Plains Indian campsites. It is possible that, during the attack, some of these objects were in the process of being carried out by their owners and then dropped within the cluster areas. It is surmised that those fleeing the camp could take only their most prized possessions, as perhaps the coffee grinder found in fragmented condition within one group; and objects needed for defense or survival, as perhaps a skinning knife and unfired rifle balls found within another group. In contrast, items that are more mundane found within cluster areas—unfinished arrow points, cone tinklers, metal scrap, and so forth—would have been left behind. An abundance of these latter artifact types strongly indicates the location of one or more tipis on the day of the attack. Artifacts found within one concentration, which encompasses a bank of Sand Creek, include tools useful for excavation. These items, intermixed with cannonball shrapnel and carbine bullets, are likely indicators of where some of the camp defenders excavated pits along the creek bank. George Bent's and other Cheyenne accounts tell of families, mainly women and children, hastily digging holes in the sand along the creek banks to provide some protection from the soldiers. But those holes or pits became a killing zone for those who occupied them. Bent saw the potential for disaster and, despite nursing a nasty hip wound, vacated the death trap.

In addition, hundreds of lead bullets (at least five hundred observed) with a range of calibers including .69, .58, .54, .50, .45, .44, and .36 have been recovered in the clusters (figure 21). Most of these are the types used by the

Colorado Volunteers and most have impact deformation. Fragments and nearly complete assemblages of at least five 12-powder howitzer case shot and shell were also present, as were three Bormann fuses for the cannon rounds (figure 22). Two are poorly cut for timed flight, but one was cut for a one-second flight before bursting into lethal shrapnel. This is a very short range, suggesting that the guns were within 400 yards or so of their intended targets (see discussion below). Other weapons recovered include eight complete or partial iron arrowheads and several complete and fired percussion caps. Also noted in the relic collection were about twenty .50-70 cartridge cases that definitely postdate the Sand Creek massacre, since they were not developed until 1866. These could relate to buffalo hide hunter activities of the late 1860s or 1870s; army scouts in the area after 1864; activities related to the Montana or Goodnight-Loving cattle trails that passed this general area; or simply later ranching activities. Other cartridge cases include .56-56 Spencers, .56-50 Spencers, .44-Henry, and a variety of other brass cartridge cases in odd calibers. The .44-Henry could have been used in the fight, but the others postdate the 1864 event by years. The .56-56 Spencer could have been at the fight, but not the .56-50-caliber Spencers,

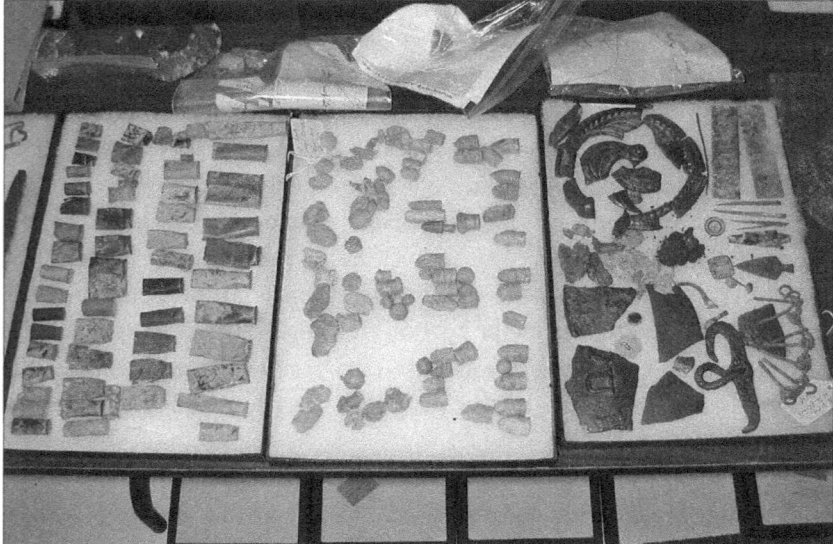

Figure 21. Bullets and cartridge cases from Bowen find area.

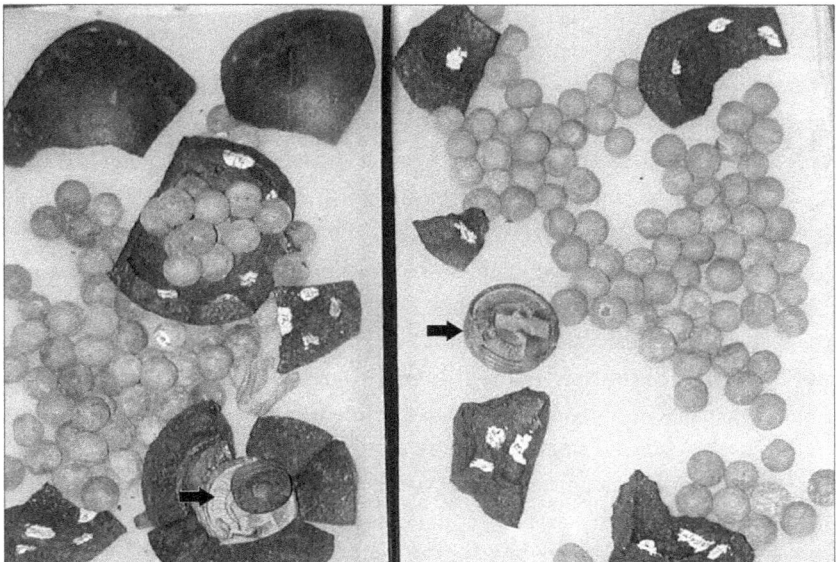

Figure 22. Lead case shot balls, cannonball shrapnel, and Bormann fuses (arrows) from Bowen find area.

since they too postdate the event. A few items of army equipment were also noted, including a carbine strap snap hook, a canteen stopper, and a trouser button that could date to the 1864 era.

Personal items include horseshoes and horseshoe nails, tack buckles, bridle ornament pieces, a bracelet, five finger rings, several pieces of trade silver, six awls, about a dozen tinklers, a spoon, an iron scraper, two hoes, another scraper made from an old gun barrel, fragments of a leather shoe, a crushed brass bucket, and several dozen cast iron kettle fragments probably from three or four separate kettles. There is also a large assemblage of miscellaneous items including wire, a coffee grinder gear, and other nondescript pieces of iron and other metals.

These relics clearly represent a mixed deposit, the artifacts dating to the 1864 event and those that were introduced from a few years to decades after the fight. Those clearly dating to 1864 include most of the lead bullets, cannonball fragments, and some of the personal items. The personal and camp items are striking in that they represent either personal adornment items (rings, bracelet, tinklers) or tools or items that could be used to dig the shelter pits. The relic assemblage of camp items is not consistent in type or quantity with those seen in the annuity lists or in the camp debris of the 1864 period found by the archaeological team in features to the southeast.

The number of cannonball fragments is significant, as are the shell, case shot, and fuse artifacts. The fuses indicate that the shells and case shot were intended to explode within a second after firing, thus indicating a range of roughly 400 yards or less.[7] For a cannon this is very close, essentially point-blank range. Historical accounts of the attack on the village indicate that the artillery went into battery 600–800 yards from the campsite, then fired a salvo, perhaps one round apiece. The artillery could not fire into the village after the soldiers entered it for fear of striking their own men. The cannoneers did fire at the fleeing Cheyennes and Arapahos before being ordered north to fire on the shelter pits.

The cannonball fragments and short-timed Bormann fuses found to the north of the camp artifact concentration are inconsistent with long-range firing on the village but consistent with firing at short range at the survivors hiding in the sand pits. Another striking element of the firearm artifact assemblage is the near absence of firearm calibers likely to have been used by the Cheyennes and Arapahos. Few bullets in trade gun calibers or firearm types known to have been issued as annuity items are present, thus supporting earlier conclusions that the Indians offered little resistance to the soldiers' attack.

Based on a preponderance of evidence, the Indian village that was attacked by Chivington's troops on November 29, 1864, is identified as the one found during the professional archaeological investigations in 1999. That site is in complete agreement with the historical documents, which include an 1868 map of the Sand Creek massacre area drawn by Lt. Samuel Bonsall, which indicates that an area north of the traditional site in the Dawson South Bend was the likely site of the village.[8] The relic evidence is consistent with some village element, perhaps the northwestern terminus of the village site, being in this location. Most important, the relic data finds and identified distributions are consistent with accounts of the tribe's flight for survival and pursuit by the Coloradans and of the decimation of those who dug and took shelter in the sand pits along the banks of Sand Creek.

A Massacre or a Battle Considered

Although most constituent groups agree that the Sand Creek affair was a massacre and not just a fight, some have argued for the latter description. Cheyenne and Arapaho oral histories and tradition clearly identify the Sand Creek affair as a massacre, even if there are disagreements about its precise location on the landscape.[9] In a vigorously argued text on the weakness of oral history and particularly oral tradition relative to well-constructed historical narrative and sound interpretation of archaeological data, Ronald Mason makes strong arguments that modern scholars often abrogate their responsibility to scholarship in the name of political correctness or deference to the feelings of other cultures.[10] He argues that no one owns the past, that it is beyond any group's control and is exempt from ownership since it is, in fact, extinct. Nevertheless, he emphatically defends the value of oral history and to a degree the value of oral tradition, especially in the cultural context in which they were created. He forcibly argues that those cultural contexts cannot be translated to another culture's view of the past without critical thought. He defines oral history as that passed down from an event participant or observer, oral tradition as that passed from one to another as secondhand recollections or retelling of tales and stories by those other than the direct participant or observer.

The crux of Mason's argument is that oral tradition should not be dismissed, but that its value is diminished over time because of its potential to be recalled improperly, enhanced, and modified in the telling and retelling. Oral tradition can be useful in the study of history, but only when corroborated by multiple sources.

The reinterpretation of all the physical evidence collected here raises the question of whether the attack and subsequent fight still fit the definition of a massacre and argue for or against the Cheyenne and Arapaho oral tradition. In the twenty-first century the words "massacre," "war crimes," and "crimes against humanity" are often seen or heard in various media reports detailing far-flung and apparent indiscriminate killings of soldiers and civilians in strife-ridden places around the world. Despite media hyperbole, these terms have modern and legal definitions that apply in international courts of law. These are systemic crimes in that they seldom involve individuals; rather, they reflect groups of people violated in a systemic manner. Crimes against humanity consist of widespread attacks against civilian populations, including murder, rape, torture, deportation, imprisonment, and other inhumane acts that intentionally cause great suffering or serious injury (physical or mental). War crimes are serious violations of international humanitarian law; in modern terms, these involve the use of poison gas or biological agents, ill treatment of civilian population and prisoners of war in violation of international law, and weapons outlawed by treaties.[11]

Applying these definitions to the Sand Creek site, based on the documentary and oral tradition evidence, is an interesting exercise, but one that must be carefully executed given that the terms and definitions are twentieth century in origin. There were, however, rules of war that existed during the Civil War as well. In April 1863, President Lincoln signed and authorized War Department General Order 100, developed by Francis Lieber, a German-born scholar. General Order 100, also known as Lieber's Code, specified the laws of warfare and required Union soldiers to honor those laws. The order was a remarkable document for its time and was one of the first of its type in the history of the world. European governments embraced the concepts laid out in the work, and over the next several years the order became the foundation on which were eventually built the Geneva Conventions on the laws of war.[12]

General Order 100 effectively governed the conduct of soldiers toward their enemy and the civilian population for the remainder of the Civil War. The rules governing conduct toward enemies, prisoners of war, partisans, and civilians are clearly laid out in the document. And though they were generally embraced and put into practice in the eastern theater, Union commanders and troops in the Trans-Mississippi West, who were forced to deal with an enemy practicing unconventional warfare and frustrated by its unrelenting and brutal nature, appear to have rationalized some components to fit their particular situation. Thus General Order 100 was not enthusiastically embraced in the West, nor universally or evenhandedly implemented.[13]

Nevertheless, General Order 100 was military law by the time Sand Creek occurred. In essence it requires that troops do not destroy or take civilian property or harm civilians even if they are sympathetic to the enemy, disclaims cruelty or bad faith toward an armed enemy, requires that prisoners of war be treated fairly, and disallows torture. The order also spells out that there are times when no quarter can be given and none expected, but Section III, part 61, states in that regard, "Troops that give no quarter have no right to kill enemies already disabled on the ground, or prisoners captured by other troops," and in part 71 states that those who kill or inflict wounds on a disabled enemy or a prisoner of war shall, if duly convicted, suffer death. Section IV of the order deals specifically with partisans and armed enemies not belonging to the enemy's forces. Partisans are defined as soldiers armed and wearing the uniform of their army, or appropriate marks to distinguish them from civilians; if detached from the main body they are entitled to be treated as enemy combatants and treated according to the rules of war. In contrast, those not part of an organized army or without formal commission (authorization) can be treated as pirates or highway robbers and summarily dealt with. The component dealing with partisans, was, in effect, a codification of Lieber's earlier work on the laws of war applied to guerrillas, which Gen. Henry Halleck had made policy in the fall of 1862. Depending on the commander's point of view, fights with Indians could fall under the partisan concept or the pirate or brigand concept.[14]

Applying the rules of war—found in the historic context of General Order 100 and its modern counterparts—to the Sand Creek events, it is clear that the attack and destruction of the village and its inhabitants meets the definition of a massacre. Wilhelm's 1881 *Military Dictionary and Gazetteer* states that a massacre is "the killing of human beings by indiscriminate slaughter, murder of numbers with cruelty or atrocity, or contrary to the usages of civilized people; cold-blooded destruction of life; butchery; carnage."[15] Whether by nineteenth- or twentieth-century standards, the affair unequivocally qualifies as a massacre.

The events that played out on Sand Creek generate differences of opinion as to whether this was a legitimate battle of giving no quarter and accepting none, or, in modern parlance, a war crime. Among the contemporary and survivor accounts of the fight, from both sides, there is little disagreement that the affair was very one-sided. Among the descriptive accounts there is general agreement that the Colorado soldiers attacked a protected camp and shot down without mercy as many inhabitants as possible.

There seems to be little disagreement among the accounts regarding the manner of death of the Cheyenne and Arapaho villagers. They were shot down without mercy and undoubtedly many were mutilated in some manner. The fact they were shot down without mercy reinforces the cruelty of the internecine features of the Indian Wars but does not, in itself, prove that a war crime or barbarous act was committed by the Colorado Volunteers. Quarter was not expected in plains warfare. Beyond that, though, the execution and mutilation of women and children is in direct contravention to the accepted laws and rules of war then in practice. Disarmed, disabled, and wounded tribespeople could be expected to be treated as prisoners of war, which did not happen in this case.

A variety of recent forensic research conducted to determine the types of wound patterns that predominate in actual combat events versus illegal mass execution injuries aid in further examining the question. One manner in which to identify combat versus extrajudicial killings is defined as the wounded-to-killed ratio.[16] It was found that in conventional warfare the wounded normally outnumber fatalities at least two to one. In the case of extrajudicial mass killings, the number killed is usually far greater than the number wounded. The authors of this research conclude that the wounded-to-killed ratio has implications for recognizing violations of internationally accepted rules of warfare. The Sand Creek massacre clearly fits the definition of extrajudicial killing and violation of the accepted rules of war in the wounded-to-killed ratio.

In addition to the wounded-to-killed ratio, a recent study rigorously looked at the ratio of fatal to nonfatal wounds that occur in conventional warfare and mass murder events by gunshot, hand grenades, artillery shelling, and aerial bombing. The study involved research into medically documented international conventional warfare death and wound patterning over a sixty-year period from World War II through the first Gulf war.[17] These researchers developed a mathematical formula of statistical probability to define objectively the difference between conventional warfare and mass murder wounding events. Their data show that for conventional warfare a wounded-to-killed ratio of five to one is normal over the sixty years of modern wars studied. Applying their formula to Sand Creek, the statistical probability that at least 25 percent of the Indians present were killed in a context of conventional warfare is very low. The percentages of soldier dead (1.4 percent) and wounded (6 percent) are far more typical of conventional war, even in a one-sided battle, thus reinforcing by scientific methods the interpretation of the Sand Creek event as a war crime and massacre.

Conclusions

Multidisciplinary investigations of the Sand Creek massacre present clear evidence that even relatively small conflicts between Plains Indians and the U.S. military left physical evidence that can be found and interpreted in light of the historical record and participant/eyewitness recollections. Applying a holistic approach to the study of Sand Creek provides an interpretive depth and breadth that cannot be attained in its study by any single discipline alone.

The Sand Creek artifact and relic finds coupled with their known distribution, and interpreted in light of the historical research, indicate that the 1st and 3rd Colorado Volunteers planned and executed a nearly flawless ambush on Black Kettle's unsuspecting village. Chivington divided his command according to a long tactical tradition and then proceeded to destroy the camp and many of its residents. This approach is a classic tactic used in insurgency operations throughout history and even today.[18]

The preponderance of scientific evidence allows a reasonable and scientifically defensible conclusion to be made. The multidisciplinary approach to the study of the site found demonstrable evidence of the Colorado Volunteer attack and destruction of the village site. The 1864 relic-collected artifacts are most likely associated with the northern terminus of the Cheyenne and Arapaho village and the survivors route of flight and with an attempt, using available tools and objects, to dig hasty shelter pits north of the main village site. The small arms and ordnance relics collected on the private land are overwhelmingly consistent with weapons used by the Colorado Volunteers. It is clear the Coloradoans poured heavy fire into the shelter pits dug by the tribespeople, and there is little evidence of corresponding return fire from the shelter pits, indicating minimal resistance by the Indians. Artillery fire is clearly evident in the relic collection, with at least five shell and case shot rounds fired into the shelter pits or at the fleeing villagers. This number of artillery rounds could not have been fired into the village because of the ongoing attack of the soldiers after the initial cannon salvo; the cannoneers would have been firing into their own men as they entered the village. Thus, the extensive evidence of small-arms fire and cannonading is nearly a priori proof that the finds north of the camp debris concentration likely represent the site of the Cheyenne and Arapaho shelter pits and the flight for survival.

NOTES

1. See the Sand Creek Relocation Study by the National Park Service (2000), and subsequently by Greene and Scott (2004). These two works are the source of statements made in this essay, except where other documentation is provided.
2. Hoig 1961; National Park Service 2000; Scott 1994.
3. Cox-Paul 2008.
4. Masich, n.d.
5. Scott 2000:75–80.
6. Ibid.
7. For artillery ranges, see Gibbon 1970:app. 42.
8. Greene 2000.
9. Roberts 2000.
10. Mason 2006.
11. Connor 2005:19–29; Ratner and Abrams 2001; Reisman and Antoniou 1994; Robertson 1999; Schabas 2000.
12. For studies and applications of General Order 100, see Birtle 2003; Veggeberg 1999.
13. See Veggeberg 1999 for extended discussions on General Order No. 100 as it applies to the Trans-Mississippi West and struggles with American Indians.
14. Additional information is found in Birtle 2003; Veggeberg 1999:154.
15. Wilhelm 1881:310.
16. Coupland and Meddings 1999.
17. Snow et al. 2008:14–28.
18. See Birtle 2003, and more recently Peters 2007.

The Mountain Meadows Massacre

Commentary

Ronald K. Wetherington

The two essays in this section, on the Mountain Meadows massacre, in many ways typify both the perspective and the methods of the associated disciplines. The anthropological approach stresses the cultural construction of perception and the material context of the researcher and the research. The historical approach stresses the careful weighing of the documentary sources and the motives behind these as partial explanations for events of the past. In this particular event, however, there are serious challenges to both disciplines that are somewhat unusual, and the authors address these in an effective and forthright manner.

For the archaeologist—in this case the bioarchaeologist—the time constraints for the study, combined with the fact that victim recovery and burial were so long delayed, reduced the potential information that might have been recovered had the bodies been examined in their original context. If we recognize, as Joanna Sofaer recommends, that "the skeleton is a point of articulation of the material and social," the bones out of context tell us less than they might, and a body in isolation from its collective subset (the massacre as a whole; the separate locales at death of male and female-plus-young) necessarily truncates the narrative of understanding the event.[1] The interpreter here is thus more handicapped than in other cases reported in this volume, and yet the meticulous and impressive study of the remains provided critical information about the massacre.

Recently, for historians (and for the Mormon Church), the challenge here is not in the narrative of what happened, although there are discrepancies in the several primary sources, but in finding an adequate explanation for the proximate motive behind the massacre, and, at least for the church, in building an elaborate and defensible assignation of blame. Motives that have been suggested, in those primary sources, include the desire for punishment for wrongs committed and laws violated (e.g., against blasphemy), historical memory of their own persecution and forced migration, the need for the settlers to replenish their beef herds, and fear that the migrants were harbingers of a U.S. military invasion. Unfortunately, the documentary records can theoretically support any of these and do not exclude any. Glenn Leonard's redaction of the documentation and his examination of its reliability are thorough and well presented.

It is tempting to explain such a mass killing as hysteria, or the inertia of violence spurred by context and opportunity (the "Lucifer effect"),[2] which has been proffered as an explanation for the Sand Creek Massacre, also discussed in this book. The forethought and planning involved here, however, make such an explanation suspect. It is also tempting to see the act of terrible violence as a fright-imbued "last stand" by Mormon settlers expecting another forced relocation. A similar last-stand effort is seen in the Adobe Walls attack.

It is interesting that the authors in this section agree that context is critical to any interpretation of cause or motive. Lars Rodseth and Shannon Novak note that the physical isolation and lack of outside witnesses made the killings feasible, and Leonard emphasizes that "chronology and context, two mainstays of any historical investigation, helped make clearer the causes of the massacre." A plural number of causes seems to be a consensus, and yet there are those, forever wishing for an Aristotelian efficient cause, who will continue to seek a single spark that ignited the violence.

Another element of context unites Paiute and Mormon in an irony of historical perspective: the history of the American Indian in the West is one of continual displacement toward the changing frontier boundary, and this was also Mormon history. In the same way the Indians resisted marginalization, so also did the Mormons. Leonard recognizes this, as does Joe Watkins in this book's final comments.

A significant point of divergence in the two essays here concerns the evidence for complicit Paiute participation. Rodseth and Novak find the evidence equivocal but suggest that Mormons "in Indian garb"—and not Paiutes—were responsible, whereas Leonard accepts the several contemporary accounts that suggest at least some direct Indian involvement. Leonard recognizes some of the contradictions in testimony, including accounts of Paiutes themselves. Rodseth and Novak, as well, recognize that people participating in the very same event may not "experience, interpret, or remember what happened in the same way." What remains curiously elusive is why the Mormons needed either to have the Paiutes participate or to masquerade as Paiute warriors themselves. Although the Indians may have been used originally as a fear factor to dissuade trespassers, the decision to kill all of the travelers appears to render this motive moot.

It is important, as Leonard notes, to examine the broader contextual history of Mormon persecution in trying to sort out the narrower context of the massacre itself. "Without the reignited emotions of the Mormon War," he writes, one could argue "that there would not have been a massacre at Mountain Meadows."[3] Rodseth and Novak emphasize that a narrative slowed to reveal the deliberate sequence of events, combined with the skeletal evidence, provides the essential contextual clarity. That the broader context has been used by some as an excuse for the crime is seen as unacceptable by all three authors.

NOTES

1. Sofaer 2006:87.
2. See, for example, Browning 1992.
3. On the history of Mormon violence as a tool of social control and on retaliation for Mormon persecution by the United States, see also Krakauer 2004.

Understanding the Mountain Meadows Massacre

Glenn M. Leonard

An important chapter in the history of the American West centers on the so-called Indian Wars of the mid to late nineteenth century. A typical armed engagement in the Southwest during that period involved U.S. military forces whose targets were the villages or encampments of local American Indians. Generally, military leaders cited a grievance to explain and justify the attack. Most often, victory was achieved through superior forces or armaments. The officers prided themselves on clever tactics to prevent defeat. Often, the triumphs of one armed force over another changed the course of history for those defeated. These raids, attacks, and massacres also defined and redefined relationships between opposing groups.[1]

The massacre at Mountain Meadows shares some commonalities with this pattern of typical military engagements between American soldiers and Indian tribes in the Southwest. But the differences greatly outweigh the similarities. Utah's most violent mass killing involved white men in the territorial militia whose leaders recruited Southern Paiutes from three or four bands to assist in killing all but the youngest members of an emigrant company on its way from Arkansas to California. The Mormon instigators of the killing first sent reluctant Paiute fighters against the emigrant wagon camp in a diversionary effort to get their cattle. The initial assault,

UNDERSTANDING THE MASSACRE 157

on Monday, September 7, 1857, met with unexpected resistance. It was followed by two more attempts and then a four-day standoff. New militia and Paiute recruits arrived at the Meadows late Thursday. On Friday, September 11, the plotters then approached the desperate emigrants with a false promise of safe escort. Low on ammunition and weakened by casualties and hunger, the emigrants gave up their arms and were marched, strung out along the sloping valley, into an ambush. The deception that preceded the killing of around 120 white American citizens sets this engagement apart from all other mass killings in the American past.

Context

The massacre at Mountain Meadows was not part of any Indian War. Rather, it might be seen as the most violent incident in an ongoing contest known at the time as the Mormon War.[2] At their respective cores, both of these "wars" centered on a contest for land and resources. People in every place and time need the things that sustain life. Most urgently they require land, water, and the living things generated by these elemental natural resources. When newcomers in large numbers seek a share of the resources from old-timers, a peaceful reallocation is seldom easy.[3] The tensions created in the Mormon War were an important part of the context that made the massacre at Mountain Meadows possible. Mormon attitudes toward local native peoples also factor into the story. Latter-day Saints approached Indians with a missionary spirit and a program for encouraging farming while many of their contemporaries could not get beyond the stereotype of "savages."[4]

The violent encounters in the Indian Wars were one of the end products of a national effort to relocate tribes from their traditional homelands. The U.S. government's removal policy was itself an outgrowth of the British attempt to draw a boundary between New England colonists and nearby Indians. The removal effort gained currency when explorers penetrated Thomas Jefferson's Louisiana Purchase. They described the vast, newly acquired plains as unsuitable for white agriculture. Native tribes were pushed out of their chosen lands and into America's undesirable properties. But, over time, those who once rejected the presumably permanent Indian territories found them attractive. Under the presidency of Andrew Jackson, and later, these reevaluations led to additional relocations, with the Indians forced into even more restrictive reservations.[5]

When Mormon leader Brigham Young selected the Great Salt Lake Valley as a new headquarters for his people in 1847, he knew what the U.S. government's removal policy meant. A decade earlier in western Missouri, strains between newcomer Mormons and their old-timer neighbors led first to verbal exchanges and then to armed conflict, with aggressive actions on both sides. The Mormons were mostly northerners, the Missourians southerners. They differed in ways cultural, economic, religious, social, and psychological. The first stage of the Mormon War ended when Missouri's governor declared the Mormons in a state of insurrection and ordered the militia to treat them as enemies who "must be exterminated or driven from the state, if necessary for the public good."[6] As ten thousand Latter-day Saints relocated in western Illinois, their Missouri neighbors took possession of Mormon farms and improvements.[7] Over the next six years, the Mormons petitioned officials at all levels of government to redress these losses, without success.[8]

In Illinois, a contest for political control of Hancock County moved gradually toward another forced removal. Once again, in their new gathering place at Nauvoo and the surrounding countryside, the Mormons found themselves in "a cultural clash between themselves and their neighbors, rumors leading to attacks, vigilantes claiming the right of majority rule and self-preservation, and Mormons attempting to defend themselves or strike back before being overwhelmed in a still larger wave of violence."[9] The established settlers were losing elections to the Mormon majority. The Anti-Mormon political party offered a solution to end the competition between the civic and covenant communities: "It is impossible that the two communities can long live together," a spokesman wrote. "They can *never* assimilate. We repeat our firm conviction that one or the other *must* leave."[10]

Mormonism's first prophet, Joseph Smith, considered suggestions to relocate in Wisconsin, on the contested Texas-Mexico borderland on the Nueces plains, in Mexican Upper California, in Oregon, or on Vancouver Island. Quietly Smith sent out explorers to seek a place among Indian peoples along the upper Missouri River, and he considered Oregon and the Great Basin region of Upper California. Unaware of these confidential inquiries—and frustrated by inaction—vigilantes assassinated Smith and subsequently set fire to rural Mormon homes and haystacks. Brigham Young, who succeeded Smith, negotiated a short delay to prepare his people for the long trek and then led them across Indian Territory and the open plains to the Great Basin (figure 23).[11]

An aggressive U.S. expansionist policy soon brought the Mormon settlements and the rest of the Southwest under the American flag. In the Compromise of 1850, Congress granted statehood to California and divided the rest of the former Mexican region between New Mexico and Utah territories.[12] Like the governments in other nineteenth-century territories, Utah's contained a mix of local and imported officers; disagreements among various factions were commonplace. The competing perspectives in Salt Lake City set territorial governor Brigham Young and other Mormon officials against outsider officeholders in judicial and other positions. This local versus outside competition was no different elsewhere in the American West.[13]

Figure 23. Brigham Young, 1858. Courtesy LDS Church History Library.

Reports from some of Utah's outsider federal justices in 1857 led President James Buchanan to appoint a new governor. The president dispatched an escort of some fifteen hundred federal troops to subdue a reported Mormon insurrection. The events that followed that year and the next would become known to history as the Mormon Conflict or, more commonly, the Utah War—the last incarnation of the midwestern Mormon War.[14] Tensions rose rapidly, in part because Buchanan failed to notify Young of his intentions. Fearing another Missouri expulsion or worse, Young reorganized the militia and stepped up drills. He ordered the Saints to scout out mountain hiding places and hoard essential goods. Nothing vital for their own survival in a wartime emergency should be sold to passing emigrants, he declared. That included beef cattle, flour, and ammunition. Young rallied his followers to prepare for a fight, hoping to prevent one. If threatened, he would implement a scorched earth policy, move off to some other place, and leave nothing but the ashes of the buildings and improvements of ten years' hard labor.[15]

When the emigrants who were later killed at Mountain Meadows entered the Salt Lake Valley in late July and early August 1857, they found themselves in this strained environment. As an emigrant party mostly from Arkansas made its way through Utah along the southern road to California, the emigrants and settlers exchanged words over minor issues. When tempers rose, cooler heads in the settlements nearest Salt Lake City calmed angry feelings. In the isolated communities of southern Utah, where communication with headquarters took days, a few overwrought community leaders reacted in haste to resolve what they perceived as real threats. Their plans to steal some beef cattle from the emigrants to replenish their herds spiraled out of control and led them to the fateful decision that 120 men, women, and children must die. For the Arkansas farmers and their families, the hopes for a better life in California ended in a bloody massacre at Mountain Meadows. Echoing the rationale of public officials in Missouri and Illinois, these victims of injustice in the early Mormon War now committed greater injustices against those they had defined as enemies.

Juanita Brooks, a groundbreaking historian of the massacre, described the dangerous perceptions involved in the decision to kill the emigrants this way: "Exaggeration, misrepresentation, ungrounded fears, unreasoning hate, desire for revenge, yes, even the lust for the property of the emigrants, all combined to give justification which, once the crime was done, looked inadequate and flimsy indeed."[16] Without the reignited emotions of the Mormon War, one could argue, there would not have been a massacre at Mountain Meadows. Gen. Daniel H. Wells, who commanded the territorial militia at the time, offered that assessment in a rare public interview in 1877. Many factors came together at the time, he said, creating "a combination of circumstances such as will probably never exist again." Somehow, a few desperate Mormons concluded that the emigrants were "leagued with the soldiers."[17]

Broader studies of religious or ethnic violence offer additional help toward an understanding of the puzzling question of why generally good people with ordinary human weaknesses do bad things to other ordinary and basically good people.[18] The social factors existing in Mormon society at that time match conditions found in other settings where violence has erupted. Potentially antagonistic situations typically feature a concentration of authority among a few local decision makers, the absence of clear orders from headquarters, and economic deprivation. In Utah's theocratic society, "civil, religious, and military power was dangerously held in the hands of a few. Impoverished settlers knew the virtues of obeying."[19] Within the context of these conditions, minor disagreements can move step-by-step toward a mass riot or killing. Aggressors first dehumanize and demonize opponents by creating an image of them as the Other. With earlier displacements fresh in mind, many Utah Latter-day Saints did just that; they viewed all outsiders with suspicion.[20] In a setting of heightened emotions such as this, rumors create false perceptions that become a new reality. This ultimately leads to violence against the created enemy.[21] The perpetrators typically perceive the minor infractions of their opponents as an exaggerated power or evil intention. Once again, the pattern fits Utah Territory in the 1850s: as untrue or exaggerated rumors circulated, the settlers felt somehow that their community values were being threatened by the emigrants.[22] From "seemingly innocent beginnings," Roy Baumeister observed, good people can "cross the line. [But] once one has done this, there are powerful forces that sweep one along into greater acts of cruelty, violence, or oppression."[23]

Settings for violence in America often matched the circumstances described by these sociological studies. Other factors also weighed in. Traditionally, the most studied are the political and economic differences that inflamed contesting parties.[24] A cultural blindness toward ethnic and religious minorities also contributed to the tension between peoples of a growing and expanding country. In a dominant Protestant, Anglo-Saxon America, prejudices against the peculiarities of Mormonism (or what religious studies scholars have termed a New Religious Tradition[25])—and against Indians and other "different" peoples, including Catholics, Irish immigrants, and blacks—would take a century and more to mollify. As a minority in American society, Latter-day Saints not only felt acted against, they developed stereotypical prejudices against others. The corrective process among multicultural communities continues yet.[26]

These and other cultural biases also tainted the way historians once viewed conquest and conflict in the American West. Written with a nationalistic emphasis, the "Old Frontier History" gloried in America's "manifest destiny"—the occupation of a supposedly virgin land beyond the Mississippi River, especially the Pacific Coast's coveted door to Asia.[27] For a generation and more, the story of the westward movement celebrated the conquest of Indian homelands. As did other Americans, the Mormons encroached on Indian lands. Euro-American outsiders brought new religions and different ways of understanding the land and its resources. They wanted to displace or remake the old. They owned the story and told it their way.

More recently, new voices have offered alternate versions of the story. Today's restatements of the past acknowledge the views of the neglected victims, among them American Indians, Hispanic Americans, women, Mormons, and the environment. The "New Western History" acknowledges the damage done in both the doing of the deed and the telling of the story.[28] An examination of borderland histories and their violent engagements now requires the usual attention to time and place, resources and circumstances. In addition, historians and anthropologists who explain the West must now pay attention to race and ethnicity, gender, and the ways people act when confronted or when asked to cooperate in the use of natural resources.[29] Today's readers and visitors to historic places increasingly expect a more complex restating of old stories. They want and deserve a fair consideration of neglected points of view.

Content

An understanding of the broader context helps explain why aggressive behavior occurs and how it has been explained by historians. Yet there remain many specific factors to consider in getting at the truth behind competing explanations of violent encounters in the American Southwest. This is especially true for attempts to unravel the controversial history of the Mountain Meadows massacre. The sources are confusing, often self-serving, and contradictory. No wonder readers seeking to understand this terrible crime encounter myriad contrasting explanations. These can be considered under three headings.

One explanation has the Paiutes killing the Arkansas Company in response to outrages committed by the emigrants. The verbal report submitted to Brigham Young a few weeks after the massacre echoed this pattern and reinforced the idea that the pioneers deserved to die. The same explanation appears in the report of an early Mormon investigation with the revealing title "The Emigrant and Indian War." Skeptics soon rightly identified the accounts of an "Indian massacre" as a cover-up crafted by Mormon leaders, the massacre's real planners.[30]

A second perspective severely limits Paiute involvement and casts Brigham Young as a behind-the-scenes supporter of local actions.[31] An expanded version of this explanation makes Young the instigator of the mass killing of innocent travelers and casts his local religionists as obedient partners in crime.[32]

Yet another explanation falls somewhere between these two extremes. This storyline faults Mormon greed and vengeance, with John D. Lee as the sole instigator and some Paiutes as helpers. Other variations of this approach identify local Mormon leaders as collaborators with Lee in making decisions based on unfolding misjudgments and missteps. In this reading of the sources, local militiamen partner with recruited Paiutes in the mass killing.

The last-noted variation is reflected in the classic 1950 account of the massacre by Juanita Brooks and in the retelling fashioned through the collaborative effort that I was involved in with my colleagues Ronald W. Walker and Richard E. Turley, Jr. In our book, we summarize the interpretive framework of the three main approaches as follows:

One approach portrays the perpetrators as good people and the victims as evil ones who committed outrages during their travel through central and southern Utah. . . . The second approach looks at the innocence of the emigrants and the evil of their killers who at best are described as followers of misguided religion. . . . The third main approach . . . attempts to navigate between the extremes of the other two. This approach is partly a commonsense recognition that both victims and perpetrators were decent but imperfect people whose paths crossed in a moment of history that resulted in a terrible tragedy.[33]

As the three of us pored over the mass of available historical evidence, we began to see ourselves as historical detectives. A crime had been committed. We wanted to solve it. Some pieces of the puzzle fit all of the traditional explanations. Some had never found a place. We committed ourselves to get as close to the truth as humanly possible by ignoring all existing explanations. We would look at original sources, weigh their validity, and seek confirming evidence from sources closest to the event and as free as possible from human bias. Chronology and context, two mainstays of any historical investigation, helped make clearer the causes of the massacre. From the outset we agreed to accept whatever conclusions our examination yielded. Cover-ups and half-truths had for too long clouded the issues surrounding this horrible event.[34]

Independently, in previous historical inquiries, each of us had faced challenging riddles.[35] None of them matched the complexity of this controversial subject. We searched out new documents, invited outside readers from varied backgrounds to critique our drafts, and consulted competent persons in fields beyond our own training. We also met with representatives of the Southern Paiutes to hear their perspective. As the project moved forward, we invited colleagues within our institutional home, the church history department of the Church of Jesus Christ of Latter-day Saints, to join the conversation by challenging every detail of our evolving conclusions.[36] After six long and exhausting years, we completed our work. In August 2008, Oxford University Press in New York City published our findings as *Massacre at Mountain Meadows: An American Tragedy*.

In a rather concise treatment (231 printed pages) we present our conclusions as narration. We believe that timeworn frames of reference centering "on personalities and conspiracies . . . are best answered by telling the story and letting events speak for themselves." For the most part we chose not to engage in scholarly arguments for or against previous interpretations, but to address general readers.[37] The following narrative summarizes our findings and serves as background for a discussion of a few specific questions and how we resolved them.[38]

The Narrative

Several emigrant companies constituted mostly of farm families from northwestern Arkansas entered the Salt Lake Valley in July and early August 1857. During a short stay, the travelers reorganized themselves as what became known as the Arkansas Company. The loosely organized body included about 140 men, women, and children, under the leadership of Alexander Fancher and Jack T. Baker.[39] The emigrants were headed to California with as many as eight hundred head of beef cattle. A second group of emigrants that became known as the Missouri Company followed the Fancher and Baker trains. The Missouri Company included several smaller groups, with families from Missouri, Arkansas, and Texas, headed by Nicholas Turner, William Dukes, and Wilson Collins. As these two amalgamated wagon companies traveled through the territory, they traded with Mormon settlers and, in central Utah, with the Pahvant and Southern Paiute peoples. For all emigrants on the southern route to California, Mountain Meadows offered water, grass, and a resting place before moving down the Magotsu and Santa Clara streams and across the desert to their destination (figures 24 and 25).[40]

Like many other Americans, some of the California-bound pioneers held negative stereotypes about members of the Church of Jesus Christ of Latter-day Saints. They saw this "peculiar people" as cultural outcasts for their clannishness, plural marriages, unusual doctrines, and suspicious friendliness with Indians. On the other side, some of Utah's Mormons still carried the emotional wounds of their clashes and forced removal from Missouri and Illinois. These settlers held deep suspicions against the nation that had rejected them. Utah in the summer of 1857 was a place for inevitable misunderstanding.

Figure 24. Mountain Meadows. Photo by Wally Barrus.

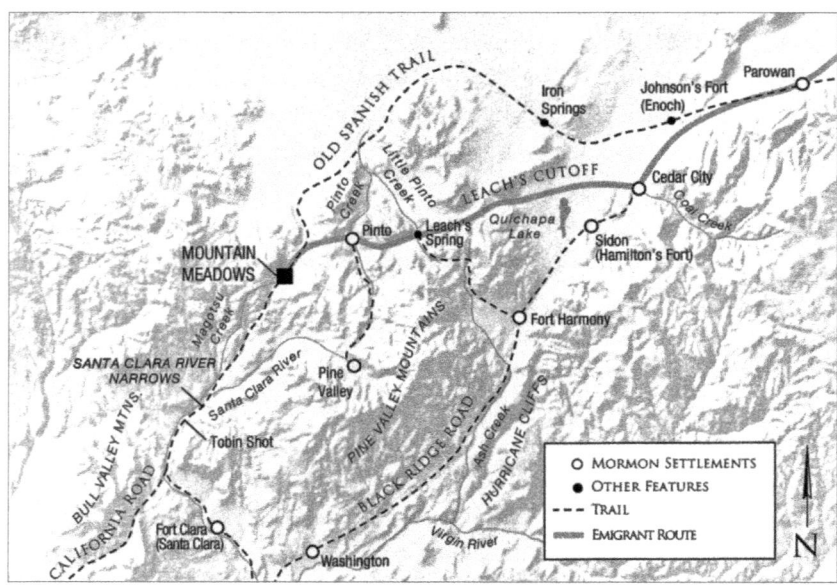

Figure 25. Southern Utah, showing Mountain Meadows location and emigrant trails. Map by Sheryl Dickert Smith and Tom Child.

When word reached Utah that President Buchanan had dispatched an army, local leaders feared the worst. Buchanan failed to inform Brigham Young of his intent, which was that the army was to escort a new governor to replace Young and put down a reported Mormon insurrection. Young prepared to defend the Mormon gathering place. He advised families to put away grain, flour, and ammunition. The territorial militia stepped up its drills and dispatched sentries to watch the mountain passes. In this time of uncertainty, Young told southern Utah's Pahvant and Paiute leaders that, if the American troops were coming to kill Mormons, they would also kill Indians. He delivered the same message to Ute and Shoshone leaders. Young wanted these tribal spokesmen on his side, but they declined, explaining, in the words of a Mormon interpreter, that "they was afraid to fight the Americans & so would raise grain & we [the Mormons] might fight."[41]

News of the approaching army increased Mormon vigilance, making it difficult for the Arkansas and Missouri parties to replenish their foodstuffs. Challenges faced them in some communities when the emigrants turned their cattle onto grasslands the settlers considered their own. From time to time tempers flared on both sides. A few troublemakers traveling with the Arkansas party created minor problems along the way, taunting and threatening the locals. Individuals in the Missouri Company triggered an exchange of gunfire between the Turner party and Pahvant Indians midway through the territory. In that instance local Mormon leaders quickly negotiated a ceasefire and escorted the men to safety. It was Mormon policy—not always realized—to develop and maintain friendly relationships with the various American Indian tribes among whom they lived.[42]

Along the route to California, some insensitive overlanders cheated Shoshone traders or fired randomly at them. In response, the Shoshone tribesmen attacked the emigrants. Mormon officials intervened to resolve the issue. This pattern of insensitive interaction was commonplace all along the California Trail, a product of what historian John Unruh called a "callous attitude of cultural and racial superiority."[43] The altercations in northern Utah Territory disappointed Governor Young, who served also as territorial superintendent of Indians. Strategically, in the tense environment of 1857, he needed the tribes as friends; he sought to win their favor with gifts. Little

Soldier and other native leaders said they preferred to stand aside until they saw what happened between the Mormons and the army.[44]

In a public speech on August 16, Young revealed his war strategy. If the army launched hostilities against the Saints, he said, the people would flee to the mountains and burn everything behind them. With the Saints fighting a guerilla war from their hiding places, there would be no one to mediate between emigrants and Indians. He announced a new policy for dealing with conditions on the migration route. "I will not hold the Indians still while the emigrants shoot them, as they have hitherto done," he said, "but I will say to them [the Indians], go and do as you please." The result, he warned, would be a halting of goods and people along that section of the transcontinental road. Perhaps this would get Washington's attention. Young did not want to fight, but he wanted "his enemies" to have a fair warning.[45]

At Cedar City, southern Utah's last major stop for resupply before heading into the desert, the emigrants bought wheat, had it ground into flour, and traded with some of the settlers. Reports of the company's six hundred or more loose stock had preceded them. In later years, settlers recalled interactions with the emigrants. Nephi Johnson, a visitor to Fort Cedar that day, said, "The company was of a mixed class, some being perfect gentlemen, while others were very boastful, and insulting, as they said that they were coming back and assist the [U.S.] army to exterminate the Mormons." Johnson observed Alexander Fancher trying to calm one of the men. A tall man on horseback approached sixty-three-year-old Barbara Morris and, according to the woman's son, "made use of the most insinuating and abusive language." One man brandished a pistol. He claimed that it had helped kill Joseph Smith. Whiskey purchased at a local distillery may have loosened the tongues of the adventurers, further predisposing them to hostility.[46]

Cedar City's mayor, Isaac C. Haight, was himself the subject of a run-in after a clerk at the local general store could not provide the goods the emigrants requested. Haight was the store's chief executive and also the city's highest-ranking religious leader, a major in the militia, and head of the Iron Mission, the area's struggling iron ore mining and processing enterprise (figure 26). Haight slipped out and ordered the city marshal to arrest the men for disturbing the peace and breaking the law against profanity. When the city marshal approached one of the emigrants, others stood with him and he refused to be taken. The marshal backed off, and the visitors left.[47]

The Arkansas people camped for the night across the valley to the west, then began a two-day trek to the grasslands of Mountain Meadows, where they intended to spend a few days resting their livestock before continuing their trek to central California's San Joaquin Valley.[48]

Unsatisfied with this turn of events, Major Haight, who headed one of Cedar City's two battalions, asked his military superior, Col. William H. Dame, living twenty miles to the north at Parowan, to authorize militia support for the marshal in arresting the offensive visitors (figure 27). Dame consulted his military council and on September 4 advised Haight to calm the citizens and let the emigrants move on. They should pay no attention to "their threats," Dame wrote, "as 'words are but wind.'"[49]

Denied the use of the militia by Dame, Haight decided to enlist Paiutes as part of his strategy to hoard grain and beef-on-the-hoof for a potential evacuation. Mary Campbell recalled Haight saying that "the people in southern Utah needed some stock just then, as if he was giving the citizens a hint to get the stock away from the company." To oversee the rustling of the stock and punishment of the offending emigrants, Haight entrusted the mission to John D. Lee, a man known for getting things done (figure 28). Lee served as a church-appointed Farmer to the Indians and as a major in the militia, overseeing men in the four settlements south of Cedar City. He lived at Harmony, a mission settlement twenty miles below Cedar.[50]

When Lee arrived in Cedar City, the pair talked into the night. Then, after breakfast on Saturday, Lee, Haight, and three of Haight's supporters recruited Paiutes from the Coal Creek band camped near Cedar City. Lee then headed home to invite participation from the Ash Creek band at Harmony. Their joint mission was to follow the emigrants when they left the Meadows. In a narrow Santa Clara River canyon ten miles south of the Meadows, the recruits were to distract the emigrants, "kill as many of the men as they could, and get away with as many cattle as possible, but not to harm the women and children."[51]

Figure 26. Isaac C. Haight. Courtesy LDS Church History Library.

Figure 27. William H. Dame. Courtesy Special Collections, Sherratt Library, Southern Utah University.

Figure 28. John D. Lee. Courtesy LDS Church History Library.

The following day, Haight raised the issue before an ecclesiastical council that he headed. That Sunday afternoon assembly was divided over his proposal to take harsh action against the emigrants. Opponents challenged his authority to involve the militia. To satisfy critics, on Monday Haight sent off a letter seeking counsel from Brigham Young. Haight also dispatched a courier to the Meadows instructing Lee to pull back. That missive arrived too late. So, too, did two other messengers, William C. Stewart and Joel White, who left Cedar City Sunday afternoon to consult with Lee.[52]

Instead of waiting for the party to leave the Meadows, Lee had launched the Paiutes on a premature attack on the emigrant camp at dawn on Monday, September 7. That first assault and two later attempts to breech a now reinforced emigrant wagon corral met stiff resistance. The firefight killed as many as seven emigrants, including the trusted coleader, Alexander Fancher, and one Paiute, the brother of Santa Clara leader Jackson. Several on each side were wounded. Paiute leaders Moqueetus and Bill from Cedar City suffered broken bones in their legs and were crippled for life. Some of the Santa Clara Paiutes took their bounty, eighteen or twenty head of cattle, and headed home.[53]

The Paiutes were upset with Lee's failed plan and his promises that the emigrants would be an easy target. Lee and a few Mormon associates took control of the grazing emigrant livestock. But the emigrants had shot at Lee, and he feared they knew he was a white man, despite his attempt at disguise. More important, two young men who had left the emigrant wagon corral to look for stray cattle on Sunday were intercepted by Haight's associates at a watering hole midway between Cedar City and the Meadows. William Stewart killed one of the emigrants, William Aden, outright. Joel White shot the other one, known to the settlers as the "Dutchman" or "German" (a Pennsylvanian of German descent). Though wounded, the young man rode to safety and reported the incident to the wounded coleader, Jack Baker.[54]

Word of the first attack reached Haight before he dispatched James Haslam with the letter for Brigham Young. Haslam informed Dame of the attack when he reached Parowan Monday afternoon. Dame convened a council that evening to consider options. The situation had moved from idle threats made by a few emigrants to a serious confrontation. The men of Parowan may have considered Brigham Young's August 16 Indian policy as they weighed options. Young had warned against interfering with disputes between Indians and emigrants. The council "decided to render aid and protection to the emigrants, should they call for assistance. Otherwise," one of the council members recalled, "it was considered just, in view of the threats and insults the company had offered to the Saints in passing through the settlements, to let them fight it out with the Indian as best they could." Dame learned from an Indian runner early Tuesday that two or three of the emigrants had been killed. Dame sent two trusted agents to investigate. They returned to Parowan Wednesday evening, disgusted with what Lee and the Paiutes had done.[55]

Meanwhile, Isaac Haight was informed of Aden's killing by the returning Stewart and White on Monday afternoon. Haight faced a new challenge. Should he let the emigrants leave and risk triggering a military response from California? Ultimately Haight concluded that anyone old enough to testify that Mormons had participated in the first attacks or in Aden's murder must die. What had started as a cattle raid and then morphed into a selective punishment in lieu of arrest would now be a mass murder. In effect, the massacre on Friday, September 11, was carried out to cover the crimes of a few and to prevent what they feared would be harsh retribution against many.[56]

Once again, Haight sought Colonel Dame's approval to call up forces. This time Haight approached Dame in person. In August, Dame had promised militia leaders in Salt Lake City he would not activate forces in the event of a crisis until he secured their agreement. Late Wednesday night, Dame's council listened to Haight's request to use militiamen and accepted it. Apparently Haight had explained the problem as an Indian-emigrant fight. The council agreed to send a company out from Parowan to call the Indians off, gather the livestock, and let the emigrants go on their way.[57]

For Haight, the council's decision was only a first step. Authorization to use the militia to rescue the emigrants did not accomplish Haight's objective. He had intentionally withheld from the council information about Aden's death. He had not explained the perceived implications of that killing. In a private meeting held near Fort Parowan's east gate after the council dispersed, Haight told Dame of his dilemma and won Dame's reluctant support. Their conversation defined the purpose of the massacre:

to prevent the outside world from learning of Mormon responsibility for the first killings. "L[ee] & the Indians had commenced it and it had to be done," Dame explained to a confidant a few days after the massacre. "For if it should come to the ears of President Buc[h]anan, it would endanger the lives of the Bretheren."[58]

For these two men—the senior military officers and top-ranking church and civic leaders in their respective communities—the midnight decision was their last chance to prevent the massacre. No one after that dared to disobey their orders. Directions were sent through military channels, indirectly backed in Utah's theocratic society by unstated ecclesiastical and civil authority. Both Dame and Haight later regretted their collaborative decision. Haight told William Barton, who was present in the initial council, "I would give a world if I had it, if we had abided by the decision of the council; but, alas, it is too late." Instead, Haight had ignored counsel that would have led to a peaceful resolution and convinced Dame to join him. Dame had gone back on his promise to senior officials that he would consult them before calling up militiamen in a crisis.[59]

When the two decision makers arrived at the Meadows late Friday night after the killing was done, they argued over ultimate responsibility and how to report the massacre. Ultimately Haight got his way; they would report the killings as an Indian massacre. Militiaman Samuel Knight overheard portions of their angry conversation. Knight said he learned that none of Salt Lake City's church leaders "had sanctioned or encouraged in any way the dastardly deed of which these fanatics were guilty."[60]

After Haight reached Cedar City Thursday morning, September 10, he set in motion new recruitment efforts. Militia captains and a few others joined the relief force, and Indian interpreter Nephi Johnson was told to invite additional Coal Creek Paiutes to accompany him to the Meadows. The Cedar City reinforcements arrived at the Meadows in groups late into the night. One of Haight's ecclesiastical and military associates in Cedar City, Maj. John M. Higbee, delivered the orders to Lee. The plan was to decoy and destroy all but the youngest in the emigrant party. All of those old enough to "tell the tale" would die.[61]

With the reinforcements now on hand at the Meadows, Major Lee, who served as commanding officer on the field, set about on Friday morning to organize the men. Nephi Johnson delivered the word to the Paiute leaders, who agreed to assist in the killing. Then Lee and the newly arrived senior militiamen held a council with their key supporters. After a hard-won agreement, Lee sent Johnson and another interpreter to share the plan with the Paiutes. Southern Paiutes lived in a society that allowed each man to make his own decision. In the Meadows situation, some must have chosen not to participate. Those who did were placed in hiding.[62]

The number of Southern Paiutes present on Friday may never be known. Militia estimates ranged from forty to as high as six hundred. Nephi Johnson said there were about 150 Indians present. In later years, some Paiutes said that if any of their people were present they watched from the hillside. Others acknowledged minimal participation. One knowledgeable Paiute said, "All the Indians there were not more than one hundred."[63]

The presence of any Indians may have reflected both a tenet of war and the settlers' true feelings about their Southern Paiute neighbors. Our conclusion was this: "The role assigned to the Paiutes was a feeble attempt on the militia leaders' part to salve their own consciences. Though reconciled to killing the emigrant men, they wanted to limit the number of women and children they would have to kill themselves—as if planning and directing the crime were not enough."[64]

With the Paiutes informed, Lee and Higbee next organized some four dozen militiamen into a hollow square and instructed them on their duties. Inwardly, some objected, but none dared challenge their superiors. Besides, Johnson later explained, most of the men considered the emigrants "as their common enemies, and under the excitement caused by the advent of the [approaching] Army they felt partly justified in distroying them." The men turned their horses out to roam and marched to within two hundred yards of the emigrant camp. Dressed in civilian clothing and armed variously—with revolvers, Jaeger rifles, "shotguns, Kentucky rifles, flint locks and every imaginable firearm"—they waited.[65]

Under a white flag of truce, Lee approached the wagon corral and presented an offer to emigrant spokesmen. Lee told them that the Indians had withdrawn and would allow Lee and his men to escort the party to safety in Cedar City. The emigrants must abandon their wagons and give up their guns. The firearms would go with the Arkansans, covered by blankets in one of two Mormon baggage wagons. The sick and young would ride atop the blankets and in the other wagon. Everyone else would walk. Weakened by thirst and fatigue over the nearly five-day siege, the emigrants ultimately set aside their skepticism and agreed. They had no real options.[66]

The loaded wagons led the procession out of the wagon corral, with Lee walking between them. The women and older children followed next, led by Haight's adjutant on horseback. The surviving men followed behind, each one accompanied by an armed Mormon escort. Major Higbee rode just ahead of the men. The distances between the three groupings widened to a quarter mile each as they moved slowly up the long valley.[67]

A mile and a half north of the wagon camp, Lee and the wagons crossed a ridge and disappeared out of sight of the women and children, who were approaching an area covered thickly with cedars and sagebrush—the hiding place of the Southern Paiutes and the Mormon militia interpreters. Higbee hesitated as the women reached, and then began moving beyond, the place of ambush. Lee would later reprimand him for the delay. When no change of orders came, Higbee shouted "Halt," the signal to begin the killing. All but a few of the militia obeyed the order, turned, and fired into the heads of the emigrant men and youths (figure 29).[68]

Figure 29. The Mountain Meadows Massacre.

As that volley echoed up the valley, Johnson and another interpreter ordered the Paiutes from their hiding places, which caused the women and children to scatter in fright. Some ran toward the wagons, some headed for the men, others ran into the brush. Meanwhile, Lee and the wagon drivers murdered those under their charge. The massacre was over in minutes. The few who escaped the initial onslaught were hunted down and killed. Among them were three scouts who sneaked out of the wagon corral before the massacre began and headed for California with a petition pleading for help. An estimated 120 men, women, and children died in the killings that week.[69]

Before nightfall, militia leaders and some of the Paiutes began taking watches, jewelry, and money off the bodies and then stripped them of their outer clothing. Paiutes also searched the emigrants' wagons for useful items. Residents in and near Cedar City described returning Paiutes with possessions they did not have previously: horses, saddles, guns, household utensils, and clothing.[70]

The following morning, as directed, the troops gave the victims a cursory burial. They had arrived ill equipped for the task. Using spades of their own and some from the emigrant wagons, they sought out softer soil in ravines. Some shallow burials were four to a grave. Other bodies were heaped and covered with a thin layer of soil. A Santa Clara missionary who was herding cattle at the Meadows said it wasn't long before wolves and coyotes "uncovered the remains and picked the bones." Widespread knowledge of this led many to believe that the militia had made no effort to bury the bodies. The next summer Jacob Hamblin reburied what he could find of the scattered remains, and in May 1859 government troops gathered up more bones for reburial at a half-dozen or more locations in the valley.[71]

On Saturday, the emigrant wagons (twelve to twenty of them), bearing the goods that had not been looted, were driven away from the Meadows and stowed. Haight later oversaw an auction of clothing and household goods at the Mormon tithing store in Cedar City. Lee took charge of the cattle that had not already been driven off or slaughtered for food. Seventeen children, from six years of age to an infant, were placed with local Mormon families. In May 1859, Brigham Young dispatched Indian missionary Jacob Hamblin to collect the orphans from their Mormon caretakers. Federal agents then returned them to relatives in Arkansas.[72]

Brigham Young's response to Isaac Haight's September 7 letter arrived in Cedar City on Sunday, September 13, two days after the massacre. On September 8, Young had learned that desertions had shrunken the U.S. army's numbers to fewer than nine hundred men, and that its mission would not result in a forced abandonment of the Mormon Zion. The crisis of uncertainty had ended. "In regard to emigration trains passing throughout settlements," he told Haight, "we must not interfere with them untill they are first notified to keep away. You must not meddle with them." Then, consistent with his new policy of noninterference, Young added, "The Indians we expect will do as they please but you should try and preserve good feelings with them. . . . While we should be on the alert, on hand and always ready[,] we should also possess ourselves in patience, preserving ourselves and property."[73]

From the outset, Haight and Lee had agreed to blame the Southern Paiutes for the cattle raid. A handful of whites would remain in the background. As events cascaded out of control during the week, Mormon involvement increased. The settlers now carried the burden of the killings. Both the participating men and their wives at home (who knew why their husbands had gone to the Meadows) were sworn to secrecy. Lee reported the mass murder to Young as an Indian massacre. He justified the killing with a recital of emigrant outrages. Lee would maintain that he had arrived on Tuesday, after the first attacks, and failed in attempts to prevent further killing. Lee did not reveal to Young or others that more than fifty Mormon militiamen had participated in Friday's killing. The Paiutes would be victimized with the full responsibility.[74]

The wheels of justice regarding the massacre moved slowly under the political standoff in territorial Utah. The new governor, Alfred Cumming, was reticent to seek out the responsible parties even when Young offered "all possible assistance" to ensure a thorough investigation. Cumming said President Buchanan's amnesty for actions during the Utah War pardoned all past Mormon offenses. Federal investigations in 1859 yielded new information that placed responsibility on Dame, Haight, Lee, Higbee, Stewart, and a few others, but the men went into hiding and could not be found.[75]

Not until after the Civil War did the courts once again tackle the job of sorting through the evidence. Of the nine men indicted in 1874, four or five were arrested and held for a time, then released. Isaac Haight spent the remaining fourteen years of his life dodging federal officers who went after him for his role in the massacre or for plural marriage. Only John D. Lee was brought to trial, convicted of murder, and executed. Officials returned Lee to the Meadows, where he died by firing squad in March 1877. Brigham Young died six months later.[76]

Case Studies

The historian's approach to understanding events in the past requires a careful evaluation of sources. That process tests the credibility of each source by certifying the authenticity of the document itself and by weighing the information it contains against other sources. Sometimes the weight of evidence is clear; other times contradictions cannot be resolved. When issues cannot be resolved, readers can be offered both probable and possible solutions.[77] This shading of conclusions was especially necessary in the case of the massacre at Mountain Meadows. For every source investigated in the preparation of *Massacre at Mountain Meadows*, we compared minor details of time and place with statements by other witnesses. We adopted proven investigative rules of evidence and relied as much as possible on firsthand reports. We gave greater credence to accounts closer to the actual event. We preferred at least two independent sources for important conclusions, if they could be found. We approached all written sources with caution, seeking to extract and use only that which made sense in the slowly unfolding scenario.

A few representative case studies illustrate how we evaluated sources and drew on studies of similar encounters to reach the conclusions presented in the book. These examples explore our responses to questions about the credibility of a group of important sources, the alleged provocations of the emigrants, and the process that led to the decision to kill innocent people.

How reliable are the sources describing John D. Lee's role in the massacre? An understanding of these sources was essential to our investigation. Though not the only person indicted for his participation in the massacre, Lee was the only one tried and executed. His trial on conspiracy in 1875 and

UNDERSTANDING THE MASSACRE 179

a second trial on a charge of murder in 1876 generated a significant body of information. Newspapers in Utah Territory and elsewhere reported the trials. Two somewhat independent stenographers took notes that eventually yielded two transcriptions for each of the trials. Letters, reports, and diaries documenting events leading up to the massacre survive, as do important affidavits prepared in later years by participants in the killing. This large body of material contains much useful information along with confusing and contradictory statements. Information prepared for Lee's defense and material used against him worked its way into several documents containing Lee's formal "confession." We gave the trial transcripts and Lee's confession special attention.[78]

To test the reliability of the minutes of Lee's 1875 and 1876 trials, a major source for information on the details of the massacre, we engaged the services of LaJean Purcel Carruth, a specialist in reading nineteenth-century Pitman shorthand. She created new transcripts of the notes taken by the official court reporter, Adam S. Patterson, for trial judge Jacob Boreman, and by a local, independent reporter, Josiah Rogerson. Carruth discovered minor errors in the original transcriptions (some important to our research), plus omissions and subtle but apparently intentional shading of information. Among other shadings was the elimination of Isaac Haight's name in Rogerson's transcription, an apparent attempt to shift responsibility to Lee. Carruth's parallel-column comparison of the original and new transcriptions helped us get accurate information.[79]

We are not alone in questioning the veracity of Lee's autobiography, *Mormonism Unveiled*, particularly the two-chapter account of the massacre titled "Confessions of John D. Lee." This section reflects the defense argument presented by Lee's attorney, William W. Bishop—namely, that Lee went to the Meadows under orders to prevent any killing but arrived after the initial attack and then was ordered by his militia superiors to organize the final mass murder. Bishop edited, expanded, and submitted the manuscript to publishers after Lee's death. Royalties from the book paid Bishop's legal fees.[80] Lee wrote an initial "Confession" for Sumner Howard, the prosecuting attorney in Lee's second trial. We judged the Lee-Howard account as more authentic in many details than either a longer extract from the "Confessions" released by Bishop to newspapers in Utah and California or the complete text in the autobiography.[81] Preliminary findings from an analysis of *Mormonism Unveiled* "reveals a pervasive pattern of inconsistencies, contradictions, and modified vocabulary."[82]

Did the Arkansas emigrants provoke the attacks against them? One of our most perplexing challenges was to figure out exactly what members of the Baker and Fancher parties said and did, if anything, as they passed through the Mormon settlements. It has been a common assumption that a small group of adventurers known as the "Missouri Wildcats" had joined the Arkansas party along the way. Supposedly these adventurous rowdies taunted Mormons and offended Indians, provoking an aggressive response from one or both. Under normal circumstances the incidents would have been passed over.[83]

Utah historian T. B. H. Stenhouse published the first known reference to what he termed "Wild-cats" from Missouri in 1873. His source was Eli Kelsey, a Mormon missionary to the Indians who traveled with the Baker group from Fort Bridger to Salt Lake City. Kelsey said a rough set of men from Missouri had joined the Bakers at some point along the overland trail, and that their camp rang with "vulgar song, boisterous roaring, and 'tall swearing.'" The men reprised the outcry from the Mormon War in Missouri that the Mormons should be wiped out. Kelsey warned the Arkansans to separate themselves from the rowdies; they agreed to take his advice. We believe it is likely that after their Salt Lake stopover the "Wild-cats" headed north and took that route to California.[84]

But that finding does not resolve the issue. The Fancher train, which had preceded the Baker group into the Salt Lake Valley by a few days, had already accepted other rough-speaking travelers from Missouri into their group while camped in the valley. This information comes from other California-bound travelers passing through Utah. As late as the Arkansas party's brief stop in Cedar City, Captain Fancher was warning troublemakers in the group to cease their boisterousness. Meanwhile, the Turner-Dukes-Collins Missouri Company, moving through Utah behind the Arkansas company, had its own frontier adventurers who created problems for that wagon train as well.[85]

After a careful analysis of the sources and a reconstruction of a reliable chronology, we concluded that a few individuals in the Arkansas party and a few in the Missouri group were responsible for some of the reported tauntings or threats at different times and different places. Some incidents involving the Missouri party were later attributed to the Arkansas train. The reverse is true as well. We were able to assign most of the incidents, but not all, correctly.[86]

It is certain that some members of the Turner party exchanged fire with Pahvants near Beaver that led to injuries on both sides. Consistent with Brigham Young's policy at the time, local Mormon officials negotiated an end to the shooting. In contrast, the response to minor incidents in Cedar City led to an overreaction that ended in the mass killing at the Meadows. The bottom line is that none of the "outrages" involving either party justified the massacre.[87]

Another aspect of the question of "outrages" involved reports of poisoning at the Pahvant Indian Farm at Corn Creek. Some accounts make the emigrants responsible for the alleged poisoning and conclude that the poisoning provoked a militant Paiute response. In the wake of the Arkansas Company's overnight stop at Corn Creek, rumors began circulating that the emigrants had poisoned the carcass of a dead ox and dumped a powdered "poison" into the springs. Early reports and investigations varied in their assessment of the impact of the supposed poisoning; some reported deaths, others illnesses or nothing at all. But the perpetrators used the story to explain the massacre at Mountain Meadows as an act of Indian revenge.[88]

To help us analyze the evidence, we consulted a veterinarian familiar with cattle diseases and several physicians. These specialists examined our sources, including reports concerning Proctor Robison, a young Mormon who died within days after tanning a cattle hide. Robison's symptoms closely matched those of anthrax infections. This is a disease borne by cattle and passed to humans. Anthrax was widely reported in pioneer Utah. The infection's transmission and typical trajectory explain the pattern of reported incidents at Corn Creek. It is likely that anthrax, poison plants, or bacterial infections—or a combination of these options—caused the reported illnesses and death(s).[89]

Placing the reports into the context of nineteenth-century medical knowledge adds another layer of understanding. There was no germ theory or science of spores, bacteria, viruses, or anthrax in America at the time. Instead, popular detective novels made poisoning a major plot theme. Some westbound emigrants blamed Indians for the deaths of their cattle. Texans during the years leading to Civil War imagined wholesale poisonings by slaves and abolitionists. With no other way to explain the Corn Creek illnesses, the people of southern Utah assumed the worst about the emigrants and saw poison as the cause. "Their reaction fit the times, as poison in America had become a popular catchall. . . . It explained the unexplainable."[90]

What role did Brigham Young and other church leaders play in the massacre—and in subsequent cover-ups, investigations, and trials? Our book focuses only on the first part of this question—Young's role in the crime committed at Mountain Meadows. Because of page limitations, we have relegated to a second volume our findings on the initial investigations of 1857–59, the indictments of Mormon participants, Lee's two trials and in the mid-1870s, and the massacre's lasting impact on the people of Arkansas and Utah.[91]

Nothing in the evidence we examined indicts Brigham Young as one who ordered, approved, or condoned the massacre. Instead, the unfolding events in southern Utah place ultimate responsibility on Isaac C. Haight and John D. Lee, who received various shades of support from others. The councils, consultations, and conspiracies at Cedar City and Parowan reveal the names and roles of the decision makers. Reports of the discussions in the councils reveal no evidence of direction from outside southern Utah.

Leaders in Salt Lake City did communicate an urgent need to prepare for a possible military conflict with the approaching army. On tour of southern settlements in August, Mormon apostle George A. Smith encouraged the southern militia to prepare themselves for battle if the army invaded the territory (figure 30). Smith carried written instructions from the territorial militia leader, Gen. Daniel H. Wells. Those instructions urged the settlers to seek Indian cooperation and to ready themselves with regular militia drills. Wells and Smith reminded the people to harvest their grain and be prepared to cache it and flee to the mountains with their families if the army invaded. They were also warned against selling grain to passing emigrants. A messenger from General Wells advised military commanders to post guards in the mountain passes. Rumors were circulating that some elements of the army might come in through southern Utah.[92]

At the time of his southern tour, Smith did not yet know about the Arkansas and Missouri emigrant parties. He left the Salt Lake Valley early on August 3, just as the first of the Arkansas emigrants were arriving. Smith visited all of the southern settlements, in each place preaching a sermon with more stress on military preparation than religion.[93] Similarly, Isaac Haight's speech, misdated September 6 in traditional accounts, and sometimes used to prove Haight's intent to kill the emigrants, actually works best when read as a defiant challenge to the federal troops. Echoing Smith's readiness sermons, Haight railed out against the injustices the Latter-day Saints had suffered from the American nation. Now, he said, "they are sending an army to exterminate us." Vowing never to be driven from his home again, Haight said, "I am prepared to feed to the Gentiles the same bread they fed to us." In August, when Smith asked Haight what he would do if the rumored dragoons descended on Cedar City, he said he would "take his battalion and use them up, . . . for . . . if they are coming here they are coming for no good."[94]

Figure 30. George A. Smith. Courtesy LDS Church History Library.

We agree with other historians that Brigham Young's war policy and his public statements did contribute to heightening tensions. These statements came in three settings. In the earliest, Young and his associates rallied church members during the Mormon Reformation of 1856–57. The Reformation was an attempt to cleanse Latter-day Saints of what Young saw as a spiritual lethargy and a laziness in personal housekeeping. Young and others spoke provocatively from the pulpit and said they witnessed a change for the good in many lives. Yet tough talk about blood atonement for sins of adultery and murder "must have helped create a climate of violence in the territory, especially among those who chose to take license from it. As the revival proceeded, church leaders in Salt Lake City began cautioning local leaders not to go beyond the preaching of righteousness." As they tried to "keep alive the spirit of the Reformation," a similar message later circulated in southern Utah encouraging firmness but quietness and without excess excitement.[95]

The second setting, discussed earlier, was Young's reaction to emigrant abuse of Shoshones on the northern trail. Young's intensely focused discourse fed already present anti-American feelings among Latter-day Saints. Young's softer side emerged later when he learned that the army's purposes were protective, not aggressive, that their numbers had dropped through steady desertions, and that the troops would winter near Fort Bridger and not enter the Salt Lake Valley until the following spring.[96]

Brigham Young's calming spirit is evident in a third setting. In response to Haight's request for counsel, the church leader's letter advised him to remain alert and ready, but patient. "God rules," Young said, in a comment on the army's delay. "He has overruled for our deliverance this once again and he will always do so if we live our religion, be united in our faith and good works."[97] Young's counsel on the emigrants camped at the Meadows was to give them a fair warning and "if [they] . . . will leave let them go in peace." A mass killing of American citizens was the last thing Young would want in the uncertain climate of the summer of 1857. He was not a man anxious to take another's life. John D. Lee himself was consistent in his admission that Brigham Young knew nothing about the massacre until the killing was over.[98]

NOTES

1. Lamar 1966.
2. Bigler 1998:26–27, 141; 2008:5–6; Winn 1989:1–5, 85–86, 152–53, 181, 208.
3. Worster 1992.
4. Christy 1979:395–96, 400–405; Walker 2002:215–37; Walker et al. 2008:63–65.
5. Lavender 1984:172–73.
6. L. W. Boggs to John B. Clark, Oct. 27, 1838, in Executive Orders, 1838, Missouri State Archives, photocopy at Church History Library, Church of Jesus Christ of Latter-day Saints, Salt Lake City [hereafter Church History Library]. Jennings 1962:1–81, 129; LeSueur 1987:16–18; Parkin 1976:56–90.
7. Walker 2008:5–55.
8. Leonard 2002:327–34.
9. Walker et al. 2008:14.
10. Thomas Sharp, *Warsaw (Ill.) Signal*, Extra, Aug. 7, 1844.
11. Leonard 2002:103–104, 280–81, 525–36; Oaks and Hill 1975.
12. Leonard 1977.
13. Cooley 1958; Lamar 1966:11–14, 308, 320–21, 338; Smith 1992:66–67; White 1991:155–56, 163–69.
14. Other terms used to describe the Utah War include the Utah Expedition, the coming of Johnston's Army, and Buchanan's Blunder; see MacKinnon 1998:1149–51.
15. For an introductory overview, see Alexander 2003:125–29, 134–36. A standard treatment is Furniss 1960.
16. Brooks 1991:59.
17. "Brigham Young: Remarkable Interview with the Salt Lake Prophet," *New York Herald*, May 6, 1877; reprinted in "Interview with Brigham Young," *Deseret Evening News*, May 12, 1877; discussed in Walker et al. 2008:114.
18. Besides the works cited below, see Peck 1983; summary discussions in Walker et al. 2008:xiii–xiv, 127, 136–37; Zimbardo 2007.
19. These factors were identified by Yale University psychologist Stanley Milgram in 1961, confirmed by others, and reported most recently in Rosa Brooks, "Good People, Evil Deeds," *Los Angeles Times*, June 9, 2006. Walker et al. 2008:127–28.
20. Schwartz 1997:5; Walker et al. 2008:128. The "right of riot" used against individuals and groups is discussed in Gilje 1996:1–86.
21. Tambiah 1996:284.
22. Staub 1989:237; Walker et al. 2008:128.
23. Baumeister 1997:254.
24. Limerick 1987:280–88.
25. Shipps 1985:ix–x; and see Bloom 1992:79–81, 96.
26. Brown 1975:30–33, 35.
27. Billington 1949; Smith 1950.

28. Limerick outlines the difference between the "Old Frontier History" and the "New Western History" in the introduction to her book *The Legacy of Conquest* (1987:17–32); and see Limerick et al. 1991. Textbooks employing this approach include Hine and Faragher 2000 and White 1991.

29. See the discussion of Patricia Limerick's 1989 "non-manifesto" in Nugent 1994; also Sanchez 1940. Another classic study is Meinig 1971.

30. Wilford Woodruff, Journals, 1833–98, Sept. 29, 1857; George A. Smith and James McKnight, "The Emigrant and Indian War at Mountain Meadows, Sept. 21, 22, 23, 24, 1857," (1858), both in Church History Library. For early suspicions of Mormon involvement, see *Los Angeles Star*, Oct. 10 and 17, 1857; and *San Francisco Daily Alta California*, Oct. 17 and 18, 1859.

31. A recent example is Bagley 2002.

32. Denton 2003.

33. Walker et al. 2008:xii–xiii.

34. Ibid., xv. Although supported by our employer, the Church of Latter-day Saints, we exercised total editorial control over the product. We alone are responsible for our conclusions.

35. Leonard 2002; Turley 1992; Walker 1998.

36. We name those who assisted us in Walker et al. 2008:233–37.

37. Ibid., xv.

38. Because the following summary is drawn from our book, here I provide only references for direct quotations but page numbers where the reader can find additional information on the topics addressed in each paragraph. A complete bibliography, the four appendices, and other information are available on our web page, www.mountainmeadows.org.

39. Others traveling with the Baker and Fancher trains (the Arkansas Company) were the Jones-Tackitt-Poteet, Mitchell, Cameron, Parker, and Duck family groups.

40. For a historical profile of the emigrants, see Walker et al. 2008:75–88. Forensic anthropologist Shannon A. Novak offers an additional perspective on the families and the event in Novak 2008, and with Lars Rodseth in this volume.

41. Walker et al. 2008: 242–53; Dimick B. Huntington, Journal 1857–59, Sept. 1, 1857, Church History Library.

42. Walker et al. 2008:101–15.

43. Unruh 1979:186, and see also 176–79, 186–89.

44. Walker et al. 2008:89–100.

45. Ibid., 116–28; Brigham Young, Discourse, Aug. 16, 1857, reported by George D. Watt, in Historian's Office, Reports of Speeches, ca. 1845–85; and Wilford Woodruff, Journals, 1833–98, Aug. 16, 1857, both in Church History Library; Cooley 1980.

46. Nephi Johnson, affidavit, July 22, 1908, First Presidency, Cumulative Correspondence, 1900–1949; and Elias Morris statement, Feb. 2, 1892, Collected Material concerning the Mountain Meadows Massacre, both in Church History Library; Walker et al. 2008:129–33.

47. Walker et al. 2008:133-34.
48. Ibid., 134, 149-52.
49. Ibid., 135-36; James H. Martineau to Susan [Martineau], May 3, 1876, James Henry Martineau Collection, Church History Library.
50. Mary S. Campbell, Andrew Jenson interviews, Jan. and Feb. 1892, Church History Library; Walker et al. 2008:137-39.
51. Walker et al. 2008:142-48; Ellott Willden, Andrew Jenson interviews, Jan. and Feb. 1892, Mountain Meadows file, Andrew Jenson, Collection, Church History Library.
52. Walker et al. 2008:155-57.
53. Ibid., 157-59, 168-69.
54. Ibid., 159-60.
55. Ibid., 166-67, 173-74, 177; William Barton, field notes of interview with Andrew Jenson, Jan. or Feb. 1892, Mountain Meadows file, Andrew Jenson, Collection, Church History Library; also published in "Selections from the Andrew Jenson Collection," in Turley and Walker 2008:96-97.
56. Walker et al. 2008:164, 174.
57. Ibid., 173-74, 177-78.
58. Extracts from Jacob Hamblin's journal, in Jacob Hamblin to Brigham Young, Nov. 13, 1871, General Office Files, President's Office Files, Brigham Young, Office Files, Church History Library.
59. Walker et al. 2008:127-28; William Barton, interview with Andrew Jenson, in "Selections from the Andrew Jenson Collection," in Turley and Walker 2008:96-101.
60. Walker et al. 2008:178-79, 212-13; conversation with Samuel Knight, in Abraham H. Cannon, Diary, 1879-95, June 13, 1895, typescript, L. Tom Perry Special Collections, Harold B. Lee Library, Brigham Young University, Provo, Utah.
61. Walker et al. 2008:179-81.
62. Ibid., 186-92.
63. Ibid., 193; Nephi Johnson, affidavit, Nov. 30, 1909, in Collected Materials concerning the Mountain Meadows Massacre, Church History Library. Nephi Johnson's 1908 and 1909 affidavits, along with other primary documents, many of them previously unavailable or ignored, are conveniently available in Turley and Walker 2009. Walker et al. 2008:192-93, 265-66; "The Lee Trial: What the Chief [of] the Beaver Indians Has to Say about It," *Los Angeles Star*, Aug. 4, 1875.
64. Walker et al. 2008:192.
65. Nephi Johnson, affidavit, July 22, 1908, First Presidency, Cumulative Correspondence, 1900-1949, Church History Library; Walker et al. 2008:191-93.
66. Walker et al. 2008:193-97.
67. Ibid., 197-98.
68. Ibid., 199-201.
69. Ibid., 201-207, 224-25; C. F. McGlashan, "The Mountain Meadows Massacre," *Sacramento Daily Record*, Jan. 1, 1875; Beadle 1878:500-501.

70. Walker et al. 2008:207–208.

71. Ibid., 214–15; Conversation with Samuel Knight, in Abraham H. Cannon, Diary, 1879–95, L. Tom Perry Special Collections, Harold B. Lee Library, Brigham Young University, Provo, Utah.; Jacob Hamblin, statement, in Carleton 1860:8.

72. Bagley 2002:171–73, 158–60; Brooks 1991:253–54, 259–60, 264–65.

73. Walker et al. 2008:181–86, 225–26; Brigham Young to Isaac C. Haight, Sept. 10, 1857, Letterpress Copybook 3:827–28, Brigham Young, Office Files, Church History Library.

74. Walker et al. 2008:181, 209, 215–16.

75. C. F. McGlashan, "Mountain Meadow Massacre," *Sacramento Daily Record*, Jan. 1, 1875; Little 1881:57; James Buchanan, *Message of the President of the United States, Communicating, in compliance with a resolution of the Senate, information in relation to the massacre at Mountain Meadows, and other massacres in Utah Territory*, 36th Cong., 1st sess., Senate Exec. Doc. 42, Serial 1033 (Washington, D.C.: Government Printing Office, 1860), 60.

76. Walker et al. 2008:227–31. Our findings concerning the aftermath of the massacre, including the investigations and Lee trials, will appear in a subsequent volume.

77. The methods of historical research and writing are discussed in many guides and handbooks, including Barzun and Graff 1957; Bloch 1953; Fischer 1970; and Nevins 1962.

78. Turley, "Problems with Mountain Meadows Massacre Sources," in Turley and Walker 2008:145, 147.

79. Ibid., 145–47.

80. Bishop 1877.

81. Howard: "Lee's Confession," *Sacramento Daily Record-Union*, Mar. 24, 1877; Bishop: "Lee's Last Confession," *San Francisco Daily Bulletin Supplement*, Mar. 24, 1877.

82. Turley, "Problems with Mountain Meadows Massacre Sources," Turley and Walker 2008:147–51; quote from ibid., 147 n. 30, describing findings in Orton 2008.

83. Brooks 1991:50–57, 219.

84. Stenhouse 1873:427–29; P., letter, Oct. 14, 1857, in "The Immigrant Massacres," *San Francisco Daily Alta California*, Oct. 17, 1857; Carpenter 1980:165–69; Parker 1902:65–67; Walker et al. 2008:87.

85. P., letter, in *San Francisco Daily Alta California*, October 17, 1857; Nephi Johnson, affidavit, July 22, 1908, First Presidency, Cumulative Correspondence, 1900–1949, Church History Library; Walker et al. 2008:113–15, 132–35.

86. Walker et al. 2008:113–15.

87. Ibid., 115, 175–79.

88. Ibid., 119–21; Brooks 1991:140–41, 214–15; John D. Lee, report to Brigham Young, in Wilford Woodruff, Journals, September 29, 1857, Church History Library.

89. Walker et al. 2008:121–23.

90. Ibid., 123; and see Essig 2000:4–5, 216–60.

91. Thomas G. Alexander's 2006 examination of the early Mormon investigations offers a fine analysis of the issue.

92. Walker et al. 2008:67–70.

93. Ibid., 68, 70–72.

94. Brooks 1991:52; Walker et al. 2008:72; George A. Smith, Sept. 13, 1857, in "Remarks," *Deseret News*, Sept. 23, 1857.

95. Walker et al. 2008:25–27.

96. Brigham Young, Discourse, Aug. 16, 1857, in Historian's Office, Report of Speeches, Church History Library; and Brigham Young to Isaac C. Haight, September 10, 1857, Letterpress Copybook 3:827–28, Brigham Young, Office Files, both in Church History Library; photo reproduction of Young's letter, in Walker et al. 2008:184–85.

97. Brigham Young to Isaac C. Haight, Sept. 10, 1857, Letterpress Copybook 3:827–28, Brigham Young, Office Files, Church History Library.

98. Walker et al. 2008:75–88, 228, 231; J. H. Beadle, "Interview with Jno. D. Lee of Mountain Meadows Notoriety," *Salt Lake Tribune*, July 29, 1872; Lee 2003, 2:164–65, 203, 369, 378, 382, 452–53, 462, ca. July 20, 1871, July 4, 1872, Sept. 24, Oct. 16, 31, Nov. 7, 1875, Apr. 6–7, 1876.

Placing the Dead at Mountain Meadows

Lars Rodseth and Shannon A. Novak

In the summer of 1999 a construction backhoe rolled up to an old memorial at Mountain Meadows, Utah. The site was dilapidated, and the plan was to establish a much larger and more dignified monument to the 120 people who had died here, back in 1857. Because many of the victims were thought to be buried in this very spot, elaborate precautions had been taken to avoid disturbing any human remains. Aerial photographs and historic maps had been carefully studied, local landowners had been duly consulted, and ground-penetrating radar had been brought in to trace the limits of the mass grave.[1] On August 3, with a light breeze upon the sagebrush, construction finally began.

A few minutes later, the backhoe driver cut his engine. His second bucket of dirt hovered just inches above the ground. It was filled with hundreds of human bones.

For more than 150 years, diverse and conflicting interpretations of what happened at Mountain Meadows have been carried along in several distinct social networks.[2] At the national level, journalists and historians have tended to tell one type of story. Quite different traditions were passed down in "Mormon country," from Salt Lake City and St. George to the outlying communities of Arizona, Nevada, Idaho, and Wyoming. Moreover, even within Utah many local and family variants of the "Mountain Meadows massacre" have survived, combined, mutated, and spread.

Only in recent decades has there been a sustained effort to reconcile the various versions of the narrative. This effort was invigorated in 1999 with the first scientific study of human remains from the massacre site. Interested observers on all sides expected modern forensics to shed some new light on this puzzling and deeply disturbing event. Our aim here is to explore how the skeletal findings actually did affect our understanding of Mountain Meadows, often in unexpected ways.

Facts and Frames

On one level, we know what happened at Mountain Meadows. There is little or no debate about basic facts such as these: (1) more than one hundred people were killed; (2) the victims included men, women, and children; (3) the men had been separated from the women and children before the massacre began; (4) most of the men were shot; (5) most of the women and children were bludgeoned or stabbed; (6) the only survivors were seventeen young children; (7) the corpses were exposed to the elements for almost two years before being buried at the massacre site by U.S. troops; and (8) the surviving children remained in Utah until summer 1859, when most of them were returned to Arkansas. Though more details could be added, these eight points constitute the factual core of the case—the key elements that are generally agreed on by all knowledgeable observers.

Yet the facts, to be understood fully, must be set within some kind of interpretive frame.[3] Indeed, to know "what happened" in any given case is to know how the facts fit together within a larger social context and sequence of events. In a relatively simple situation, all interested observers share a large body of background knowledge about the historical setting, the participants, and the events leading up to the moment of interest. Such generally shared knowledge allows the act of interpretive framing to proceed without contention—sometimes without conscious effort at all. In a more complex situation, however—especially in a frontier zone[4]—there may be sharp asymmetries in what is known or believed about a critical sequence of events. The massacre at Mountain Meadows is an exemplary case of people participating in one and the same historical sequence without necessarily sharing the background knowledge that would enable them to experience, interpret, or remember what happened in the same way.

How many distinct social groups were brought together at Mountain Meadows? It depends on what is meant by a "distinct group." The perpetrators of the massacre were members of the Church of Jesus Christ of Latter-day Saints. In 1847 the church leadership had fled the United States, gathering thousands of followers in what was then Mexican territory.[5] From this integrated and rather insulated community, with its own worldview and sense of purpose, the Iron County militia was formed. The massacre would be carried out by some fifty militiamen who had drilled for weeks in preparation for a disastrous encounter with the U.S. Army.[6]

The victims of the massacre, by contrast, were Baptist and Methodist families who had set out from northwest Arkansas in at least three large parties.[7] Though often portrayed as a unified group, the emigrants had been widely dispersed on the overland trail and were probably acquainted with just a subset of those who died beside them.

At least two other "communities" were involved in the case: the U.S. Army and the Southern Paiutes. Two months before the massacre, troops had been dispatched from Fort Leavenworth, Kansas, to bring the Utah Territory under federal control and remove Brigham Young from power. Mormon fears of a U.S. invasion culminated in the "war hysteria" that is often said to have triggered the massacre.[8] Ironically, the only federal authorities to show up at the massacre site were the soldiers who buried the victims, twenty months after the fact.[9] Meanwhile, in the run-up to the massacre, Southern Paiutes and other Utah tribes had been encouraged by Mormon leaders to attack and pillage wagon trains bound for California.[10] Though there is no credible evidence that the massacre was planned or directed by American Indians, for decades they would be treated as scapegoats for the crime.[11] Not until 2007 did the church acknowledge that any Indians at the scene of the massacre had been recruited and manipulated by local Mormon leaders.[12]

Utah militiamen, Arkansas farmers, U.S. soldiers, and Southern Paiutes did not see the world in the same way. Even if they witnessed the same event or participated in the same historical sequence, they would have relied on quite different assumptions and cultural-historical "landmarks" to understand what was happening.¹³ To take one obvious example, many Utah Mormons, with firsthand experience of religious persecution in Missouri and Illinois, feared the U.S. Army as an extermination force.¹⁴ At the same time, federal authorities seem to have imagined that "the Mormon people would hail the army as saviors, especially, they believed, women oppressed by polygamous marriages" and others who had been bullied by Brigham Young's regime.¹⁵ To oversimplify only slightly, whereas the federal government saw itself engaged in a rescue mission, the Mormons were preparing for a holocaust.

Remote Possibilities

Mountain Meadows is remote. Almost 300 miles from Salt Lake City, the site is surrounded by rugged hills and ranchland. The nearest town of any size, St. George, did not exist in 1857. Indeed, at the time of the massacre the Mormon colonization of southern Utah had only just begun. What is now Cedar City, some 35 miles from Mountain Meadows, was a struggling outpost with fewer than a thousand residents.¹⁶ Passing through "Fort Cedar" in early September, the Arkansas emigrants were soon beyond the fringe of Mormon settlement, heading into the Mojave Desert.

The remoteness of the setting helps to explain both the massacre itself and the extremely murky history that surrounds it. To some extent, the case of Mountain Meadows fits the pattern of criminal "opportunism" described by Charles Tilly: "Most opportunistic collective violence occurs when, as a consequence of shielding from routine surveillance and repression, individuals or clusters of individuals use immediately damaging means to pursue ends that would be unavailable or forbidden to them under other circumstances."¹⁷ The fact that only the killers and their victims were there to witness the event surely made the massacre feasible, whether the idea originated with the militiamen themselves or with some higher authority in Salt Lake City.

In any case, when the killing was done and the corpses were abandoned in the wilderness, Mountain Meadows quickly became "a historical maze built of lies, folklore, popular myth, justifications, and a few facts."¹⁸ For 150 years this maze has confounded attorneys, historians, and archaeologists alike.

What facts there are to go on have often been extracted from quite dubious sources—"the testimony of known killers, the reconstructed memories of seventeen young children, and reams of propaganda."[19] Personal documents in connection with the case are remarkably scarce; most of the surviving diaries and letters are not by the victims themselves but by the perpetrators or their accomplices. According to church-appointed historians with extraordinary access to the Mormon archives, a number of critical documents have been "lost, suppressed, or destroyed."[20]

Nevertheless, how the massacre happened would be described in some detail by militiamen Philip Klingensmith (1871), John D. Lee (1877), and John M. Higbee (1894), among others. At least four of the survivors, all of whom had been small children at the time of the massacre, later provided statements to newspapers or magazines.[21] Some of the best documentary evidence was offered by overland travelers and U.S. military personnel who had visited Mountain Meadows between autumn 1857 and spring 1859. Throughout this period, the bodies of the victims were exposed to the elements—and to the gaze of passers-by. The sight of the killing field shocked and horrified emigrants such as John Aiken, whose wagon train passed through the site about one week after the massacre. In an affidavit filed in San Bernardino, California, Aiken reported seeing a large pack of wolves "feasting on the carcasses of the murdered," whose number included women and children as well as men.[22]

When U.S. troops finally arrived at the Meadows, they found thousands of sun-bleached human bones still scattered over the ground, along with "locks and masses of women's hair" and the tattered remains of "little children's dresses." According to Rogers, "In places the bones of small children were lying side by side with those of grown persons, as if parent and child had met death at the same instant and with the same stroke." Such accounts clearly testified to the magnitude of the crime but could only speculate on how it was planned or carried out, and why.[23]

Perhaps the bones themselves could "testify." This was certainly the hope (or perhaps the fear) of some observers when human remains returned to the surface, 140 years after they had been buried by U.S. troops. In those 140 years, archaeology had emerged as a modern science. Forensic techniques had been developed to reconstruct crime scenes, identify victims, and

PLACING THE DEAD AT MOUNTAIN MEADOWS 195

prosecute murderers, even decades after the fact. The mass graves of two world wars and innumerable ethnic and nationalist conflicts had served as the training grounds for a new kind of scientist. The "forensic anthropologist" had begun to emerge in the public consciousness as a specialist in violent death and its often subtle material traces.[24] Yet Mountain Meadows poses a unique challenge to forensic investigation. More than a crime scene, the site is fraught with social and historical significance of the kind usually associated with a battlefield. It seems a strange battle, however, in which only one army takes the field and the civilian targets are hardly aware of the war. Perhaps the closest parallel to Mountain Meadows would be certain war crimes, such as the Banka Island massacre, in which civilians seeking safe passage through hostile territory encounter soldiers in an isolated location.[25] The very concept "war crime," however, is a twentieth-century invention and would never have been applied in the context of Mountain Meadows.

In the 140 years since the massacre, the landscape itself has been transformed. The once lush valley that served as an oasis on the Spanish Trail is now a dusty graveyard, reputed to be cursed.[26] Overgrazing and erosion may have caused the valley to go brown, but the very thought of the place had been spoiled already by blood and desecration. Hovering somewhere between a battlefield and a crime scene, Mountain Meadows is, to those who know it, a little reminder of hell.

Lifting the Fog

"To those who know it" is the operative phrase here. For how can we *know* what happened so long ago in such an out-of-the-way place, without living witnesses or candid testimonials to silence the doubters? Among residents of southern Utah, as among Germans and Poles in the shadow of Auschwitz, there has always been skepticism about the mainstream historical accounts.[27] The "hard" evidence for the massacre, as we have seen, is rather slim, and as the twentieth century wore on and the last survivors passed away it became easier in some quarters to dismiss the whole story as anti-Mormon propaganda. Short of such outright denial, many journalistic and some scholarly accounts of Mountain Meadows tend to follow certain "formulas of erasure"—omitting crucial details, euphemizing the murders, or otherwise downplaying the horror of the event.[28] Thus the massacre is rendered abstract and unsurprising—just another case of "frontier violence," for example, in a less civilized time and place.[29]

This kind of complacency was starkly challenged by the disinterred bones of the victims. Suddenly the massacre was not a propaganda point, not a mere abstraction, and not entirely of another time and place. "The past is never dead," as William Faulkner put it. "It's not even past."[30] What Faulkner did not mention, however, is the role of material objects in "reactivating" the past on a regular basis. Perhaps the past is always with us, but only because something has survived the comings and goings of human beings.[31] And when objects as enduring and intimate as human bones are brought vividly to consciousness, after so much else has crumbled away, the past is made present once again. In the case of Mountain Meadows, this is exactly what happened in the late summer of 1999.

Confronted with real human skulls, many with bullet holes or other signs of violent death, the "massacre deniers" were placed on the defensive. To this day, some descendants of the militiamen deny that their ancestors were responsible for the crime, but the more extravagant claim that the massacre never happened seems, for now, to have disappeared from public discourse. (The persistence of such a claim "underground"—in particular family traditions, for example—is of course difficult to detect or measure.) More important, the "resurrection" of the victims served as a powerful check on the widespread tendency to gloss over or euphemize the historical details of the event.

Perhaps the most disturbing aspect of the Mountain Meadows massacre, and what makes it such a touchstone for social and moral reflection to this day, is not the brutality or ferocity of the murders but, on the contrary, their rational efficiency and coordination. Most of the emigrants did not die in the initial assault, which came just before dawn on September 7. This was indeed a fierce battle, enveloped by the proverbial "fog of war." The militiamen seem to have counted on this fog to cover their tracks and allow the blame to be placed elsewhere. What they did not expect was the spirited defense mounted by the emigrants. Despite being taken by surprise and suffering several losses in the first volley, these Arkansas farmers managed to withstand a four-day siege. It was only at this point that the emigrants, dehydrated and low on ammunition, surrendered their arms and agreed to be escorted back to Cedar City.

The massacre had not yet happened. To understand how it did happen, we must *slow down* the narrative, providing something like a play-by-play description of the last inning of a pivotal game.[32] It was late afternoon, September 11. The ninety or so women and children of the company were traumatized and thirsty but otherwise unharmed. Some of their husbands and fathers were dead or wounded, but perhaps forty of the men were still able to walk. At this point, only a few militiamen—John D. Lee, Samuel Knight, Samuel McMurdy, and possibly William Bateman—were directing the operation, while the bulk of their force waited up the trail and out of sight.

The smallest children, their mothers, and a few wounded men were loaded into two wagons. With Knight and McMurdy driving, Lee directed the older children and the remainder of the women to walk immediately behind. The wagons pulled out of the siege site. At the very rear of the procession were the ambulatory men, who were drawn out in single file along the trail.[33] When they saw the column of militiamen up ahead, some of the emigrants cheered, believing they were saved. The wagons, however, were driven right past the formation, and all the women and children soon followed. What happened next is vividly described by Will Bagley: "The men marched until they were opposite Capt. Joel White's Company D and a Mormon soldier fell in by the side of each unarmed man. . . . Perhaps a quarter mile behind the women, Maj. John Higbee . . . fired a shot and gave the crucial order, 'Halt! Do your duty!' . . . At the command, the guards turned and shot down the men. . . . [Philip] Klingensmith, at the back of the ranks, did not hear who gave the order, but it 'was passed down the column; the emigrants were then and there shot down.'"[34]

How the women and children were killed is known with less certainty and in less detail. Yet Bagley, Juanita Brooks, and other authorities agree on this much: Several men, some in Indian garb, had been waiting in the brush along the trail. At the sound of gunshots, they rushed out of their hiding places with knives and blunt instruments. Within minutes, all of the women and most of the children were dead.[35]

A Thoroughly Modern Massacre?

The just-mentioned version of the story, though it hews close to the "factual core" of the case, may be inaccurate in some details. It goes out on an interpretive limb as well, and could always be criticized from other points of view. Yet some such narrative that slows the action down and provides a sense of *contingency*—of how things might have been different—is indispensable to the task at hand. For the underlying strategy of most "formulas of erasure" is to make the past seem unsurprising, perhaps inevitable—a natural expression of the time, the culture, or the world in general. What gets erased, in other words, are the "inconvenient complications" of real historical sequences, allowing problematic or puzzling events to be covered by a relatively few, vastly simplified schemes of cause and effect.[36] Even the term "massacre" tends to misrepresent what happened at Mountain Meadows, as it conjures up one or another clichéd scenario that turns out to be entirely inappropriate to the case.

First, as James W. Loewen points out, any so-called massacre on the American frontier will be commonly presumed to be an Indian act: "Across the United States historic markers and monuments use 'massacre' when American Indians kill European Americans, even when as few as one white died! Utah alone has five historical markers that use 'massacre' for Indian attacks on whites and none for any white attack."[37] Thus, the "Indian massacre" is the default scenario that tends to swallow up the case of Mountain Meadows, even if one has never heard the traditional (i.e., white, Mormon, Utah-based) accounts of American Indian involvement in the crime.

Second, there is a strong tendency among casual narrators (and some professional ones as well) to blur together two events: the initial attack on the wagon train, and the subsequent massacre of its riders. Yet a clear distinction between these two events, as we have seen, is indispensable to any genuine understanding of what happened at Mountain Meadows. Indeed, if a massacre is assumed to be an act of ferocity and "blood-lust" (spilling over from "ordinary" warfare, for example, as combatants get carried away in the heat of the moment), then Mountain Meadows was no massacre. The emigrants were killed not in a pitched battle with an enemy gone berserk but at close range by remarkably determined and disciplined soldiers.

As Brooks stated unequivocally, "a military group under military orders" was responsible for the murders.[38] By 1857 the Mormons had a long tradition of "amateur militarism" and were quite familiar with what William McNeill calls "muscular bonding"—the enhancement of soldierly discipline and solidarity through coordinated drills and maneuvers.[39] In fact, the militiamen who carried out the massacre were probably divided into two squads, each with its modus operandi: the escorts, who presented themselves as friendly authorities and defenders of the peace; and the ambushers, who presented themselves as "savages" intent on bloody mayhem. Though the two squads displayed utterly different behaviors, they were carrying out the same plan. Their "division of labor," it may be argued, was just one indication of their bureaucratic efficiency—their determination to get the job done through carefully coordinated activities.

In each squad, furthermore, the militiamen engaged in elaborate "impression management" or "face-work."[40] For their part, the escorts had a seemingly straightforward task: maintain a "poker face" before a beleaguered but still suspicious audience. What this must have entailed, however, is difficult to comprehend, given the stakes they were playing for. An analogy might be drawn with the role playing of professional contract killers, as analyzed by Randall Collins:

> The victim may be forced into a car and driven to a remote location to be killed; or lured to a supposed meeting, surrounded by a carload of companions who turn out to be his executioners. How do killers overcome confrontational tension in these cases? Their chief technique seems to be to try to keep the victim calm, to lull him into believing he will not be killed. This subterfuge is not just a way of keeping the victim under control; it is also a way of keeping the killer calm, upholding the pretense for himself as well that he is not about to kill someone.[41]

In the case of Mountain Meadows, the question of how the escorts managed to overcome their "confrontational tension" (not to mention pangs of conscience) has been explicitly raised by Bagley: "None of the men in the Mormon guard ever described their feelings as they received the cheers of the Arkansas men and escorted them up the field. None of them ever described what it was like to accept the trust of men they would soon murder in cold blood."[42]

Meanwhile, the ambushers were engaged in a dramatically different kind of face-work. Rather than maintain a calm façade, the members of this squad were required to whip themselves into a frenzy—perhaps using what Collins calls "emotional self-manipulation techniques," such as "making oneself angry by recalling past insults."[43] Indeed, those lying in wait for the women and children seem to have engaged in the fantasy that they were, for the moment, not civilized men but "free" and "savage" Indians: "To the militiamen at Mountain Meadows, whose identities had been formed by both real and imagined persecution, their performance must have been liberating.... Wild Indianness, after all, had always been attractive as well as repulsive, a way of crossing the boundaries of civilized behavior to engage in the most dramatic kind of political theater."[44]

Like the participants in the Boston Tea Party, the militiamen probably donned Indian costumes not just to disguise their identities but to unleash their emotions. Yet the emotions themselves had to have been, in a sense, contrived or engineered. Whatever bitterness or rage the Mormons harbored toward their enemies back east, to project it onto *these* people, these women and children who could do them no harm, was indeed a formidable task. Like good soldiers, however, the militiamen carried it out.

Why the killers did not adequately bury or otherwise dispose of the bodies remains an intriguing question. Perhaps they shrank from the task, once they realized what they had done; this would support an interpretation of the massacre as an opportunistic act that went terribly wrong, even in the eyes of the perpetrators. An alternative hypothesis, however, is that the corpses were meant to be discovered and observed, "to warn and intimidate any challengers to Mormon sovereignty."[45] In this case, the massacre would have to be seen as an act of coordinated destruction—the implementation of a "program of damage" by well-organized and ideologically motivated conspirators.[46] Again we are struck by the curiously *modern* quality of the massacre. Hardly a stereotypical case of "frontier violence," let alone a throwback to "primitive savagery," Mountain Meadows begins to look more like a premonition of the twentieth century, complete with political machines, paramilitary units, and campaigns of ethnic cleansing. Indeed, a question first raised by the Holocaust now spills into many other contexts, including Mountain Meadows:[47] is this horrific "aberration," this detour from modernity, actually a symptom *of* modernity—of the increasingly efficient pursuit of ideological ends by means of bureaucratic rationality?

CS IRONIES

When the bones were disinterred at Mountain Meadows, the television program *CSI* was still in the planning stage. Its creator wanted to put a new spin on the cop show formula, presenting stories in which "the heroes would solve crimes with smarts and microscopes rather than fists and guns"[48] One year later, in the fall of 2000, the series went on the air and American society immediately began to feel the "CSI effect"—an exaggerated sense of the technical wizardry and infallibility of forensic science.[49] "Any sufficiently advanced technology," as Arthur C. Clark observed, "is indistinguishable from magic." This applies as much to forensic as to rocket technology. As Zoë Crossland observes, "Popular accounts of forensic anthropology often talk of the 'testimony' or mute 'witness' of bones and describe human remains as 'speaking for themselves' in the service of justice and truth."[50] DNA analysis in particular has gained a certain occult quality in the popular imagination. The notion, after all, that invisible traces of one's self are left behind in blood, hair, semen, or bone, and that these traces can be not only recovered and revealed but made to "speak one's name"—this indeed smacks of fetishism and other forms of sympathetic magic, however rationally deployed. Less advanced technology such as fingerprinting or ballistic analysis is still impressive, but perhaps on the order of alchemy rather than true magic.

Yet none of these technologies would be applied in the case of Mountain Meadows. The 2,605 skeletal fragments from the massacre site were examined and documented by Shannon A. Novak at the University of Utah.[51] After one month, however, the analysis was abruptly terminated and the bones were returned to Mountain Meadows. The new monument at the site, designed and funded by the Church of Jesus Christ of Latter-day Saints, was to be formally dedicated on September 11, 1999. As part of the ceremony, all the disinterred remains were to be sealed beneath the foundation. The reburial had been expedited through the intervention of Utah governor Mike Leavitt, himself a descendant of one of the Iron County militiamen.[52]

Though the skeletal analysis had been cut short, it did produce some important findings. The sample represented at least twenty-eight individuals, including men, women, and children. Eighteen skulls were delineated and partially reconstructed. Bludgeoning was evident in six of these skulls.[53] At least one mature female, two young adult males, and three juveniles had suffered powerful blows to the head. The children's crania in particular had extensive crushing. The older woman and two young men exhibited more localized blunt-force impacts to their foreheads.

The most common injury observed in the victims was a single gunshot wound to the head. The trauma pattern was consistent with point-blank, execution-style killing as opposed to long-distance firing under battlefield conditions.[54] The locations of the gunshot wounds indicated that some of the victims were shot from behind; others would have been directly facing their assailants. All the shooting victims were adult males, with the exception of one juvenile of indeterminate sex.[55] In this case, the ten- to fifteen-year-old victim was shot in the top of the head from above and behind his or her right side.

Extensive postmortem damage suggested that the corpses had been left on or near the surface, where they had been subjected to feeding and disarticulation by wolves or other carnivores. Most of the small bones of the hands, feet, vertebrae, and joint surfaces were missing entirely. The long bones in the sample were generally covered with punctures, pits, scoring, and furrows, indicating long-term carnivore activity.[56] Bleaching and other signs of weathering suggested that the scattered remains had been exposed on the surface for many months.

If more time had been allowed for the study, advanced forensic techniques might have shed some new light on what happened at Mountain Meadows. X-rays of skeletal lesions, for example, might have allowed the identification of lead wipe—microscopic fragments of metal sometimes left on gunshot wounds, especially in bone. Chemical analysis of such fragments can be used in turn to trace the elemental signature of the metal, suggesting where the ore had originated. If the source could be matched to a known mine that was controlled by local Mormons, for example, this would be circumstantial evidence for the culpability of the militiamen.

DNA analysis, often seen as the highest form of the forensic art, would have added little to our understanding of the massacre itself. Unlike a recent crime scene, the massacre site offers no organic trace of the perpetrators. The only surviving DNA, 140 years after the fact, would be that contained in bones and teeth. What we are left with, then, is genetic information about the victims only. Although such information might have allowed the identification of individuals (or at least family lines) within the mass grave, this by itself would seem to tell us nothing about how or why the massacre took place.

The most vexed questions surrounding Mountain Meadows have always involved the perpetrators. Who gave the order? Who pulled the trigger? Why did they do it? How many Indians were present? Who absconded with the cattle, gold, and other property on the train? High forensic technology, for all its mystique in the popular imagination, is surprisingly powerless to answer such questions.

Yet the skeletal findings have been inexorably drawn into the public arena, covered in the local and national media, incorporated into school textbooks, and used to bolster the plotline of at least one historical novel.[57] Though some scientific evidence shows up in these accounts, they are prone to focus on the usual hot-button issues of culpability and exoneration. The question of American Indian involvement in particular has received a fair amount of press, renewing debate about how the massacre is portrayed in state history texts.[58] The tendency has been for journalists and other authors to look to the forensic analysis for proof that Mormons rather than Indians committed the massacre.

Yet no such proof is likely to emerge from a study of this kind. First, the disinterred bones from Mountain Meadows represented no more than 25 percent of the massacre victims.[59] As a result, an absence of evidence for x in the sample cannot settle the question of x's presence in the population as whole. Still, the limitations of such "negative evidence" were seldom appreciated in popular treatments, and the absence of scalping or arrow wounds, for example, was widely understood to clear the Indians of the crime. Second, skeletal injuries in general can be used to profile victims, but usually not perpetrators. If the bodies at Mountain Meadows had been scalped, this would not prove that American Indians were responsible, any more than gunshot wounds, by themselves, could prove that the militiamen did it. Nevertheless, Novak's study has been widely portrayed as a scientific refutation of traditional (white, Mormon, Utah-based) accounts.

Conclusion

The real significance of the skeletal analysis had little to do with "smoking guns" or the people who wielded them. Forensic anthropology has indeed shed new light on Mountain Meadows, but not in the ways one might have expected. Scientific study of the victims' remains has had at least three salutary effects.

First, by considering these remains in their own right, anthropology draws attention to those who *died* at Mountain Meadows, and not just the murderers and their reputed accomplices. When the bodies are taken seriously, the people are taken seriously—in some quarters for the first time. From the perspective of Mormon Utah, the victims have long been portrayed as anonymous ruffians who were more than a little responsible for their own demise. This kind of depiction had been questioned by a long series of authors from Bancroft to Bagley, yet it took the bones themselves to humanize the victims, endow them with individual identities, and thus "bring them to the table" of the ongoing conversation about the massacre.

Second, the skeletal analysis has raised the consciousness of many living descendants of the massacre victims, helping in some degree to unite and mobilize the extended families and local organizations that have some stake in how the massacre is remembered. "Although the bones cannot settle the matter of what *really* happened at Mountain Meadows, or who is to blame, or what is to be done, they are a powerful catalyst for the ongoing process of forming and reforming communities on the basis of historical evidence."[60] With the victims' descendants organized to take on the Church of Latter-day Saints, there have been renewed attempts to bring all the stakeholders, including the Southern Paiutes, under one big tent for the first time.[61] At its best, this process aims not to smooth over or bury the past but to allow the full range of stories and historical voices to be heard—however uncomfortable that could prove to be for all concerned.[62]

Third, the human remains have proved to be a mnemonic device of subtle but undeniable power. In a sense, as noted above, we *know* what happened at Mountain Meadows. The historical record, though patched together and warped by many gales of propaganda, still shelters much that can be called knowledge. By reminding us of what we already had, the bones arrested the process of erasure and once again made the past present.

If this was a case of forensic anthropology, it was less about the forensics and more about the anthropology. An anthropology of Mountain Meadows would approach the human remains as significant in their own right. It would recognize that these bones were once inside bodies and that each of the bodies was shaped by a unique sequence of biographical events. It would try to reconstruct the social and economic matrix that produced these bodies, their ways of living, and their ways of suffering.[63] Human remains, in short, would be precious historical artifacts, rich with information, and not just evidence at a crime scene.

NOTES

1. Baker et al. 2003.
2. Novak and Rodseth 2006.
3. E.g., Goffman 1974; Goodin and Tilly 2006; Trouillot 1995.
4. Rodseth and Parker 2005.
5. Bagley 2002; Brooks 1962; Walker et al. 2008.
6. Bigler 1998.
7. Novak 2008.
8. Brooks 1962.
9. Carleton 1995 [1859]; Hunt 1958:171–86.
10. Bagley 2002:91–94; Farmer 2008:96.
11. Knack 2001; Tom and Holt 2000.
12. Jessica Ravitz, "LDS Church Apologizes for Mountain Meadows Massacre," *Salt Lake Tribune*, Sept. 11, 2007; see also Walker et al. 2008:265.
13. E.g., Harrison 2004; Hirsch and O'Hanlon 1995.
14. Walker et al. 2008:42–49.
15. Alexander 2003:125.
16. Shirts and Shirts 2001.
17. Tilly 2003:131.
18. Bagley 2002:99.

19. Novak 2008:9.
20. Carrie A. Moore, "LDS Researchers Call Massacre Documents a 'Web of Conflicting Information,'" *Deseret News* (Salt Lake City, Utah), May 24, 2008; Walker et al. 2008:xi.
21. Cates 1875; Evans 1897; Greenhaw 1938; Mitchell 1940; see also Bagley and Bigler 2008.
22. John Aiken, Affidavit made before Marcus Kate, Notary Public, Nov. 24, 1857, San Bernardino, Calif.
23. Carleton 1995 [1859]:36; Rogers 1962 [1860]:267.
24. Komar and Buikstra 2008; Stewart 1979.
25. Tanaka 1996:81–88.
26. Seefeldt 2001.
27. Lipstadt 1993; Shermer and Grobman 2000.
28. Bagley 2002:365–67; Trouillot 1995:96.
29. E.g., Walker et al. 2008:xiii–xiv.
30. Faulkner 1951.
31. Trouillot 1995:29; see also Carsten 2007.
32. Sahlins 2004:131–32.
33. Brooks 1962:74.
34. Bagley 2002:146–47.
35. Ibid., 147–51; Brooks 1962:75.
36. Tilly 2006:64–65.
37. Loewen 1999:80.
38. Brooks 1962:xviii.
39. Bagley 2002:13; McNeill 1995; see also Gardner 2007.
40. Goffman 1959, 1967.
41. Collins 2008:432.
42. Bagley 2002:146.
43. Collins 2008:451.
44. Novak 2008:177.
45. Ibid., 179.
46. Tilly 2003:103.
47. Bauman 1989.
48. Hayes 2004.
49. E.g., Houck 2006; Kruse 2010; Schweitzer and Saks 2007.
50. Clark 1962; Crossland 2009:75.
51. Novak 2008; Novak and Kopp 2003.
52. Bagley 2002:374; Brooks 1973; Novak 2008:7.
53. Novak 2008:168.
54. Gill 1994; Scott et al. 1998; Willey and Scott 1991.
55. Novak 2008:162–63.
56. Ibid., 179.

57. On school texts, see Hatch 2004; Hopper et al. 2007. The novel is *Destroying Angel* (Larson 2008).

58. On the press, see, e.g., Christopher Smith, "Mormon Massacre at Mountain Meadows: Forensic Analysis Supports Paiute Tribe's Claim of Passive Role," *Salt Lake Tribune*, Jan. 21, 2001. For debate on texts, see Hatch 2004; Holsted 2007; Shane Johnson, "Read No Evil: Students Aren't Learning the Darker Side of Utah's History. Should They?" *City Weekly*, Salt Lake City, Sept. 25, 2003.

59. Novak 2008:10.

60. Holsted 2007; Novak and Rodseth 2006; quote from Novak 2008:xiv–xv.

61. Jessica Ravitz, "LDS Church Apologizes for Mountain Meadows Massacre," *Salt Lake Tribune*, Sept. 11, 2007.

62. Borneman 1997; Ross 2003.

63. E.g., Robb 2008; Scarry 1985; Sofaer 2006.

Afterword

AMERICAN INDIANS AND THE FORMALITIES OF HISTORY

Joe Watkins

The concept of a "frontier" as a margin of developed or settled country is more often examined from the perspective of the "developed" or "settled" country—that is, from the perspective of those attempting to settle a particular area. Though the "frontier" in America has always been a moving line, the more common perception situates it in the American West or Southwest. The more common period examined by disciplines that depend on chronology—such as history and archaeology—is that of the seventeenth, eighteenth, and nineteenth centuries when expanding European and then American cultures commonly encountered American Indian cultures.

As the European and American empires expanded, American Indians served as constant reminders of the things that needed conquest and taming. Nature required taming, but only when the Indians were conquered, civilized, exterminated, or assimilated could the frontier be "safe" for occupation. Once "civilization" had been established, and the Indians pushed farther and farther into the "wilderness," the frontier advanced again until it reached another "obstacle" that needed removal. This process was repeated time and time again, with generally similar results. American Indians defined the frontier as much by their physical and social presence as reminders of what stood in the way of "progress" as by the distinct cultural entities they represented.

As the beneficiaries of much of the actions on which American history has been based, American Indians have the questionable "honor" of being the fodder of historical research. They have often been presented as not-so-passive hindrances to "manifest destiny" or the last (but hardly least) obstacle to America's rise to greatness as it strove to unify the continent from "sea to shining sea." Perhaps this is an oversimplification of perspective—and I admit to not having recently conducted a survey of many American history textbooks—but Indians do not feel a sense of empowerment knowing when "America" became the "land of the free" but *not* "the home of the (Indian) brave." Because of the manner in which Indians have often been portrayed, many academicians cannot understand why they do not jump at the opportunity to present "their side of the story" when it comes to the history of the western frontier, specifically, and "history" more generally. Why would they not want to be involved in presenting alternative histories to those within mainstream disciplinary texts?

I am not a historian but an archaeologist. I am not even an archaeologist of the historical period but what some have called a "prehistorian," an archaeologist who deals primarily with time periods prior to written records. There is often a considerable period of overlap between the "prehistoric" and "historic" periods, creating a gray area as to which discipline better suits the interpretive process and the needs of academicians.

This essay presents mostly my opinion, drawn from experiences within social science concerning the reluctance of American Indians to be active participants in the discourse of history. It is somewhat circular in that I discuss some of the reasons Indians do not participate in academic discourse when such participation might alleviate some of the issues that feed their hesitancy to participate.

History as Propaganda, History as Nation Building

American history often serves political ends, for it combines accounts and creates a story of the struggle to forge the nation within which we live. It is often told in heroic narrative, as "founding fathers" struggled to throw off the shackles of colonial England while carving civilization out of wilderness.

This trope of history instills in the young American student a national propaganda that emphasizes the best and minimizes the least desirable aspects of that past.

W. E. B. Du Bois, in his essay "The Propaganda of History," writes:

> If . . . we are going to use history for our pleasure and amusement, for inflating our national ego, and giving us a false but pleasurable sense of accomplishment, then we must give up the idea of history as a science or as an art using the results of science, and admit frankly that we are using a version of historic fact in order to influence and educate the new generation along the way we wish.
>
> It is propaganda like this that has led men in the past to insist that history is 'lies agreed upon'; and to point out the danger in such misinformation.[1]

The establishment of a national social identity through promotion of a shared history is one of the most important means by which a nation-state enlists the loyal support of its citizens. But it is extremely difficult for American Indians to embrace a "shared history" that is neither shared nor their history. What good is a history that alienates while supposedly trying to build? Must the building blocks of that nation be formed from the living tissue of descendants of the "losers," people who are continually taught about their "failure"? Adobe Walls is an appropriately ironic example, because, as Cruse notes (this volume), the "attack on the Adobe Walls compound . . . was the primary catalyst that prompted the U.S. Army to wage all-out war against the southern Plains tribes," even though the twenty-eight non-Indian defendants held off more than two hundred Comanche, Kiowa, and Cheyenne warriors. What might have happened had the Indians won is anybody's guess, but the results would probably still have been no less catastrophic to the long-term history of Indian cultures of the southern plains.

Whose History Is It? Whose History Should Be Taught?

The nonobjective nature of "history" of non-European cultures has been presented by various authors, and yet authors continue to question whose history is "right" as well as whose is "valid."[2] In *Telling the Truth about History*, the authors argue that "a comprehensive national history is not now an educational option for the country; it is a cultural imperative."[3] But how comprehensive can such histories actually be? As reviewer Bonnie Smith notes, the authors of *Telling the Truth about History* recognize that historians "now engage in and produce a democratic version of history that includes minorities, underclasses, and women, while the more or less totalitarian kind of objectivity adhered to by professional historians of other generations recedes."[4] And yet the question still persists: whose history should be taught?

James Wilson writes about the problems involved in trying to integrate American Indian oral traditions into a written historical narrative: "It is often very difficult to interpret the surviving oral tradition: the written English version of a story not only translates it into another language but also transposes it from the cultural context in which it was originally told." Such interpretation may be necessary in order to "document" the events described by the speaker (such as the oral traditions by the Indian victors at the Battle of the Little Bighorn). "But, even with these limitations," Wilson continues, "it still tells us unmistakably that we are in touch with a world very different from Euro-America's: a world in which Indians are the central characters, rather than simply bit players; in which the importance of their history lies in its significance to *them* rather than for us; and in which the very concepts of history itself is [sic] radically at odds with Western assumptions and beliefs."[5]

It is this shift in perspective from that of an outsider to that of a central character that would be welcome within reflexive histories created by American Indians. Lakota chief Gall's story of the Battle of Greasy Grass has a more powerful meaning for Indian victors of the Battle of the Little Bighorn than an army-oriented presentation of "Custer's Last Stand." Why then, shouldn't American Indians want to participate in telling that story to a wider and more supportive audience?

Perhaps one of the reasons American Indians do not participate more fully in the academic discourses that revolve around history is that there are few who need, or have the time, to pursue academic validation of their histories. "History" is important to them, but it is not so important that other people accept the "truth" of that history as it is that other people accept its "validity." Perhaps, as well, some American Indians are hesitant to speak out from fear that they will be thought to be "the" expert on tribal histories or deemed to speak for the entire group, something they may not be culturally allowed to do.

In May 2005 the Washington State Legislature passed House Bill 1495 encouraging school districts to develop a history and culture curriculum that would include information on the culture, history, and government of the nearest federally recognized tribes in the required Washington state history and government courses. Although this move would likely be welcomed by all involved, it creates a question not only of inclusion but also of segregation. How does one integrate competitive histories of two cultures in such a way that neither culture is seen as the loser or the winner in a situation where clearly the actual winner maintains social, economic, and political control? Can such local histories compete with standardized texts that create an encyclopedic presentation of continental American history, or do they become merely anecdotal whispers of historic also-rans? It remains to be seen whether such a program will contribute to the involvement of American Indians in the discipline, or whether it will create an uneasy truce between cultures whose concepts and uses of history diverge. In addition, there arises another issue: whose version of the history should be used—the version crafted by the academician or that held within oral traditions?

Enter Archaeology

Archaeology is as concerned about inclusivity of American Indian oral histories and tradition as history is, it is just that the time range archaeology investigates is perhaps deeper and the "documents" less defined. The conflict between the historical record and oral history is as strong within archaeology as it is within history, even though archaeology does not rely as strongly on the written record.

Ronald Mason examines some of the conflicts between the use and utility of Indian oral history within the practice of "scientific archaeology." He considers *oral history* "the memories and recollections of the individuals who experienced or witnessed in their own lives the event they relate" and defines *oral tradition* as information "believed by their narrators to be more less faithful renderings of the older happenings to which they refer."[6] Some might equate oral history to an "eyewitness account" while relegating oral tradition to that of "hearsay." Some American Indians dismiss the utility of archaeology, and some archaeologists dismiss the utility of Indian oral histories and traditions, but each can serve as a complement to the other when applied in a consistent manner and when the limitations of each are recognized.

The participants in this volume have used archaeology to supplement and elucidate the historical record. As Gorenfeld notes, "Historians must view the mass of material they gather in connection with a particular event with a degree of suspicion and with a willingness to embrace archaeological evidence, especially when it calls into question the written and oral record." This caveat is one that is justly appropriate for the archaeology of the historic period as well as the archaeology of the frontier.

Two other chapters raise important points for consideration: Kelman details Chivington defending his actions at Sand Creek by making "the native people killed at Sand Creek enemies not just of whites in Colorado Territory but of the Union more broadly, the bloodshed not just a triumph in the Indian Wars but of the Civil War." In a more general description of ways that one culture can create a situation where conflict becomes easier to justify, Leonard writes, "Aggressors first dehumanize and demonize opponents by creating an image of them as the Other." Both of these methods were used in a general campaign against Indians on the frontier and are appropriate for the discussion of the impacts on the Cheyennes and Arapahos of Colorado, the Jicarillas of Cieneguilla, as well as the Arkansas Company at Mountain Meadows, even though the victims at Mountain Meadows were not Indian. These thoughts speak to the universality of war, hate, and distrust and contribute to the not-so-modern idea of "massacres" and perhaps the role that written history has often played in campaigns to downplay the treatment of the American Indian on the American frontier.

Battles and Massacres

The authors of this volume provide discussion of four historic events that had varying degrees of impact on the local Indian groups.

AFTERWORD

The Battle of Cieneguilla, little known to most Americans, occurred in 1854, only six and a half years after the acquisition of New Mexico Territory under the Treaty of Guadalupe Hidalgo. It is highly unlikely that the dragoons involved in the battle actually *knew* their opponents other than as a general menace to the continued Americanization of the area. But, as with other aspects of the general American response to its "Indian problem," perhaps it seemed necessary to equate "military action" with "military might." The deep context of the conflict—the withholding of food from the Jicarillas by the commissioner of Indian affairs—is lightly mentioned even though it was likely the underlying cause of the events that led to the battle.

The results of the battle are perhaps less memorable than the resultant court of inquiry over the actions of Lieutenant Davidson. Gorenfeld discusses the issues associated with the cavalry style of war as well as the implications of the Jicarilla victory at Cieneguilla: "One by one the scattered Jicarilla bands surrendered, dispossessed of their land and impoverished to starvation," leading to their exile to the Mescalero Apache Reservation in southeastern New Mexico.

In Johnson's essay the Jicarillas are presented as the tactical experts in a terrain suited to their style of warfare. Though both Gorenfeld and Johnson recognize and draw attention to the blunders of Lieutenant Davidson, Johnson fleshes out the role of the Indians in the battle, whereas Gorenfeld presents the long-term effects of the battle on the tribe. In this regard, as the Indians are moved more toward center stage in the recounting of the history of the battle, it is easier to give acknowledgment to the Indian victors than to make excuses for the cavalry's missteps.

The Battle of Adobe Walls is much better known by the general populace, although still not to the extent of other battles in the West. As noted by Cruse, Adobe Walls created a convenient excuse for the U.S. Army to wage a punitive war on *all* the Indians of the southern Great Plains and not merely the individual Comanche, Kiowa, and Cheyenne participants. It provided a starting point from which the U.S. Army launched its Indian Campaign of 1874 and rolled over the Indians of the southern Great Plains. Cruse's essay provides a discussion of the general background of the battle, and he uses archaeological methods on the battlefield to gather insights into the locations of the protagonists and the weapons each group used. But although this is a generally objective recounting of the events at Adobe Walls, something many people *expect* history to be, its conclusions about the poor state of the armament of the Indians offer reason to pause concerning the army's overzealous reactions.

Baker offers the social and chronological setting for the battle and even offers an Indian perspective of the "defenders" as intruders and the Indian attackers as "warriors who lost their lives trying to rid the plains of the detested buffalo hunters." He recounts as much the method he used for garnering the story as the story itself, but the inclusion of Indian perspectives (e.g., that of Comanche Frank Yellow Fish) is welcome indeed. Additionally, as Baker notes, the fact that some of the Indian participants returned to Adobe Walls in commemoration adds an emotional element that seems to demonstrate that, at least to these individuals, the connection to the past is still strong.

But the battle at Adobe Walls is but a small part of relationships that existed between the settlers/intruders of the West and the Indian populations impacted by them. Jacki Thompson Rand, in her book *Kiowa Humanity and the Invasion of the State*, calls attention to the effects of U.S. colonialism as evidenced by U.S. Indian policy and the disruptions it created among the institutions that had served tribal groups well before contact. Though writing specifically about the Kiowas, Rand describes armed resistance by the Indians and U.S. responses, often hyperbolic in reaction—a story shared by most other American Indian tribes on the southern Great Plains at this time, including Comanches and Cheyennes.[7]

The discussions of the Sand Creek massacre certainly are weakened by the lack of an Indian (Cheyenne and Arapaho) voice, resulting in the very situation suggested here—a missed opportunity to deepen our understanding of historical and emotional ties to the past. The authors who wrote on Sand Creek present two perspectives that illuminate different aspects of the event, with Kelman providing a more in-depth discussion of the social and cultural milieu within which the event happened. Scott's piece establishes the geographic milieu of the event by utilizing archaeologically derived data to better place the various participants within the landscape but also offers a detailed discussion of whether the event was indeed a "massacre" or a "battle." These two essays complement each other and offer a well-reasoned background for the events that led up to and culminated in the attack on the Cheyenne and Arapaho village. The deeper context of the event is described by Kelman as he offers glimpses into the state of mind with which the Colorado Volunteers carried out the massacre as well as the general culture within which they operated. Scott's discussion of the event in relation to the rules of war that existed during that time further supports the label "massacre" to the actions of the Colorado militia at that site.

These essays are well written, and, as Scott notes, the area continues to reverberate with sacredness for the descendants of the Indians who fought and died there, especially as it "embodies disenfranchisement and the loss of life they suffered because of U.S. government policy toward them in the nineteenth century." In this regard, the massacre reflects an ethos similar to that of the Adobe Walls battle, but its interpretation lacks the color and depth that could be afforded by comments and stories of those whose ancestors were "vanquished."

Finally, in the discussions of the Mountain Meadows massacre, American Indians are represented in another role within the western historical drama. Though the Paiutes were originally blamed in entirety for the action, their complicity as coconspirators with the local Mormon populace marks them as somewhat different actors in this event. Perhaps some Paiutes took part in running off the livestock of the emigrant wagon camp, and perhaps some took part in ambushing and killing the emigrants themselves, but we have no idea what truly drove them to participate beyond a promise of some of the spoils. Leonard likens the relationship of the federal government to the Mormons with that of the United States toward the Indians—relocation, expulsion, and discrimination—and it was this distrust of the federal government that sent reverberations through Utah that contributed to the massacre.

Rodseth and Novak do not stop at the facts of the Mountain Meadows massacre as they are known but instead delve into the social context as well as the scientific evidence to help tell the story. In this instance, Mountain Meadows certainly lives up to the full meaning of the term "massacre." As they note, the events at Mountain Meadow were as if "only one army takes the field and the civilian targets are hardly aware of the war." As I have noted elsewhere, words bring with them an implied judgment already made.[8] By making particular word choices, we as researchers can color anyone's perception of reality, a point shared by Rodseth and Novak: "Even the term 'massacre' tends to misrepresent what happened at Mountain Meadows, as it conjures up one or another clichéd scenario that turns out to be entirely inappropriate to the case.... Thus, the 'Indian massacre' is the default scenario that tends to swallow up the case of Mountain Meadows, even if one has never heard the traditional (i.e., white, Mormon, Utah-based) accounts of American Indian involvement in the crime."

Conclusions

The above discussion does not imply that American Indians are not interested in the historical fabrics that have created the nation within which we now live. Indians carry with them segregated and integrated histories of their "genetic" nations (e.g., Choctaw histories, Comanche histories, Navajo histories) as well as that of the political nations within which they exist. These histories intersect in many different places and diverge as often, and yet each history carries with it the truth of the group that holds it dear.

John Powers notes, "History is not static; it changes in accordance with shifting perceptions and changing needs." Additionally, as anthropologist Peter Whiteley writes, "All accounts of the past . . . involve politics, and this may be the most difficult stumbling block against intercultural consensus."[9] These points, taken in conjunction, might be a call to the discipline to heed: American Indians need the discipline to change with the shifting perceptions and changing needs of those about whom the history is written—not from a postmodernist perspective that equalizes all perceptions rather than weaving "facts," chronology, and interpretation into a logical and defendable fabric, but from a perspective that recognizes the needs to which such information can be put as a tool for gaining better understanding about the *politics* of the events and issues of the past that continue to shape our present and our future.

But, as Leonard notes in this volume, perspectives on "history" are changing:

For a generation and more, the story of the westward movement celebrated the conquest of Indian homelands. . . . Euro-American outsiders . . . owned the story and told it their way.

More recently, new voices have offered alternate versions of the story. Today's restatements of the past acknowledge the views of the neglected victims—among them American Indians, Hispanic Americans, women, Mormons, and the environment. The 'New Western History' acknowledges the damage done in both the doing of the deed and the telling of the story.

American Indian tribal members were invited to participate in the conference that led to this volume, but they did not do so. I am unsure why they chose not to, but I cannot help but wonder at what might have been said had they chosen to do so. The "old" western history is built largely on the successful ability of the winners to write the textbooks; in other instances it is built on the silences of the losers. Occasionally, even the best-intended actions of those involved create issues that seem to reinforce the resultant disconnect between both sets of participants.

Scott writes in this volume that "the Indian village that was attacked by Chivington's troops on November 29, 1864, is identified as the one found during the professional archaeological investigations in 1999." Twenty years earlier, however, as a result of the actions of Cheyenne Arrow Keeper Red Hat, the "Cheyennes' determination of where the village stood and the massacre began" was the South Bend of Sand Creek. Though the location described by Scott might be more "scientifically correct," the other location remains "of transcendent significance" to the Cheyenne.[10]

This volume and the larger discipline of history would have benefited greatly by a series of American Indian voices outside of those whose words were recorded during the original events; perhaps soon those voices will respond and strengthen the stories presented here.

NOTES

1. Du Bois 2007 [1935]:584–85.
2. See Brown 1971, and Loewen 1996, regarding American Indian histories; Clark et al. 2004 for women in history; and Davis 2005 for more general relationships regarding alternative histories.

3. Appleby et al. 1994:295.
4. Smith 1995:661.
5. Wilson 1998:xxviii.
6. Mason 2000:240.
7. Rand 2008.
8. Watkins 2006:105.
9. Powers 2004:155; Whiteley 2002:408.
10. Greene and Scott 2004:115.

References

Abel, Annie Heloise. 1916. The Journal of John Greiner. *Old Santa Fe* 3(11): 202.

Adams, Christopher D., David M. Johnson, and Diane E. White. 1998. *Research Design for the Investigation at a Mescalero/Cavalry Battle Site*. Lincoln National Forest Cultural Resource Report 1998-08-043. Alamogordo, N.Mex.

Adams, Christopher D., Diane E. White, and David M. Johnson. 2000a. *Last Chance Canyon Apache/Cavalry Battle Site, Lincoln National Forest, New Mexico*. Albuquerque: U.S. Department of Agriculture, Forest Service.

———. 2000b. *Dark Canyon Apache Rancheria Battle Site*. Albuquerque: U.S. Department of Agriculture, Forest Service.

Aldrich, Virgil C. 1955. Mr. Quine on Meaning, Naming, and Purporting to Name. *Philosophical Studies: An International Journal for Philosophy in the Analytic Tradition* 6:17–26.

Alexander, Thomas G. 2003. *Utah: The Right Place*, rev. ed.. Salt Lake City: Gibbs Smith.

———. 2006. *Brigham Young, the Quorum of the Twelve, and the Latter-day Saint Investigation of the Mountain Meadows Massacre*. Leonard J. Arrington Mormon History Lecture Series 12, Sept. 21, 2006. Logan: Special Collections and Archives, Merrill Library, Utah State University; distributed by Utah State University Press.

Altshuler, Constance W. 1991. *Cavalry Yellow and Infantry Blue: Army Officers in Arizona between 1851 and 1886*. Tucson: Arizona Historical Society.

Appleby, Joyce O., Lynn A. Hunt, and Margaret Jacob. 1994. *Telling the Truth about History*. New York: W. W. Norton.

Bagley, Will. 2002. *Blood of the Prophets: Brigham Young and the Massacre at Mountain Meadows*. Norman: University of Oklahoma Press.

Bagley, Will, and David L. Bigler, eds. 2008. *Innocent Blood: Essential Narratives of the Mountain Meadows Massacre*. Norman: University of Oklahoma Press.

Baker, Shane A., Richard K. Talbot, and Lane D. Richens. 2003. *Archaeological Remote Sensing Studies and Emergency Data Recovery at 42WS2504, Washington County, Utah*. Brigham Young University Museum of Peoples and Cultures Technical Series 03-8. Provo, Utah: Office of Public Archaeology.

Baker, T. Lindsay. 1987. Beaver to Buffalo Robes: Transition in the Fur Trade. *Museum of the Fur Trade Quarterly* 23(1): 1–8 and (2): 4–13.

Baker, T. Lindsay, and Billy R. Harrison. 1986. *Adobe Walls: The History and Archeology of the 1874 Trading Post*. College Station: Texas A&M University Press.

Ball, L. Durwood. 2001. *Army Regulars on the Western Frontier, 1846–1861*. Norman: University of Oklahoma Press.

Bancroft, Hubert Howe. 1889. *History of Utah, 1540–1886*. San Francisco: History Co.

Barbero, Alessandro. 2003. *The Battle: A New History of Waterloo*. New York: Walker and Co.

Barr, Juliana. 2011. Geographies of Power: Mapping Indian Borders in the "Borderlands" of the Early Southwest. *William and Mary Quarterly* 68:5–46.

Barzun, Jacques, and Henry F. Graff. 1957. *The Modern Researcher*. New York: Harcourt, Brace and World.

Bauman, Zygmunt. 1989. *Modernity and the Holocaust*. Ithaca, N.Y.: Cornell University Press.

Baumeister, Roy F. 1997. *Evil: Inside Human Cruelty and Violence*. New York: W. H. Freeman.

Beadle, J. H. 1878. *Western Wilds, and the Men Who Redeem Them*. Cincinnati: Johns Brothers.

Bennett, James A. 1996. *Forts and Forays*. Ed. Clinton Brooks and Frank Reeve. Albuquerque: University of New Mexico Press.

Bent, George, and George Hyde, eds. 1905–1906. Forty Years with the Cheyennes. *The Frontier: A Magazine of the West* 4, October–March.

Berthrong, Donald J. 1979. Legacies of the Dawes Act: Bureaucrats and Land Thieves at the Cheyenne-Arapaho Agencies of Oklahoma. *Arizona and the West*. 21:335–54.

Bigler, David L. 1998. *Forgotten Kingdom: The Mormon Theocracy in the American West, 1847–1896*. Spokane, Wash.: Arthur H. Clark.

———. 2008. "A Lion in the Path": Genesis of the Utah War, 1857–1858. *Utah Historical Quarterly* 76:4–21.

Billington, Ray Allen, with James Blaine Hedges. 1949. *Westward Expansion: A History of the American Frontier*. New York: Macmillan.

Birtle, Andrew J. 2003. Army Counterinsurgency and Contingency Operations Doctrine, 1860–1941. Center of Military History, U.S. Army, Washington, D.C.

Bishop, William W., ed. 1877. *Mormonism Unveiled; or The Life and Confessions of the Late Mormon Bishop, John D. Lee: (Written by Himself)*. St. Louis: Bryan, Brand.

Blight, David. 2001. *Race and Reunion: The Civil War in American Memory*. Cambridge, Mass.: Harvard University Press.

———. 2011. *American Oracle: The Civil War in the Civil Rights Era*. Cambridge, Mass.: Belknap Press of Harvard University Press.

Bloch, Marc. 1953. *The Historian's Craft*. Trans. Peter Putnam. New York: Alfred A. Knopf.

Bloom, Harold. 1992. *The American Religion: The Emergence of the Post-Christian Nation*. New York: Simon and Schuster.

Bode, Emil, A. 1994. *A Dose of Frontier Soldiering: The Memoirs of Corporal E. A. Bode, Frontier Regular Infantry, 1877–1882*. Ed. Thomas T. Smith. Lincoln: University of Nebraska Press.

Bodnar, John. 2010. *The Good War in American Memory*. Baltimore: Johns Hopkins University Press.

Borneman, John. 1997. *Settling Accounts: Violence, Justice, and Accountability in Postsocialist Europe*. Princeton: Princeton University Press.

Bourdieu, Pierre. 1989. Social Space and Symbolic Power. *Sociological Theory* 7:14–25.

Boyer, Jack K. 1965. Battle of Cieneguilla. Paper presented to the Taos Historical Society, Taos, N.Mex.

Brackett, Albert G. 1965. *History of the United States Cavalry, from the Formation of the Federal Government to the 1st of June 1863*. New York: Argonaut Press.

Brooks, Juanita. 1962. *The Mountain Meadows Massacre*. Norman: University of Oklahoma Press.

———. 1973. *On the Ragged Edge: The Life and Times of Dudley Leavitt*. Salt Lake City: Utah State Historical Society.

———. 1991. *The Mountain Meadows Massacre*. 2nd ed., rev. Norman: University of Oklahoma Press.

Brown, Dee. 1971. *Bury My Heart at Wounded Knee: An Indian History of the American West*. New York: Holt, Rinehard and Winston.

Brown, Richard Maxwell. 1975. *Strain of Violence: Historical Studies of American Violence and Vigilantism*. New York: Oxford University Press.

Browning, Christopher R. 1992. *Ordinary Men: Reserve Police Battalion 101 and the Final Solution in Poland*. New York: Harper Collins.

Byers, John R., Jr. 1969. Helen Hunt Jackson (1830–1885). *American Literary Realism* 2:143–48.

———. 1975–76. The Indian Matter of Helen Hunt Jackson's "Ramona": From Fact to Fiction. *American Indian Quarterly* 2:331–46.

Carleton, James Henry. 1860. *Report on the Subject of the Massacre at the Mountain Meadows, in Utah Territory, in September, 1857, of One Hundred and Twenty Men, Women and Children, Who Were from Arkansas*. Little Rock, Ark.: True Democrat Steam Press.

———. 1995 [1859]. *Special Report of the Mountain Meadows Massacre*. Spokane, Wash.: Arthur H. Clark.

Carpenter, Helen. 1980. A Trip across the Plains, in an Ox Wagon, 1857. In *Ho for California! Women's Overland Diaries from the Huntington Library*, ed. Sandra L. Myres, 165–69. San Marino, Calif.: Huntington Library.

Carroll, John M., ed. 1985. *Sand Creek Massacre: A Documentary History, 1865–1867.* New York: Amereon Limited.

Carson, Christopher. 1966. *Kit Carson's Autobiography.* Ed. Milo Quaife. Lincoln: University of Nebraska Press.

Carsten, Janet, ed. 2007. *Ghosts of Memory: Essays on Remembrance and Relatedness.* Malden, Mass.: Blackwell.

Cates, Nancy Huff. 1875. Letter. In "The Mountain Meadow Massacre: Statement of One of the Few Survivors." *Daily Arkansas Gazette*, Sept. 1.

Chalfant, William Y. 1989. *Cheyenne and Horse Soldiers: The 1857 Expedition and the Battle of Solomon's Fork.* Norman: University of Oklahoma Press.

Christy, Howard A. 1979. The Walker War: Defense and Conciliation as Strategy. *Utah Historical Quarterly* 47(5): 395–420.

Clark, Arthur C. 1962. *Profiles of the Future.* New York: Harper and Row.

Clark, Roger, Jeffrey Allard, and Timothy Mahoney. 2004. How Much of the Sky? Women in American High School History Textbooks from the 1960s, 1980s, and 1990s. *Social Education* 68:57–62.

Collins, Randall C. 2008. *Violence: A Micro-Sociological Theory.* Princeton, N.J.: Princeton University Press.

Connor, Melissa A. 2005. Landscapes of Conflict. Ph.D. dissertation, Department of Geography, University of Nebraska, Lincoln.

Cooley, Everett L. 1958. Carpetbag Rule: Territorial Government in Utah. *Utah Historical Quarterly* 26:107–28.

———, ed. 1980. *Diary of Brigham Young, 1857.* Salt Lake City: Tanner Trust Fund/ University of Utah Library.

Coupland, R. M., and D. R. Meddings. 1999. Mortality Associated with Use of Weapons in Armed Conflicts, Wartime Atrocities and Civilian Mass Shootings: Literature Review. *British Medical Journal* 319:407–410.

Cox-Paul, Lori. 2008. John M. Chivington The "Reverend Colonel", "Marry Your Daughter", "Sand Creek Massacre." *Nebraska History* 88:126–37, 142–45.

Coyle, Clarence C. 1911. Stories of Quanah Parker. *Texas Magazine* 4(5): 64–66.

Crane, R. C. 1925. The Settlement in 1874-5 of Indian Troubles in West Texas. *West Texas Historical Association Year Book* 1:3–14.

Crimmins, M. L. 1947. General Nelson A. Miles in Texas. *West Texas Historical Association Year Book* 23:36–45.

Crossland, Zoë. 2009. Of Clues and Signs: The Dead Body and Its Evidential Traces. *American Anthropologist* 111(1): 69–80.

Cruse, J. Brett. 2008. *Battles of the Red River War: Archeological Perspectives on the Indian Campaign of 1874.* College Station: Texas A&M University Press.

Cullum, George W. 1850. *Register of the Officers and Graduates of the U.S. Military Academy at West Point.* New York: J. F. Trow.

———. 1858. *Register of the Officers and Graduates of the U.S. Military Academy at West Point.* 2 vols. New York: D. Van Nostrand.

Davidson, Homer K. 1974. *Blackjack Davidson: A Cavalry Commander on the Western Frontier.* Glendale, Calif.: Arthur H. Clark.
Davis, Matu B. 1996. *Native America in the Twentieth Century.* New York: Garland.
Davis, M. Elaine. 2005. *How Students Understand the Past: From Theory to Practice.* Walnut Creek, Calif.: AltaMira Press.
Davis, W. W. H. 1982. *El Gringo, New Mexico and Her People.* Reprinted. Lincoln: University of Nebraska Press.
Denton, Sally. 2003. *American Massacre: The Tragedy at Mountain Meadows, September 11, 1857.* New York: Alfred A. Knopf.
Dixon, Billy D. 1902. A Story of Adobe Walls When Indians and Buffaloes Roamed in Texas. *Denver (Colo.) Times*, June 9.
Dixon, Olive K. 1914. *Life and Adventures of "Billy" Dixon of Adobe Walls, Texas Panhandle.* Ed. Frederick S. Barde. Guthrie, Okla.: Co-Operative Publishing.
Du Bois, W. E. B. 2007 [1935]. The Propaganda of History. In *Black Reconstruction in America*, 582–97. New York: Oxford W. E. B. Du Bois Reader Press.
Dunlay, Tom W. 2000. *Kit Carson and the Indians.* Lincoln: University of Nebraska Press.
Dunn, William R. 1985. *"I Stand by Sand Creek": A Defense of Colonel John M. Chivington and the Third Colorado Calvary.* Fort Collins, Colo.: Old Army Press.
Eiselt, B. Sunday. 2005. Letter Report Concerning the Results of Morphological Analysis and Instrumental Neutron Activation Analysis of 15 Cimarron Micaceous Sherds from the Cieneguilla Battle Site. Unpublished manuscript on file, Carson National Forest, Taos, N.Mex.
Eisley, Loren. 1973. The Leaf Pile. In *The Innocent Assassins.* New York: Charles Scribner's Sons.
Essig, Mark Regan. 2000. Science and Sensation: Poison Murder and Forensic Medicine in Nineteenth-Century America. Ph.D. dissertation, Cornell University.
Evans, Rebecca Dunlap. 1897. Mountain Meadows Massacre . . . Related by One of the Survivors. *Fort Smith Elevator*, August 20, 2:1–3.
Faller, Lincoln. 2000. Making Medicine against "White Man's Side of Story." *American Indian Quarterly* 24:64–90.
Farmer, Jared. 2008. *Mormons, Indians, and the American Landscape.* Cambridge, Mass.: Harvard University Press.
Faulkner, William. 1951. *Requiem for a Nun.* New York: Random House.
Felstiner, William L., Richard L.Abel, and Austin Sarat. 1980–81. The Emergence and Transformation of Disputes: Naming, Blaming, Claiming. *Law and Society Review* 15:631–54.
Fischer, David Hackett. 1970. *Historians' Fallacies: Toward a Logic of Historical Thought.* New York: Harper and Row.
Foster, Gaines M. 1988. *Ghosts of the Confederacy: Defeat, the Lost Cause and the Emergence of the New South, 1865–1913.* Oxford: Oxford University Press.
Fox, Robert A. 1993. *Archaeology, History, and Custer's Last Battle: The Little Big Horn Reexamined.* Norman: University of Oklahoma Press.

Frazer, Robert W. 1963. *Mansfield on the Condition of the Western Forts, 1853–54.* Norman: University of Oklahoma Press.

———, ed. 1968. Colonel George Archibald McCall. *New Mexico in 1850: A Military View.* Norman: University of Oklahoma Press.

———. 1980. The Battle of Cieneguilla. *La Cronica de Nueva Mexico* 9 (Mar.).

Furniss, Norman. 1960. *The Mormon Conflict, 1850–1859.* New Haven, N.J.: Yale University Press.

Garavaglia, Louis, and Charles Worman. 1998. *Firearms of the American West, 1803–1865.* Niwot: University of Colorado Press.

Gardner, Andrew. 2007. *An Archaeology of Identity: Soldiers and Society in Late Roman Britain.* Walnut Creek, Calif.: Left Coast Press.

Gengenbach, Heidi. 2000. Naming the Past in a "Scattered" Land: Memory and the Powers of Women's Naming Practices in Southern Mozambique. *International Journal of African Historical Studies* 33:523–42.

Gibbon, John. 1970 [1860]. *The Artillerist Manual, Compiled from Various Sources and Adapted to the Service of the United States.* Glendale, N.Y.: Benchmark.

Gilje, Paul. 1996. *Rioting in America.* Bloomington: Indiana University Press.

Gill, George W. 1994. Skeletal Injuries of Pioneers. In *Skeletal Biology in the Great Plains: Migration, Warfare, Health, and Subsistence,* ed. Douglas W. Owsley and Richard L. Jantz, 159–72. Washington, D.C.: Smithsonian Institution Press.

Goddard, Pliny Earle. 1911. *Jicarilla Apache Texts.* Anthropological Papers of the American Museum of National History, Vol. 3. New York.

Goffman, Erving. 1959. *The Presentation of Self in Everyday Life.* New York: Doubleday.

———. 1967. *Interaction Ritual: Essays in Face-to-Face Behavior.* Chicago: Aldine.

———. 1974. *Frame Analysis: An Essay on the Organization of Experience.* Cambridge: Harvard University Press.

Gonzalez, John M. 2004. The Warp of Whiteness: Domesticity and Empire in Helen Hunt Jackson's "Ramona." *American Literary History* 16:437–65.

Goodin, Robert E., and Charles Tilly, eds. 2006. *The Oxford Handbook of Contextual Political Analysis.* New York: Oxford University Press.

Gorenfeld, Will, and John Gorenfeld. 1998. The Springfield Musketoon: The Gun That Almost Lost the West. *Wild West,* June.

Greene, Jerome A. 2000. Report on the Historical Documentation of the Location and Extent of the Sand Creek Massacre Site. In Sand Creek Massacre Site Location Study, Intermountain Regional Office, National Park Service, Denver.

Greene, Jerome A., and Douglas D. Scott. 2004. *Finding Sand Creek: History, Archaeology, and the 1864 Massacre Site.* Norman: University of Oklahoma Press.

Greenhaw, Clyde R. 1938. Survivor of a Massacre: Mrs. Betty Terry of Harrison Vividly Recalls Massacre of Westbound Arkansas Caravan in Utah More Than 80 Years Ago. *Arkansas Gazette,* Sept. 4, Sunday mag., 6.

Gregory, Tony, and Andrew J. G. Rogerson. 1984. Metal Detecting in Archaeological Excavation. *Antiquity* 58:179–84.

Grinnell, George Bird. 1955 [1915]. *The Fighting Cheyennes*. Norman: University of Oklahoma Press.
———. 1972 [1923]. *The Cheyenne Indians*, Vol. 1: *History and Society*; Vol 2: *War, Ceremonies, and Religion*. Lincoln: University of Nebraska Press.
Haecker, Charles, M. 1998. *Archaeological Remote Sensing Survey of the Civil War Site of Camp Lewis, Pecos National Historic Park, San Miguel, New Mexico*. Cultural Anthropology Projects PECO-01. Intermountain Support Office, National Park Service, Santa Fe, N.Mex.
Haecker, Charles M., and Jeffery G. Mauck. 1997. *On the Prairie of Palo Alto*. College Station: Texas A&M University Press.
Halaas, David F., and Andrew E. Masich. 2005. *Halfbreed: The Remarkable True Story of George Bent, Caught between the Worlds of the Indian and the White Man*. New York: De Capo Press.
Haley, James L. 1976. *The Buffalo War: The History of the Red River Indian Uprising of 1874*. New York: Doubleday.
Hanson, David. 2001. *Carnage and Culture: Landmark Battles in the Rise of Western Power*. New York: Doubleday.
Harrison, Simon. 2004. Forgetful and Memorious Landscapes. *Social Anthropology* 12(2): 135–51.
Hatch, Mallorie A. 2004. Finding a Voice after Violence: Portrayals of the Mountain Meadows Massacre in Utah History Textbooks. Honors thesis, Department of Anthropology, University of Utah.
Hawk, Charles C. 2005. The Battle of Cieneguilla: Historical Clues to Questions about the Battle. Taos County Historical Society. Unpublished manuscript on file, Carson National Forest, Taos, N.Mex.
Hayes, Jonathan. 2004. "Exquisite Corpses." *New York* magazine, September 27.
Heitman, Francis B. 1903. *Historical Register and Dictionary of the U.S. Army from Its Organization, September 20, 1789, to March 2, 1903*. 2 vols. Washington, D.C.: Government Printing Office.
Hendricks, Rick, and John P. Wilson. 1996. *The Navajos in 1705, Roque Madrid's Campaign Journal*. Albuquerque: University of New Mexico Press.
Herr, John K. 1953. *The Story of the U.S. Cavalry*. Boston: Little, Brown.
Higbee, John M. 1962 [1894]. Appendix 2. In *The Mountain Meadows Massacre*, by Juanita Brooks, 226–35. Norman: University of Oklahoma Press.
Hine, Robert V., and John Mack Faragher. 2000. *The American West: A New Interpretive History*. New Haven, Conn.: Yale University Press.
Hirsch, Eric, and Michael O'Hanlon, eds. 1995. *The Anthropology of Landscape: Perspectives on Place and Space*. Oxford: Clarendon Press.
Hobsbawm, Eric, and Terence Ranger, eds. 1992. *The Invention of Tradition*. Cambridge: Cambridge University Press.
Hoig, Stan. 1961. *The Sand Creek Massacre*. Norman: University of Oklahoma Press.
Holsted, David. 2007. Woman Set to Rewrite Local History. *Harrison (Ark.) Daily Times*, Sept. 27.

Hopper, Shay E., T. Harri Baker, and Jane Browning. 2007. *An Arkansas History for Young People*, 4th ed. Fayetteville: University of Arkansas Press.

Horgan, Paul. 1954. *Great River.* 2 vols. New York: Rinehart.

Houck, Max M. 2006. CSI: The Reality. *Scientific American* 295:85–89.

Hoxie, Frederick. 2001 [1984]. *A Final Promise: The Campaign to Assimilate the Indians, 1880–1920*. Lincoln: University of Nebraska Press.

Hunt, Aurora. 1958. *Major General James Henry Carleton, 1814–1873: Western Frontier Dragoon*. Glendale, Calif.: Arthur H. Clark.

Hyde, George E. 1968. *The Life of George Bent, Written from His Letters.* Ed. Savoie Lottinville. Norman: University of Oklahoma Press.

Jackson, Helen Hunt. 1881. *Century of Dishonor: A Sketch of the United States Government's Dealings with Some of the Indian Tribes.* New York: Harper and Brothers.

Jennings, Warren A. 1962. Zion Is Fled: The Expulsion of the Mormons from Jackson County, Missouri. Ph.D. dissertation, University of Florida.

Johnson, David M. 2003. A Preliminary Report on the Battle of Cieneguilla: A Jicarilla Apache Victory against the U.S. Dragoons, Carson National Forest, Taos County, New Mexico. Paper presented at the Apache Archaeology Conference May 15–17, 2003, Carlsbad, N.Mex.

———. 2009. Apache Victory against the U.S. Dragoons, the Battle of Cieneguilla, New Mexico. In *Fields of Conflict: Battlefield Archaeology from the Roman Empire to the Korean War*, ed. Douglas Scott, Lawrence Babits, and Charles Haecker. Dulles, Va.: Potomac Books.

Johnson, David M., and Chris Adams. 2005. The Battle of Cieneguilla: A Jicarilla Apache Victory over the United States Dragoons near Taos, New Mexico, March 30, 1854. Report submitted to the National Park Service, American Battlefield Protection Program, Washington, D.C.

Johnson, David M., Chris Adams, Charles Hawk, and Skip Keith Miller. 2009. *A Jicarilla Apache Victory over the U.S. Dragoons at Cieneguilla, New Mexico, March 30, 1854*. U.S. Department of Agriculture, Forest Service, Southwestern Region, Research Report 20, Albuquerque, N.Mex.

Johnson, David M., Chris Adams, Larry Ludwig, and Charles Hawk. In press. Taos, the Jicarilla Apache, and the Battle of Cieneguilla. In *Voices of Taos: A Topical History*, Albuquerque: University of New Mexico Press.

Johnson, David M., Chris Adams, and Diane White. 2002. A Research Design for the Investigation of the Battle of Cieneguilla between the Second Dragoons and the Jicarilla Apache on March 29, 1854. Unpublished manuscript. Carson National Forest, Taos, N.Mex.

Jones, Charles Irving, ed. 1944. William Kronig, New Mexico Pioneer; from His Memories of 1849–1860. *New Mexico Historical Review* 19(3): 185–210.

Kammen, Michael. 1993. *Mystic Chords of Memory: Transformations of Tradition in American Society*. New York: Vintage.

Keegan, John. 1976. *The Face of Battle*. New York: Viking Press.

Klingensmith, Philip. 1962 [1871]. Appendix 4. In *The Mountain Meadows Massacre*, by Juanita Brooks, 238–42. Norman: University of Oklahoma Press.

Knack, Martha C. 2001. *Boundaries Between: The Southern Paiutes, 1775–1995*. Lincoln: University of Nebraska Press.

Komar, Debra A., and Jane E. Buikstra. 2008. *Forensic Anthropology: Contemporary Theory and Practice*. New York: Oxford University Press.

Krakauer, Jon. 2004. *Under the Banner of Heaven*. New York: Random House.

Kruse, Corinna. 2010. Producing Absolute Truth: CSI Science as Wishful Thinking. *American Anthropologist* 112:79–91.

LaDuke, Winona. 2005. *Recovering the Sacred: The Power of Naming and Claiming*. Cambridge, Mass.: South End Press.

Lamar, Howard. 1966. *The Far Southwest, 1846–1912: A Territorial History*. New Haven, Conn.: Yale University Press.

Larson, Charles M. 2008. *Destroying Angel*. Irvine, Calif.: Zyrus Press.

Lavender, David. 1984. *The Southwest*. Reprint. Albuquerque: University of New Mexico Press (Harper and Row, 1980).

Leckie, William H. 1956. The Red River War 1874–1875. *Panhandle-Plains Historical Review* 29:78–100.

———. 1963. *The Military Conquest of the Southern Plains*. Norman: University of Oklahoma Press.

———. 1967. *The Buffalo Soldiers: A Narrative of Negro Cavalry in the West*. Norman: University of Oklahoma Press.

Lee, John D. 2001 [1877]. *Mormonism Unveiled; or the Life and Confessions of the Late Mormon Bishop, John D. Lee*. Ed. William Bishop. Albuquerque, N.Mex: Sierra Blanca.

———. 2003. *A Mormon Chronicle: The Diaries of John D. Lee, 1848–1876*. 2 vols. Ed. Robert Glass Cleland and Juanita Brooks. San Marino, Calif.: Huntington Library.

Leonard, Glen M. 1977. Southwestern Boundaries and the Principles of Statemaking. *Western Historical Quarterly* 8:39–53.

———. 2002. *Nauvoo: A Place of Peace, a People of Promise*. Salt Lake City: Deseret Book; Provo, Utah: Brigham Young University Press.

LeSueur, Stephen C. 1987. *The 1838 Mormon War in Missouri*. Columbia: University of Missouri Press.

Limerick, Patricia. 1987. *The Legacy of Conquest: The Unbroken Past of the American West*. New York: W. W. Norton.

Limerick, Patricia Nelson, Clyde A. Milner II, and Charles E. Rankin, eds. 1991. *Trails: Toward a New Western History*. Lawrence: University Press of Kansas.

Linenthal, Edward T. 1995. *Preserving Memory: The Struggle to Create America's Holocaust Museum*. New York: Columbia University Press.

Lipstadt, Deborah E. 1993. *Denying the Holocaust: The Growing Assault on Truth and Memory*. New York: Free Press.

Little, Edward C. 1958. The Battle of Adobe Walls. *Pearson's Magazine* 19(1): 75–85.

Little, James A., ed. 1881. *Jacob Hamblin: A Narrative of His Personal Experience*. Salt Lake City: Juvenile Instructor.

Loewen, James W. 1996. *Lies My Teacher Told Me: Everything Your American History Textbook Got Wrong*. New York: Touchstone Books.

———. 1999. *Lies across America: What Our Historic Sites Get Wrong*. New York: Simon and Schuster.

Lowe, Percival. 1985. *Five Years a Dragoon and Other Adventures on the Great Plains*. Norman: University of Oklahoma Press.

Ludwig, Larry L., and James L. Stute. 1993. *The Battle at K-H Butte*. Tucson: Western Lore Press.

MacKinnon, William P. 1998. Utah Expedition, or Utah War. In *New Encyclopedia of the American West*, ed. Howard R. Lamar, 1149–51. New Haven, Conn.: Yale University Press.

Marsden, Michael T. 1979. A Dedication to the Memory of Helen Hunt Jackson: 1830–1885. *Arizona and the West* 21:109–12.

Marshall, S. L. A. 1947. *Men against Fire: The Problem of Battle Command*. New York: William Morrow.

Masich, Andrew E. n.d. Russville Archaeology Project: A Preliminary Report on Ammunition and Ammunition Components. Manuscript on file, Office of the State Archaeologist, Colorado Historical Society, Denver.

Mason, Ronald. 2000. Archaeology and Native American Oral History. *American Antiquity* 65(2): 239–66.

———. 2006. *Inconstant Companions: Archaeology and North American Indian Oral Traditions*. Tuscaloosa: University of Alabama Press.

Mathes, Valerie Sherer. 1989. Helen Hunt Jackson and the Ponca Controversy. *Montana: The Magazine of Western History* 39:42–53.

———. 1997. *Helen Hunt Jackson and Her Indian Reform Legacy*. Norman: University of Oklahoma Press.

Mathes, Valerie Sherer, and Richard Lowitt. 2003. *The Standing Bear Controversy: Prelude to Indian Reform*. Urbana-Champaign: University of Illinois Press.

Matson, Daniel S., and Albert H. Schroeder. 1957. Codero's Description of the Apache—1876. *New Mexico Historical Review* 32(4): 345–46.

Mawson, Anthony R. 2007. *Mass Panic and Social Attachment: The Dynamics of Human Behavior*. London: Ashgate.

McMurtry, Larry. 2005. *Oh What a Slaughter: Massacres in the American West, 1846–1890*. New York: Simon and Schuster.

McNeill, William H. 1995. *Keeping Together in Time: Dance and Drill in Human History*. Cambridge, Mass.: Harvard University Press.

Meinig, Donald W. 1971. *Southwest: Three Peoples in Geographical Change, 1600–1970*. New York: Oxford University Press.

Méndez-Gastelumendi, Cecilia. 2001. The Power of Naming, or the Construction of Ethnic and National Identities in Peru: Myth, History and the Iquichanos. *Past and Present* 171:127–60.

Michno, Gregory. 2003. *Encyclopedia of Indian Wars: Western Battles and Skirmishes, 1850–1890*. Missoula, Mont.: Mountain Press.
———. 2004. *Battle at Sand Creek: The Military Perspective*. El Segundo, Calif.: Upton and Sons.
Miles, Nelson A. 1896. *Personal Recollections and Observations*. Chicago: Werner.
Miller, Skip Keith. 2003. Notes on Ceramic Analysis. Unpublished manuscript on file, Carson National Forest, Taos, N.Mex.
Min, Anselm K. 2006. Naming the Unnameable God: Levinas, Derrida, and Marion. *International Journal for Philosophy of Religion* 60:99–116.
Mitchell, Sallie Baker. 1940. The Mountain Meadows Massacre—An Episode on the Road to Zion. *American Weekly*, Sept.
Mooar, J. Wright. 1932. Buffalo Days. Ed. James Winford Hunt. *Holland's, the Magazine of the South* (Dallas, Tex.) 52:8, 24, 28.
Moses, L. G. 2002. *The Indian Man: A Biography of James Mooney*. Lincoln: University of Nebraska Press.
National Park Service. 2000. Sand Creek Massacre Site Location Study. Intermountain Regional Office, National Park Service, Denver.
Nevins, Allan. 1962 [1938]. *The Gateway to History*. Rev. ed. New York: Doubleday Anchor.
Nolan, Louis. 2007 [1853]. *Cavalry: Its History and Tactics* Yardley, Pa.: Westholme.
Novak, Shannon A. 2008. *House of Mourning: A Biocultural History of the Mountain Meadows Massacre*. Salt Lake City: University of Utah Press.
Novak, Shannon A., and Derinna Kopp. 2003. To Feed a Tree in Zion: Osteological Analysis of the 1857 Mountain Meadows Massacre. *Historical Archaeology* 37:85–108.
Novak, Shannon A., and Lars Rodseth. 2006. Remembering Mountain Meadows: Collective Violence and the Manipulation of Social Boundaries. *Journal of Anthropological Research* 62:1–25.
Nugent, Walter. 1994. Western History, New and Not So New. *OAH Magazine of History* 9:5–9.
Oaks, Dallin H., and Marvin S. Hill. 1975. *Carthage Conspiracy: The Trial of the Accused Assassins of Joseph Smith*. Urbana: University of Illinois Press.
Opler, Morris E. 1971. Jicarilla Apache Territory, Economy and Society in 1850. *Southwestern Journal of Anthropology* 27:309–329.
Ortiz, Alfonso, ed. 1983. *Handbook of North American Indians,* vol. 10. Washington, D.C.: Smithsonian Institution.
Orton, Chad M. 2008. W. W. Bishop Unveiled: An Analysis of John D. Lee's Confessions. Paper presented at the annual Mormon History Association Conference, Sacramento, Calif., May 23, 2008.
Parker, Basil B. 1902. *The Life and Adventures of Basil G. Parker*. Plano, Calif.: Fred W. Reed.
Parkin, Max H. 1976. A History of the Latter-day Saints in Clay County, Missouri, from 1833 to 1847. Ph.D. dissertation, Brigham Young University.

Peck, M. Scott. 1983. *People of the Lie: The Hope for Healing Human Evil.* New York: Simon and Shuster.
Peters, Dewitt C. 1874. *Kit Carson's Life and Adventures, from Facts Narrated by Himself, Embracing Events in the Life Time of America's Greatest Hunter, Trapper, Scout and Guide.* Hartford, Conn.: Dustin, Gilman.
Peters, Ralph. 2007. Myths of Counterinsurgency. *Armchair General,* Sept.
Peterson, Merrill D. 1995. *Lincoln in American Memory.* Oxford: Oxford University Press.
Pettis, Capt. George A. 1908. *Kit Carson's Fight with the Comanche and Kiowa.* Santa Fe: New Mexican Printing Company.
Phillips, Christopher. 1990. *Damned Yankee: The Life of General Nathaniel Lyon.* Baton Rouge: Louisiana State University Press.
Phillips, Kate. 2003. *Helen Hunt Jackson: A Literary Life.* Berkeley: University of California Press.
Pickerill, William. 1865. *History of the Third Indiana Cavalry.* Indianapolis, Ind.: Aetna Printing.
Poinsett, J. R. 1856. *Cavalry Tactics, First Part: School of the Trooper—Of the Platoon and of the Squadron—Dismounted.* Philadelphia: J. B. Lippincott.
Powers, John. 2004. *History as Propaganda: Tibetan Exiles versus the People's Republic of China.* New York: Oxford University Press.
Pritzker, Barry. 2000. *A Native American Encyclopedia: History, Culture and Peoples.* New York: Oxford University Press.
Prucha, Francis Paul. 1984. American Indian Policy in the Twentieth Century. *Western Historical Quarterly* 15:4–18.
Punke, Michael. 2007. *Last Stand: George Bird Grinnell, the Battle to Save the Buffalo, and the Birth of the New West.* Washington, D.C.: Smithsonian Institution Press.
Rand, Jacki Thompson. 2008. *Kiowa Humanity and the Invasion of the State.* Lincoln: University of Nebraska Press.
Ratner, Steven R., and Jason S. Abrams. 2001. *Accountability for Human Rights Atrocities in International Law: Beyond the Nuremberg Legacy.* 2nd ed. Oxford: Oxford University Press.
Reisman, W. Michael, and Chris T. Antoniou. 1994. *The Laws of War: A Comprehensive Collection of Primary Documents on International Laws Governing Armed Conflict.* New York: Vintage Books.
Robb, John. 2008. Meaningless Violence and the Lived Body: The Huron-Jesuit Collision of World Orders. In *Past Bodies: Body-Centered Research in Archaeology,* ed. Dusan Boric and John Robb, 89–99. Oxford, U.K.: Oxbow Books.
Roberts, Alexa. 2000. *Cheyenne and Arapaho Tribal Oral Histories and Traditional Tribal Methods Regarding the Location of the Sand Creek Massacre.* Sand Creek Massacre Site Location Study, Intermountain Regional Office, National Park Service, Denver.

Roberts, Gary L. 1984. Sand Creek: Tragedy and Symbol. Ph.D. dissertation, Department of History, University of Oklahoma.
Roberts, Gary Leland, and David Fridtjof Halaas. 2001. Written in Blood: The Soule-Cramer Sand Creek Letters. *Colorado Heritage*, Winter, 22–32.
Robertson, Geoffrey. 1999. *Crimes against Humanity: The Struggle for Global Justice*. New York: New Press.
Rodenbough, Theophilus F. 2000. *From Everglade to Canyon with the Second United States Cavalry: An Authentic Account of Service in Florida, Mexico, Virginia and the Indian Country, 1836–1875*. Reprinted with a forward by Edward G. Longacre. Norman: University of Oklahoma Press.
Rodenbough, Theophilus F., and William L. Harkin, eds. 1966 [1896]. *The Army of the United States, Historical Sketches of Staff and Line with Portraits of Generals-in-Chief.* Reprinted. New York: Argonaut Press.
Rodseth, Lars, and Bradley J. Parker. 2005. Theoretical Considerations in the Study of Frontiers. In *Untaming the Frontier in Anthropology, Archaeology, and History*, ed. Bradley J. Parker and Lars Rodseth, 3–21. Tucson: University of Arizona Press.
Rogers, William H. 1962 [1860]. Appendix 11: Statement of Mr. Wm. H. Rogers. In *The Mountain Meadows Massacre*, by Juanita Brooks, 265–78. Norman: University of Oklahoma Press.
Ross, Fiona C. 2003. *Bearing Witness: Women and the Truth and Reconciliation Commission in South Africa*. Sterling, Va.: Pluto Press.
Rye, Edgar. 1909. *The Quirt and the Spur: Vanishing Shadows of the Texas Frontier*. Chicago: W. B. Conkey.
Sabin, Edwin L. 1995. *Kit Carson Days*. 2 vols. Lincoln: University of Nebraska Press.
Sahlins, Marshall. 2004. *Apologies to Thucydides: Understanding History as Culture and Vice Versa*. Chicago: University of Chicago Press.
Sanchez, George I. 1940. *Forgotten People: A Study of New Mexicans*. Albuquerque: University of New Mexico Press.
Scarry, Elaine. 1985. *The Body in Pain: The Making and Unmaking of the World*. Oxford: Oxford University Press.
Schabas, William A. 2000. *Genocide in International Law*. Cambridge: Cambridge University Press.
Schwartz, Barry. 2000. *Abraham Lincoln and the Forge of National Memory*. Chicago: University of Chicago Press.
———. 2009. *Abraham Lincoln in the Post-Heroic Era: History and Memory in Late-Twentieth Century America*. Chicago: University of Chicago Press.
Schwartz, Regina M. 1997. *The Curse of Cain: The Violent Legacy of Monotheism*. Chicago: University of Chicago Press.
Schweitzer, N. J., and Michael J. Saks. 2007. The *CSI* Effect: Popular Fiction about Forensic Science Affects Public Expectations about Real Forensic Science. *Jurimetrics* 47:357.

Scott, Bob. 1994. *Blood at Sand Creek: The Massacre Revisited*. Caldwell, Idaho: Caxton Printers.

Scott, D. D., R. A. Fox, Jr., M. A. Conner, and D. Harmon. 1989. *Archaeological Perspectives on the Battle of the Little Bighorn*. Norman: University of Oklahoma Press.

Scott, Douglas, Lawrence Babits, and Charles Haecker, eds. 2007. *Fields of Conflict: Battlefield Archaeology from the Roman Empire to the Korean War*. 2 vols. Westport, Conn.: Greenwood.

Scott, Douglas D. 2000. Identifying the 1864 Sand Creek Massacre Site through Archeological Reconnaissance. In Sand Creek Massacre Site Location Study, Intermountain Regional Office, National Park Service, Denver.

Scott, Douglas D., and Robert A. Fox, Jr. 1987. *Archaeological Insights into the Custer Battle: An Assessment of the 1984 Field Season*. Norman: University of Oklahoma Press.

Scott, Douglas D., P. Willey, and Melissa A. Connor. 1998. *They Died with Custer: Soldiers' Bones from the Battle of the Little Bighorn*. Norman: University of Oklahoma Press.

Seefeldt, W. Douglas. 2001. Constructing Western Pasts: Place and Public Memory in the Twentieth-Century American West. Ph.D. dissertation, Department of History, Arizona State University.

Sellars, Wilfrid. 1962. Naming and Saying. *Philosophy of Science* 29:7–26.

Senier, Siobhan. 2003. *Voices of American Indian Assimilation and Resistance: Helen Hunt Jackson, Sarah Winnemucca, and Victoria Howland*. Norman: University of Oklahoma Press.

Sheehan, James. 1981. What Is German History? Reflections on the Role of the Nation in German History and Historiography. *Journal of Modern History* 53:3–5.

Shermer, Michael, and Alex Grobman. 2000. *Denying History: Who Says the Holocaust Never Happened and Why Do They Say It?* Berkeley: University of California Press.

Shipps, Jan. 1985. *Mormonism: The Story of a New Religious Tradition*. Urbana: University of Illinois Press.

Shirts, Morris A., and Kathryn H. Shirts. 2001. *A Trial Furnace: Southern Utah's Iron Mission*. Provo, Utah: Brigham Young University Press.

Skelton, William B. 1992. *An American Profession of Arms: The Army Officer Corps, 1784–1861*. Lawrence: University of Kansas Press.

Smith, Bonnie G. 1995. Whose Truth, Whose History? *Journal of the History of Ideas* 56:661–68.

Smith, Duane A. 1992. *Rocky Mountain West: Colorado, Wyoming, and Montana, 1859–1915*. Albuquerque: University of New Mexico Press.

Smith, Henry Nash. 1950. *Virgin Land: The American West as Symbol and Myth*. Cambridge, Mass.: Harvard University Press.

Smith, Steven D., Christopher Ohm Clement, and Stephen R. Wise. 2003. GPS, GIS, and the Civil War Battlefield Landscape: A South Carolina Low Country Example. *Historical Archaeology* 37(3): 14–30.

Snow, Clyde Collins, Jose Pablo Baraybar, and Herbert Spirer. 2008. Estimating War Crimes from the Wounded to Killed Ratio: The Japanese Embassy. In *Skeletal Trauma: Identification of Injuries Resulting from Human Rights Abuse and Armed Conflict*, ed. Erin H. Kimmerle and Jose Pablo Baraybar. Atlanta, Ga.: CRC Press.

Sofaer, Joanna R. 2006. *The Body as Material Culture: A Theoretical Osteoarchaeology*. Cambridge: Cambridge University Press.

Stark, Dolores. 1963. Terror at Adobe Walls! *Gasser* (Colorado Springs, Colo.) 20(10): 7–10.

Staub, Ervin. 1989. *The Roots of Evil: The Origins of Genocide and Other Group Violence*. Cambridge: Cambridge University Press.

Steffen, Randy. 1977. *The Horse Soldier 1776–1943*. 4 vols. Norman: University Oklahoma Press.

Stenhouse, T. B. H. 1873. *The Rocky Mountain Saints: A Full and Complete History of the Mormons*. New York: D. Appleton.

Stewart, T. Dale. 1979. *Essentials of Forensic Anthropology, Especially as Developed in the United States*. Springfield, Ill.: Charles C. Thomas.

Swanton, John R. 1969. *The Indian Tribes of North America*. Washington, D.C.: Smithsonian Institution Press.

Tambiah, Stanley J. 1996. *Leveling Crowds: Ethnonationalist Conflicts and Collective Violence in South Asia*. Berkeley: University of California Press.

Tanaka, Yuki. 1996. *Hidden Horrors: Japanese War Crimes in World War II*. Boulder, Colo.: Westview Press.

Tate, Michael. 1999. *The Frontier Army in the Settlement of the West*. Norman: University of Oklahoma Press.

Taylor, Morris F. 1969. Campaigns against the Jicarilla Apache, 1854. *New Mexico Historical Review* 44:269–91.

Thayer, William M. 1887. *Marvels of the New West. A Vivid Portrayal of the Stupendous Marvels in the Vast Wonderland West of the Missouri River. Six Books in One Volume, Comprising Marvels of Nature, Marvels of Race, Marvels of Mining, Marvels of Stock-Raising, and Marvels of Agriculture*. Norwich, Conn.: Henry Hill.

Thornton, Thomas F. 1997. Anthropological Studies of Native American Place Naming. *American Indian Quarterly* 21:209–228.

Tiller, Veronica E. Velarde. 1983. *The Jicarilla Apache Tribe: A History, 1846–1970*. Lincoln: University of Nebraska Press.

Tilly, Charles. 2003. *The Politics of Collective Violence*. Cambridge: Cambridge University Press.

———. 2006. *Why?* Princeton, N.J.: Princeton University Press.

Tom, Gary, and Ronald Holt. 2000. The Paiute Tribe of Utah. In *A History of Utah's American Indians*, ed. Forrest S. Cuch, 123–66. Salt Lake City: Utah State Division of Indian Affairs/Utah State Division of History.

Trouillot, Michel-Rolph. 1995. *Silencing the Past: Power and the Production of History*. Boston: Beacon Press.

Tuan, Yi-Fu. 1991. Language and the Making of Place: A Narrative-Descriptive Approach. *Annals of the Association of American Geographers* 81:684–96.
Turley, Richard E., Jr. 1992. *Victims: The LDS Church and the Mark Hofmann Case.* Urbana: University of Illinois Press.
———. 2007. The Mountain Meadows Massacre. *Ensign of the Church of Jesus Christ of Latter-day Saints* 37:14–21.
———. 2008. Problems with Mountain Meadows Massacre Sources. In *Mountain Meadows Massacre Documents,* Special issue, *BYU Studies* 47(3): 142–57.
Turley, Richard E., Jr., and Ronald W. Walker, eds. 2008. *Mountain Meadows Massacre Documents.* Special issue, *BYU Studies* 47(3):1–184.
———, eds. 2009. *Mountain Meadows Massacre: The Andrew Jenson and David H. Morris Collections.* Provo, Utah: Brigham Young University Press.
Unruh, John D., Jr. 1979. *The Plains Across: The Overland Emigrants and the Trans-Mississippi West, 1840–60.* Urbana: University of Illinois Press.
Urwin, Gregory J. W. 1983. *The United States Cavalry: An Illustrated History.* Dorset, U.K.: Blandford Books.
Utley, Robert. 1967. *Frontiersmen in Blue: The United States Army and the Indian, 1848–1865.* New York: Macmillan.
———. 1973. *Frontier Regulars: The United States Army and the Indian, 1866–1891.* New York: Macmillan.
———. 2007. Red River War: Last Uprising in the Texas Panhandle. *Military Historical Quarterly* 20(1): 74–83.
Van Sickel, S. S. [1890]. *A Story of Real Life on the Plains Written by Capt. S. S. Van Sickel, Born Sept. 6, 1826: A True Narrative of the Author's Experience.* N.p.
Veggeberg, Vernon T. 1999. Laws of War on the American Frontier: General Orders No. 100 and Cheyenne-White Conflict. MA thesis, Department of History, Colorado State University, Fort Collins.
von Clausewitz, Carl. 1993. *On War.* English trans. New York: Alfred A. Knopf.
Walker, Jeffrey N. 2008. Mormon Land Rights in Caldwell and Daviess Counties and the Mormon Conflict of 1838: New Findings and New Understandings. *BYU Studies* 47(1): 5–55.
Walker, Ronald W. 1998. *Wayward Saints: The Godbeites and Brigham Young.* Urbana: University of Illinois Press.
———. 2002. Walkara Meets the Mormons, 1848–52: A Case Study in Native American Accommodation. *Utah Historical Quarterly* 70(2): 215–37.
Walker, Ronald W., Richard E. Turley, Jr., and Glen M. Leonard. 2008. *Massacre at Mountain Meadows: An American Tragedy.* New York: Oxford University Press.
Watkins, Joe. 2006. Communicating Archaeology: Words to the Wise. *Journal of Social Archaeology* 6(1): 100–18.
Weber, Kent, and Douglas Scott. 2003. Firearms Identification Procedures in the Analysis of Percussion Caps from the Battle of Cieneguilla, New Mexico. Manuscript on file, Carson National Forest, Taos, N.Mex.

———. 2006. Uncapped Potential: Applying Firearms Identification Procedures in the Analysis of Percussion Caps. *Historical Archaeology* 40(3): 131–43.

Wetherington, Ronald K. 2006. Cantonment Burgwin: The Archaeological and Documentary Record. *New Mexico Historical Review* 81:391–411.

Weyeneth, Robert R. 2001. The Power of Apology and the Process of Historical Reconciliation. *Public Historian* 23:9–38.

Whipple, Lt. A. W., and Lt. J. C. Ives. 1853–54. *Reports of Explorations for a Railroad Route Near the Thirty-Fifth Parallel of North Latitude from the Mississippi River to the Pacific Ocean.* Washington. D.C.: War Department, A. O. P. Nicholson.

White, Richard. 1991. *"It's Your Misfortune and None of My Own": A History of the American West.* Norman: University of Oklahoma Press.

Whiteley, Peter. 2002. Archaeology and Oral Tradition: The Scientific Importance of Dialogue. *American Antiquity* 67(3): 405–415.

Wiener, Philip P. 1963. James Gregory: On Power. *Journal of the History of Ideas* 24:241–68.

Wilhelm, Thomas. 1881. *A Military Dictionary and Gazetteer.* Philadelphia: L. R. Hamersly.

Wilke, Philip, and Harry Lawton, eds. 1976. *The Expedition of Capt. J. W. Davidson from Fort Tejon to the Owens Valley in 1859.* Socorro, N.Mex.: Ballena Press.

Wilkinson, Charles. 2005. *Blood Struggle: The Rise of Modern Indian Nations.* New York: W. W. Norton.

Willey, P., and Douglas D. Scott. 1991. "The Bullets Buzzed like Bees": Gunshot Wounds in Skeletons from the Battle of the Little Bighorn. *International Journal of Osteoarchaeology* 6:15–27.

Wilson, James. 1998. *The Earth Shall Weep: A History of Native America.* New York: Grove Press.

Winders, Richard Bruce. 1997. *Mr. Polk's Army: The American Military Experience in the Mexican War.* College Station: Texas A&M University Press.

Winn, Kenneth H. 1989. *Exiles in a Land of Liberty: Mormons in America, 1830–1846.* Chapel Hill: University of North Carolina Press.

Winthrop, William. 1920. *Military Law and Precedents.* Washington, D.C.: Government Printing Office.

Worman, Charles. 2005. *Gunsmoke and Saddle Leather: Firearms in the Nineteenth-Century American West.* Albuquerque: University of New Mexico Press.

Worster, Donald. 1992. *Under Western Skies: Nature and History in the American West.* New York: Oxford University Press.

Yenne, Bill. 2006. *Indian Wars: The Campaign for the American West.* Yardley, Pa.: Westholme.

Zimbardo, Philip. 2007. *The Lucifer Effect: Understanding How Good People Turn Evil.* New York: Random House.

Contributors

T. Lindsay Baker holds the W. K. Gordon Endowed Chair in Texas Industrial History at Tarleton State University in Stephenville, Texas, and directs the W. K. Gordon Center for Industrial History of Texas at Thurber, Texas. He is on the faculty of the Department of Social Sciences at Tarleton State. Baker has authored more than twenty books on the history of the American West, among them *Adobe Walls: The History and Archeology of the 1874 Trading Post* (1986), with Billy R. Harrison. A fellow of the Texas State Historical Association and a member of the Texas Institute of Letters, he actively researches and writes on both nineteenth- and twentieth-century topics.

J. Brett Cruse is Sites Supervisor in the Historic Sites Division of the Texas Historical Commission. Before joining the THC in 1995, he served as Archaeologist for several private resource management firms. He received his B.A. in anthropology/sociology from West Texas State University and his M.A. in anthropology from Texas A&M University. In 1993 he received the Journalistic Achievement Award, for excellence in the field of print media, from the Texas Historical Foundation. His most recent book, *Battles of the Red River War: Archeological Perspectives on the Indian Campaign of 1874*, was published in 2008.

Will Gorenfeld is a practicing attorney and popularizer of American western history. He received his B.A. in sociology from California State University at Northridge and his J.D. from Loyola University School of Law in Los Angeles. He is a member of the California and federal bars and currently serves as pro bono attorney for the Legal Aid Society of Marin, San Rafael, California; California Indian Legal Services in Ukiah; and the California Court of Appeals in Ventura. He has published numerous articles in magazines and professional journals, lectured on military history at the University of California at Santa Barbara, and served as docent at Fort Tejon State Park. For several summers he was employed as a forest ranger for the U.S. Forest Service at Inyo National Forest.

David M. Johnson serves as Regional Heritage Program Manager for the U.S. Forest Service in Albuquerque, New Mexico. He has also worked at the Cibola, Carson, Lincoln, and Kisatchie National Forests, and for the U.S. Army Corps of Engineers. His B.A. in anthropology is from the University of Missouri, and he received his M.A. in anthropology from Washington State University. He has authored and coauthored numerous publications on nineteenth-century engagements between the U.S. military and American Indians, including several on the Battle of Cieneguilla.

Ari Kelman is Associate Professor of History at the University of California, Davis, where he teaches courses ranging from the Civil War and Reconstruction, to the politics of memory, to environmental history. He is the author of *A River and Its City: The Nature of Landscape in New Orleans* (2003), which won the Abbott Lowell Cummings Prize in 2004, and *A Misplaced Massacre: Struggling over the Memory of Sand Creek* (2013). Kelman's essays and articles have appeared in *Slate*, *Christian Science Monitor*, *The Nation*, *Times Literary Supplement*, *Journal of Urban History*, *Journal of American History*, and many other magazines, newspapers, and scholarly publications.

Glen M. Leonard, recently retired as Director of the Museum of Church History and Art, Church of Jesus Christ of Latter-day Saints, is currently an independent historian living in Farmington, Utah. He received his B.A. and M.A. degrees in history and journalism and his Ph.D. in history and American studies from the University of Utah. He was Managing Editor for the *Utah Historical Quarterly* for three years and on its advisory board of editors for fifteen years thereafter. His numerous books and articles have won five awards. His most recent book, coauthored with Ronald Walker and Richard Turley, Jr., is *Massacre at Mountain Meadows* (2008).

Frances Levine is Director of the New Mexico History Museum. The New Mexico History Museum includes the Palace of the Governors, the oldest museum in the Museum of New Mexico system, the Fray Angélico Chávez History Library and Photo Archives, the Palace Print Shop, and the Native American Portal Artisans Program. She received her B.A. in anthropology from the University of Colorado, Boulder, and her M.A. and Ph.D. in anthropology from Southern Methodist University, Dallas. She came to the museum from her position as the assistant dean of academic affairs for arts and sciences at Santa Fe Community College, in Santa Fe, New Mexico. She is the author of *Our Prayers Are in This Place; Pecos Pueblo Identity over the Centuries* (1999) as well as coeditor of the award-winning books *Telling New Mexico: A New History* (2009) and *The Threads of Memory: El Hilo de la Memoria* (2010). She has contributed chapters to many publications in historical archaeology and ethnohistory.

Shannon A. Novak is Associate Professor of Anthropology at Syracuse University. Trained in human osteology at the Smithsonian Institution, she received her Ph.D. in anthropology at the University of Utah. Her field research includes archaeological and osteological studies in Jordan, England, Croatia, Guatemala, and the United States. As a biocultural anthropologist, her research interests include historical memory, political and domestic violence, and the materiality of dead bodies. She is the author of *House of Mourning: A Biocultural History of the Mountain Meadows Massacre* (2008). More recently, she coedited (with Kelly Dixon and Julie Schablitsky) *An Archaeology of Desperation: Exploring the Donner Family Camp at Alder Creek* (2011). Both books received the James Deetz Award from the Society for Historical Archaeology.

Lars Rodseth is Associate Professor of Anthropology at Syracuse University. He received his B.A. in philosophy from the University of Maryland and M.A. and Ph.D. degrees in anthropology from the University of Michigan. With research interests in social and cultural theory, political ideology, religion, nationalism, and kinship, he has conducted field research in Nepal and the United States. He has authored numerous book chapters and professional papers and coedited (with Bradley Parker) *Untaming the Frontier in Anthropology, Archaeology, and History* (2005).

Douglas D. Scott currently serves as Adjunct Professor for the Department of Anthropology and Geography at the University of Nebraska and Adjunct Professor for the Masters of Forensic Science Program at Nebraska Wesleyan University. From 1983 to 2006 he was supervisory archaeologist at the Midwest Archeological Center for the National Park Service in Lincoln, in which capacity he received the Department of Interior's Distinguished Service Award. Scott has been a pioneer in developing the science of battlefield archaeology, reflected in his many papers and books, including *Finding Sand Creek: History, Archeology, and the 1864 Massacre Site* (2004). He coedited (with Charles Haecker and Lawrence Babits) the two-volume *Fields of Conflict: Battlefield Archaeology from the Roman Empire to the Korean War* (2009).

Joe Watkins, Director of the Native American Studies Program at the University of Oklahoma and Supervisory Anthropologist and Chief of the Tribal Relations and American Cultures Program for the National Park Service, has been involved in archaeology for more than forty years. Before moving to the University of Oklahoma he was an Associate Professor of Anthropology at the University of New Mexico. He received his B.A. in anthropology from the University of Oklahoma and his M.A. and Ph.D. in anthropology from Southern Methodist University. He studies anthropology's relationships with descendant communities and aboriginal populations and has published numerous articles on these topics. His book *Indigenous Archaeology: American Indian Values and Scientific Practice* (2000) is a seminal work in indigenous archaeology, and his second book, *Reclaiming Physical Heritage: Repatriation and Sacred Sites* (2005), is written toward creating an awareness of major Native American issues among high school and early college students.

Ronald K. Wetherington is Professor of Anthropology and former Director of Graduate Studies at Southern Methodist University. He received his B.A. in zoology from Texas Tech University and his M.A. and Ph.D. in anthropology from the University of Michigan. He has conducted excavations at both prehistoric and historic sites, the latter at the Fort Burgwin Research Center in Taos, New Mexico, where he was the Center's director in the mid-1970s. He has published articles and books in both physical anthropology and archaeology. His *Readings in the History of Evolutionary Theory* was published in 2011. His most recent book, *Ceran St. Vrain: American Frontier Entrepreneur* (2012), includes the archaeological report of his excavation of St. Vrain's first mill. His first novel, *Kiva*, was published in the fall of 2013.

Index

Adobe Creek, 101
Adobe Walls: accuracy of account, 4; artifacts at, 2, 99–100, 102, 104–105, 108; casualties at, 81; eyewitness accounts at, 80, 86, 88; fervor of attack, 3; first battle of, 79, 82; and Red River War, 81, 86, 97, 106–107, 211, 215
Anthony, Maj. Scott, 121
Anthrax, 181
Anton Chico, New Mexico, 27
Apache, 2, 24; Jicarilla, 9, 10, 12, 15, 18, 37, 37n34, 39n81, 43–51, 54–55, 57–59, 62–63, 66, 69–71, 73, 75, 75n9; Llaneros, 13–14, 62; Mescalero, 27, 215; Olleros, 13–17
Apodaca trail, 55
Aqua Caliente: creek, 17; trail, 55
Arapaho (tribe), 114–15, 126–27, 148, 216–17; camp at Sand Creek, 135; claimed depredations by, 118–19, 214; desire for peace, 121–22, 124; oral history, 145; sacredness of Sand Creek to, 134, 136; Sand Creek artifacts of, 138, 140, 144, 149–50
Arkansas Company (migrants), 156, 160, 163, 165, 167, 169, 176, 180–83, 186n39, 191–93, 196, 199, 214

Baker, Jack T. (Arkansas Company), 165, 171, 180, 186n39
Banka Island. *See* Massacre
Bateman, William (militiaman), 197
Beall, Col. Benjamin (dragoon), 34
Bell, Lt. David (dragoon): and Chief Chacon, 26–27; conflict with Lt. Davidson, 10, 20, 28–30, 34, 36n16, 47; death of, 33; and Lobo Blanco, 14–15, 32
Bent, Charles, 13, 35n4; Bent Creek, 100; Bent, St. Vrain & Company, 79; George, 117, 119, 125–26, 129–30, 131n4, 132n21, 141; William, 119
Black Kettle (Cheyenne), 114, 118–19, 121–24, 126, 140, 149
Blake, George A. H. (dragoon): campaign against Olleros, 15–16; and drinking, 17, 20, 25; mutiny against, 29–30, 32
Bonneville, Col. Benjamin (3rd Infantry), 31
Bonsall, Lt. Samuel, 144
Borman (fuse), 142, 144
Breenwald, George (dragoon), 23
Bronson, Pvt. James (a.k.a. Bennett), 25, 31–32

Brooks, Juanita, 160, 163, 197, 199
Buchaan, Pres. James, 160, 167, 173, 177, 185n14
Buffalo Wallow, battle of, 106
Burgwin, Cantonment, 16–17, 25, 31, 36n16, 43, 75
Byers, Ned (editor), 117, 124
Byrnes, Cpl. Richard (dragoon), 18, 32

Campbell, Sen. Ben Nighthorse, 129–30
Canadian River, 82–83, 94, 100
Cannonball, 114, 137, 139–41, 143–44
Cantonment Burgwin, 16, 17, 25, 31, 36, 43
Carbine, 16, 19, 29, 38n61, 99, 107–108, 141, 143; Henry, 103n105, 107; Sharps, 38n54, 80, 95, 104–105, 138–39; Spencer, 99–100, 104–105, 107, 142; Starr, 138–39; Winchester, 99, 103–105, 107. *See also* Musketoon
Carleton, Cap. James H. (dragoon), 31
Carson, Kit, 14–15, 17, 22, 25–27, 31–32, 62, 79
Carson National Forest, 43–45
Case shot, 139–42, 144, 150
Cedar City, Utah, 168–69, 171, 173–74, 176–77, 180–83, 193, 197
Chacon (Apache), 26
Cheyenne: at Battle of Solomon River, 81; dehumanization of, 214; leaders at Adobe Walls, 95; and Medicine Lodge Treaties, 86; at Sand Creek, 114–15, 118–19, 121–22, 124, 126–27, 134–36, 138–41, 144–45, 148–50, 216, 219; union with Comanches and Kiowas, 82–83
Chispa (fire striker), 57
Chivington, Col. John M. (Sand Creek), 3, 113–14, 116–27, 130, 131n2, 131nn6–7, 135, 144, 149, 214, 219
Cieneguilla: artifact patterns at, 4–5, 52; biased official reports of, 10, 28–29, 34, criticism of Davidson at, 30; Davidson's obsession at, 3; failed leadership at, 11, 24; inadequate weapons at, 38n54; Jicarilla bravery at, 26; tactics at, 70; village, 16–17, 25, 43, 55
Cimarron River, 14
Clinton, Pres. Bill, 129
Colorado, 3, 5, 17, 117, 119–20, 123–24, 126–31, 135, 214; Indian War, 3, 79; Pioneers Association, 126; State Historical Society, 127–28; Volunteer Cavalry, 113, 116–18, 121, 135, 138–40, 142, 148–49, 217
Colt (revolver), 16, 23, 47, 52, 100
Comanches: battle at Adobe Walls, 79; domination of plains by, 13; and Medicine Lodge Treaties, 86; segregated history of, 218; union with Cheyennes and Kiowas, 82–83. *See also* Quanah Parker; Frank Yellow Fish
Conrad, Charles M. (Secretary of War), 14
Cooke, Lt. Col. Philip (dragoon), 26–28, 33, 36n16, 40n106
Coscojos. See Tinklers
Court-martial, 29–32
Cumming, Gov. Alfred, 177
Curtis, Gen. Samuel, 118, 122–23
Custer, Lt. Col. George, 24, 80, 130, 212. *See also* Little Bighorn

Dame, Col. William H. (militiaman), 169, 171–73, 177
Darlington Indian Agency, 84, 86
Davidson, Lt. (dragoon): account of Cieneguilla battle, 15–34, 57, 71, 73; Lt. Bell on, 36n16; bias of, 9, 12; court of inquiry for, 75, 215; obsession of, 3, 12; poor leadership of, 9–10, 13
Debitage, 46, 48, 51, 62
Dempsey, Benjamin (dragoon), 25

INDEX

Dixon, William ("Billy"), 80, 85, 87, 88–89, 94, 96–97, 102
Dodge City, Kansas, 82, 84–85, 07
Downing, Maj. Jacob (Colorado Volunteers), 117, 126
Drunkenness, 10, 20, 29, 34, 37n45

Embudo, 17, 25, 43, 47, 85
Era of Assimilation, 125
Evans, Gov. John, 122, 135

Fancher, Alexander, 165, 168, 171, 180, 186n39
Fog of war, 1, 4, 196
Forensic science, 148, 186n40, 191, 194–95, 201–205
Fort Burgwin. *See* Cantonment Burgwin
Fort Fillmore, 27
Fort Laramie, 29
Fort Leavenworth, 16, 28, 30, 192
Fort Lyon, 118, 120, 122–24, 126, 135
Fort Sill, 84, 86
Fort Union, 15, 36n16, 45
Fort Wise, Treaty of, 135
Frank Yellow Fish (Comanche), 86, 88, 92n25, 216
Frontier: army, 13, 34; concept of, 209; Indian displacement on, 154; manifest destiny and, 162, 186n28; Turner on, 125; violence and, 196, 198, 200
Frontier (newspaper), 117, 126

Garland, Gen. John (Dept. Commander), 27–28, 32
Geneva Convention, 146
Goodnight-Loving trail, 146
Grattan, Lt. John, defeat of, 24, 29
Greasy Grass, battle of, 212. *See also* Little Bighorn
Great Plains, 20, 82, 86, 215–16; Indian Wars, 113

Great Sioux War, 125
Greiner, John (Indian agent), 14, 18
Grier, Capt. William (dragoon), 37nn37–38
Guadalupe Hidalgo, Treaty of, 215
Gunnison Democrat (newspaper), 125

Hafen, Leroy, 128–29, 132n24
Haight, Isaac C. (mayor, Cedar City), 168–69, 171–73, 175–77, 179, 182–84
Harrison, Billy (Adobe Walls), 84, 87, 97
Henry. *See* Carbine
Higbee, Maj. John M. (militiaman), 173–75, 177, 194, 197
Holbrook, Sgt. William (dragoon), 18–19, 22–25, 37n38
Horse pistol, 16, 23, 47, 52
Howitzer: field, 79; mountain, 135, 139, 141–42
Hutchinson, Pvt. John (dragoon), 33

Indians: agents and agencies, 14, 18, 86; apprehensions of, 3; attacks by, 2, 5, 11, 14; Department of Indian Affairs, 14; opinion on history, 2, 210–214; treaties with, 2, 5, 83, 86, 135
Iron County militia (Utah), 192, 202
Isatai (medicine man), 79–80, 81n3, 83, 95–96, 108

Jackson, Andrew (president), 28, 158
Jackson, Helen Hunt, 117, 123–25, 131n3
Jingles. *See* Tinklers

Kearny, Stephen W., 15
Kent, Sgt. William (dragoon), 19–20, 62
Kiowa (tribe) 3, 79, 82–83, 86, 95, 211, 215–16; County, 127, 129
Klingensmith, Philip (militiaman), 194, 195

Knight, Samuel (militiaman), 173, 187n60, 188n71, 197
Kronig, Sgt. William (dragoon), 34

Lamar Daily News, 128
Leavitt, Gov. Mike, 202
Lee, John D. (sheriff), 163, 168–69, 171–79, 182, 184, 188n71, 197
Left Hand (Arapaho), 118, 121, 123
Lieber's Code, 146–47
Lincoln, Abraham (president): and Sand Creek, 123, 128; and Lieber's Code, 146; National Forest, 45
Little Bighorn (battle), 9, 80, 125, 130, 212. *See also* Custer
Lobo Blanco (Apache), 14–15, 32
Lone Wolf (Kiowa), 95
Lucifer effect, 154
Lyman's Wagon Train, battle of, 106

Madrid, Roque, 55
Magruder, Lt. David (surgeon), 16, 19, 32, 38n54, 38n61, 57
Maloney, Jeremiah (dragoon), 17
Mansfield, Joseph (inspector general), 19, 22
Mason, Ronald, 145, 213
Massacre: at Banks Is., 195; versus Battle, 116, 119, 127–28, 156; at Cieneguilla, 12; denial of, at Mountain Meadows, 196; George Bent on (Sand Creek), 126; at Little Bighon, 130; at Mountain Meadows, 2, 173, 176–79, 181, 192–94, 217; at Mountain Meadows, motive of, 154, 157, 163–64, 172–73, 200; nature of, 1, 3, 4, 145, 154, 149, 198, 214; of Pomo Indians, 16
Masterson, Bat (Adobe Walls), 96
McCall, George (inspector general), 18, 42n138
McGrath, Henry (dragoon), 23
McGunnegle, George (dragoon), 22–23
McMurdy, Samuel (militiaman), 197

Medicine Lodge (treaties of), 83, 86
Mescalero. *See* Apache
Messervy, W. S. (governor), 15, 17, 27
Metal detectors, 45–46, 51, 84, 105–106
Mexican War, 16, 19
Micaceous (ceramics), 46–48, 51, 59
Missouri Company (migrants), 165, 167, 180
Missouri Republican (newspaper), 26
Modoc War, 125
Mormon: church, 153–54, 164–65, 192, 201, 204; Reformation, 184; settlers and settlements, 2, 154–55, 158–59, 165, 167, 180, 190, 193, 217; War, 155, 157, 160–61
Mountain Meadows: locale of, 165, 169, 193; massacre at, motives and causes, 3, 157, 161, 178, 181, 190, 193, 198, 203, 214; Paiutes and, 2, 156, 181, 200, 204, 217; war crimes and, 195
Musketoon, 15–16, 19, 21–22, 26n17, 38n51, 38n54, 38n57, 47, 52. *See also* Carbine
Mutiny. *See* Taos
Muzzle-loaders, 16, 99, 105, 107–108
Myers and Leonard Store, 87, 95, 98, 100

Ogg, Billy (Adobe Walls), 94
O'Keefe, Tom (Adobe Walls), 98
Old Whirlwind (Cheyenne), 95
Oral record, 34, 38, 87, 93, 115, 136, 140, 145–46, 212–14
Owl Woman (William Bent's wife), 119

Pahvant (Ute band), 165, 167, 181
Paiute, 2, 33, 154–57, 163–65, 167, 169, 171–77, 181, 192, 204, 217
Palo Duro Canyon, battle of, 106
Panhandle-Plains Historical Museum, 84–85, 97
Parker, Quannah, 79–80, 81n3, 83, 86, 95
Patterson, Thomas (senator), 127

Pecos: pueblo, 45; river, 27
Percussion cap, 16, 21, 24, 33, 46, 48, 51–52, 54, 62–63, 66, 69, 73, 75, 142
Picuris: Mountain, 39n81, 69; pueblo, 43; trail, 48, 55
Pike's Peak Pioneers, 120
Plains: region, 13, 20, 33, 79–80, 82–83, 86, 93, 97, 113, 118–19, 121, 157–58, 211, 215–16; tribes, 3, 14, 93, 97, 141, 149, 211
Pomo (tribe), 15, 36n20
Post traders, 45
Propaganda, 2, 194, 196, 205, anti-Mormon, 195; history as, 211

Rath and Company, 87, 95–96, 98
Rath (settlement), 3
Raton pass, 27
Red Hat (Cheyenne), 219
Red River War, 80, 86, 93, 97, 105–107, 109n10, 125
Revenge, as motive: Mountain Meadows, 161, 181; Sand Creek, 3
Rio Caliente Canyon, 26
Rio Grande, 9, 15–18, 43, 62
Rio Pueblo, 69
Rocky Mountain News, 117, 124
Round Timber Creek, battle of, 106

San Pascual, battle, 15
Sand Creek: massacre at, 2–4, 79, 113, 115–17, 120, 126, 131n2, 134–35, 145–49, 154; physical evidence at, 5, 118–19, 123, 136–44; relation to Civil War, 119–20, 124, 126–28, 214
Sand Creek National Historic Site, 117, 129–30
Santa Fe, conquest of, 15
Santa Fe Gazette, 14, 26, 32
Santa Fe–Taos trail, 17, 55
Santa Fe Trail, 79
Scalps: Jicarilla prohibition, 26; at Sand Creek, 119–20, 123–24

Schurz, Carl (secretary of the interior), 124
Scott, Douglas D.: analysis, at Adobe Walls, 102–103, 106–107; at Sand Creek, 114, 217
Scott, Gen. Winfield, 30
Sharps. *See* Carbine
Sheridan, Gen. Philip, 105
Sherman, Gen. William T., 97, 105, 120, 140
Shoshone (tribe), 167, 184
Silva, Jesus (scout), 17
Sioux (Lakota), 29; Great Sioux War, 125
Smith, George A. (Mormon), 182–63
Smith, Joseph (Mormon), 158–59, 168
Smoky Hill River, 122
Solomon River (battle of), 81n3
Soule, Silas (Colorado Cavalry), 113, 116–17, 119–23, 126, 129, 131n2
Spencer. *See* Carbine
Standing Bear (Ponca), 123–24
Starr. *See* Carbine
Stone Calf (Cheyenne), 95
Strawbridge, James (dragoon), 22, 25, 32
St. Vrain, Ceran: Bent, St. Vrain & Co., 79, 82; Taos mill, 17, 25, 38n47
Sumner, Col. Edwin V. (commander, Dept. of New Mexico), 18, 30
Sweetwater Creek, battle of, 106

Taos: Kit Carson in, 14; mutiny in, 29–30, 32, 37n45; Pueblo, 25; trail, 17; valley, 18
Thompson, Maj. Philip (dragoon), 20, 38n47
Tinklers, 46, 51, 57, 59, 62, 141, 143
Trade fair, Indian, 45
Tribune (newspaper), 124
Turner, Frederick Jackson, 125
Turner, Nicholas (Missouri Company), 165, 167, 180–81

Tyler, Billy (Adobe Walls), 95–96

Ute (tribe), 45, 167

War Bonnet (Cheyenne), 121
Weldon, Peter (dragoon), 22, 24
Wells, Gen. Daniel H. (militiaman), 161, 182
White, James and Ann, murders of, 14, 37n37
White Antelope (Cheyenne), 121
White Shield (Cheyenne), 95

Williams, Lt. Robert (dragoon), 28–29, 36
Winchester. *See* Carbine
Wounded-to-killed ratio, 148
Wynkoop, Maj. Ned (Sand Creek), 120–23, 126

Yellow Fish, Frank (Comanche), 86, 88, 92n25, 216
Young, Brigham, 158–60, 163, 167–68, 171–72, 176–78, 181–82, 184, 192–93

www.ingramcontent.com/pod-product-compliance
Lightning Source LLC
Chambersburg PA
CBHW031433160426
43195CB00010BB/717